Alabama 1840 Census Index

The Counties formed from the Creek and Cherokee Cessions of the 1830's

Counties included are Barbour, Benton, Chambers, Cherokee, Coosa, Dekalb, Macon, Marshall, Randolph, Russell, Talladega and Tallapoosa

Transcribed and compiled by:
Betty Sue Drake

Indexed by:
Seth A. R. Posey

Southern Historical Press, Inc.
Greenville, South Carolina

This volume was reproduced
from a personal copy located in
the Publishers private library

Please direct all correspondence and book orders to:
SOUTHERN HISTORICAL PRESS, Inc.
PO Box 1267
Greenville, SC 29602-1267

Copyright 1973 by: Betty Sue Drake
Copyright Transferred 1991 to:
    Southern Historical Press, Inc.
ISBN #0-89308-331-3
Printed in the United States of America

TABLE OF CONTENTS

FOREWORD
MAP OF ALABAMA, 1840
BARBOUR COUNTY 1
BENTON COUNTY 9
CHAMBERS COUNTY 22
CHEROKEE COUNTY 32
COOSA COUNTY 41
DEKALB COUNTY 47
MACON COUNTY 54
MARSHALL COUNTY 60
RANDOLPH COUNTY 68
RUSSELL COUNTY 73
TALLADEGA COUNTY 80
TALLAPOOSA COUNTY 89

SURNAME INDEX i

FOREWORD

When President Andrew Jackson took office in 1829, almost one-fourth of present-day Alabama was still occupied by Indians, mostly Cherokees and Upper Creeks. The population of Alabama had more than doubled in the decade between 1820 and 1830 and white settlers were demanding more land.

In 1832, the Treaty of Cusseta was concluded. In this agreement, the Creeks ceded all their lands east of the Mississippi. Out of these lands, nine counties were created. By legislative action in 1836, three others were made from lands vacated by the Cherokees. These counties represent the last major land areas acquired by the state of Alabama.

The 1840 census was the first to be taken of the population in the new counties. Only heads of household were actually named. Members of the household were designated by males and females in the following age ranges: under 5, 5-10, 10-15, 15-20, 20-30, 30-40, 40-50, 50-60, 60-70, 70-80, 80-90, and 90-100. The number of slaves owned by each head of household were listed similiarly. In addition, the 1840 census named military pensioners, number of persons engaged in agriculture, mining, manufacturing and trade, commerce, navigation of the oceans, lakes, rivers, and canals, and the learned professions and engineers. The deaf, dumb, blind, and insane were indicated.

In reading any transcription of an original census, the reader is reminded that surnames must be looked for under all possible spellings. Many census takers were poorly educated and often spelled phonetically, that is, as a name sounded. Some of them used the "long s" which appears to be a "p" or "pp". Thus a name like Bass may look like Bap. Some films are dim and difficult to read; therefore errors in reading the names are inevitable.

The names in this transcription are listed in the order in which they appear on the original census rolls. This is preferable to an alphabetical arrangement as it is useful to know the neighbors of a family. Often, the neighbors were relatives as related groups tended to migrate together.

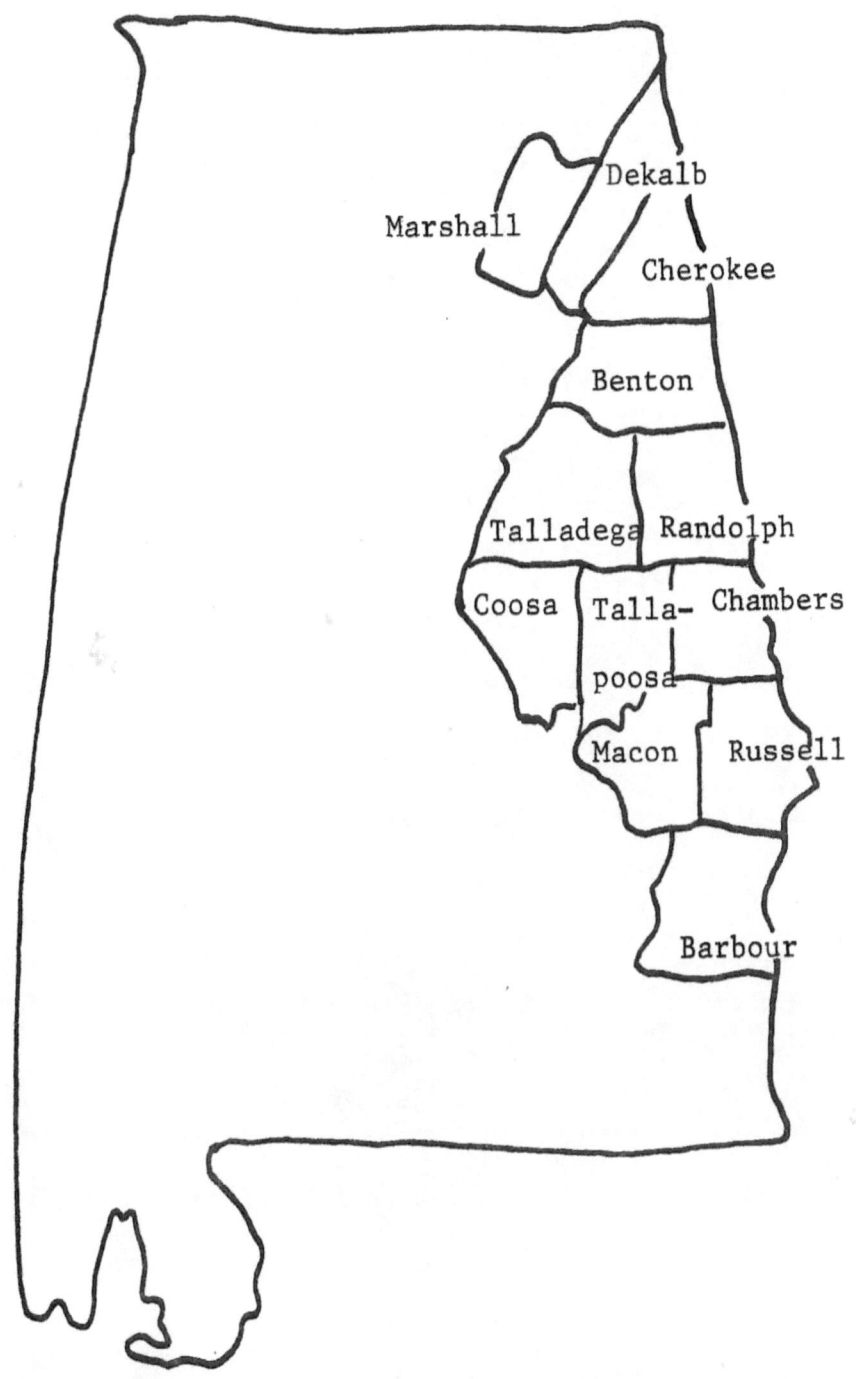

Counties made from the Indian cessions of 1832-1836

INDEX, 1840 CENSUS OF THE CREEK & CHEROKEE CESSION COUNTIES OF ALABAMA

BARBOUR COUNTY

Page 46
ARNOLD, D S.
TEAL, ROBERT
THIGPEN, JOSEPH
LEWIS, NICY
CRAWFORD, A.P.
BOOTH, JOHN P.
WHITE, WILLIS
HARDMAN, JACK
McPHAIL, A.
McBRYDE, JOHN
TAYLOR, W. S.
McDONALD, ALEX
CROSBY, JANE
STORS, ANTHONY
HALL, JOHN
CARGILE, THOMAS
McLEAN, O/D
GUNNERSON, CHARLES
NOLIN, AVERY
SPURLOCK, JOHN
RYAN, HAMPTON
BROWN, CHARLES
CAISON, JAMES
GODWIN, RANSOM
ROBERTSON, JOHN
HAMMIL (?), ZADOC J.
HARDIN, WILLIAM S.
HARRISON, L. C.
ELLIOTT, J.T.
MACKAY, JOHN
TOMSERY (?), V.R.

Page 47
BETTS, ELISHA
TREADWELL, A,
HANSON, G.J.C.
SAULSBURY, J.
POWELL, T.
SAMPLY, T.
HAMILTON, R.P.
MORRISON, JOHN M.
COWAN, W.
QUINN, E. A.
JACKSON, F. S.
HOOLE, B. J.
McCACHRAN, GEORGE

BATES, M. H.
NELSON, E. H.
McLEAN, D. C.
MANN, J. W.
DAVIS, W.L.M.
BARRY, GEORGE S.
HOWARD, JAMES
DALE, R.O.
TURNER, JOHN
McGRUDER, J.T.
REIVES, HENRY
PETTIT, J.W.A.
PACKER, A.
COLBY, JOHN
McKENZIE, W. A.
McKENZIE, A.
PARKER, THOMAS

Page 48
AYMAN, GEORGE M.
McINTOSH
WATTY, M.T.
SPEARMAN, G. H.
GUTHRE, C.F.
ROBISON, A.V.
MOSELY, M.F.
STOWE, S.F.
PARISH, RICHARD
WILLIAMS, J. E.
CATTERVILLE, A.
CANNON, S. R.
SHORTER, R. C.
EMARY, W. J.
OCHTERTONE (?), D.
STOVALL, GEORGE M.
ALEXANDER, EZEKIAL
ALEXANDER, C. M.
KIRKLAND, ASA
McGOWAN, A.
HINES, SAMUEL
DRISKEL, D.
SMITH, R.
ROACH, NATHANIEL
McLEOD, DANIEL
BROWDER, M.A.
MERRIL, A.K.

HARRISON, MOSS
LEDBETTER, JOHN
CHAVIN, JOHN

Page 49
BROWN, L.N.
SANDERS, L.B.
WINSTETTE, J.C.
HALL, JULIUS
CLARK, JOHN
HOLLAND, MOSES
CLARKE, JAMES
VENTRESS, F.
BLANCHET, HENRY
WAYD, JOHN
HALL, NATHANIEL
GRAHAM, JAMES
ATKINSON, W.M.
GALLOWAY, JAMES
HELIMS, AARON
HEARTSUGG, D.
THOMAS, H.
BENTLY, JOHN
GRAHAM, J.H.
McNEIL, HECTOR
CARROL (?), JOHN
MATTHEWS, JOHN
BAILY, JAMES
BENTON, JOHN
THOMAS, JOEL
GOOLSBY, WILLIAM
BASS, ALLIN
SHEPHERD, THOMAS

Page 50
CONDRY, DENNIS
GRIMES, WILLIAM R.
DYKES, SHADRACK
McCALE, DANIEL
BUSH, WILLIAM R.
McKINNON,
RED, ARCHIBALD
BURGESS, DEMPSEY
FLOWERS, ABNER
HAM, JESSE
McRAE, DUNCAN
KIRKLAND, SNOWDON

-1-

BARBOUR COUNTY

MOON, JOHN W.
BISSEL, CURTIS
BINSON, GEORGE W.
HERRING, GRADY
COOPER, WILLIAM
WOOTON, A.
CONDREY, JAMES
HARRISON, JOSIAH
HEATH, ISAAC
HARGROVES, HENRY
PERKINS, JOHN
DAVIS, WILLIAM
DUBOSE, JAMES
BOYLSTON, JOSEPH
MATTHEWS, JAMES
DAY, RODELIN
WILLIAM, O.J.
HELEMS. JOHN
 Page 51
LEWIS, CHARLES
LEONARD, LEO
SHEPHERD, JAMES
VANN, LEONARD
BENTON, RIGHT
WHITE, J. H.
CREAL, WILLIAM
CURRIE, JOHN
YOUNG, WILLIAM
JACKSON, JOHN W.
CURRIE, LAUCHLIN
McLENDON, JOHN G.
RIDGELL, W. J.
WINDHAM, ELIJAH
SQUIRES, WILEY
CHANCE, ARTHUR
SYLVESTER, D.
HAYS, JOHN W.
SPENCER, LEVI
McKAY, STEPHEN
McKAY, C.
ELMORE, SUKE
GUNN, WILLIAM
KAY, HIRAM
BEASON, JOHNATHAN
RANDALL, T. B.
GLOVER, W. C.
WELLBORN, LYCURGUS
 Page 52
BROWN, L---
McINTYRE, JOHN

HICKS, J. B.
ROBERTS, J.W.
COLE, JOSIAH
BARFIELD, GRADY
THOMAS, JOHN
MOORE, JOHN M.
WELLBORN, W. J. M.
MOON, LUCY
McMURRAY, JOHN M.
TICKNOR, J. H.
YOUNG, EDWARD
GEORGE, DANIEL
WALKLY, S. S.
DANFORTH, J. H.
WOODS, CLAYTON R.
DANFORTH, J. C.
CURIE, C. M.
MARTIN, J. G. L.
KIRKPATRICK, E.
BAUGHTON, S. M.
BATTLE, CULLIN
HOPKINS, BANGS
SHEPHERD, EDWARD
SWINNEY, J. L.
PATTERSON, JOHN M.
MATHIAS, JOHN B.
TILLEY, WILLIAM
WILLIS, JOEL
 Page 53
MASSY, J.
LAID, S. J.
HARPER, JESSE
BROWN, N. L.
MADKING, WILLIAM
SUMMERKAMP, F. J. C.
NASH, M. B.
McALLISTER, A.
WILKINSON, SAMUEL
JOHNSON, ARCHIBALD
LITTLE, JOSIAH
ALBRITTON,
MILLER, IRWING
CURRINGTON, H.
CHISNAT, GIBSON
McDOWELL, L. C.
WELLBORN, WILLIAM
FIELD, H. N.
COWART, J. E. F.
HUNTER, J. L.
NOLIN, DANIEL

STARR, JOHN M.
HERRON, THOMAS
MORGAN, JOHN
STONE, WESLY
HICKMAN, JOHN
CREAL, LEVI
GIBBINS, ROBERT
SAMPLY, JONATHAN
BRANTLY, G. W.
 Page 54
BRYANT, WILLIAM
BRITT, MATHEW
HAM, JOHN B.
HARDY, JAMES
CAVINESS, MATTHEW
ABNEY, WILLIAM
WELLBORN, LEVI T.
SHAW, WILLIAM
WELLS, HOWELL
MORRISON, JAMES N
HOOKS, THOMAS J.
SINSON, GEORGE
McSWAN, R. C.
LYSTER, DAVID
STEWART, ALLEN
HALL, JOSIAH A.
*COWAN, W. R.
JAMES, EDWIN
FARLY, J. C.
CASE, GREEN S.
HERROD, JACOB
RAINES, JOHN M.
SMITH, RIDDOCK
CHISNUT, ABRAHAM
GILLIS, DONALD
LEWIS, JAMES M.
SON, GEORGE W.
BECK, STPHEN
HEAD, WILLIAM
ODOM, LEWIS
 Page 55
NASH, ACTON
STALS, SAMUEL
BUSH, MOSES E.
JOHNSON, JOEL J.
SMITH, JAMES B.
HOLLAND, ALLEN
WILSON, A. J.
NORTON, D. A.
NORRIS, GUIN (?)
HITSON, W. R.

*military pensioner -2-

BARBOUR COUNTY

TERRIL, A. H.
SMITH, SION
OTT, WIHLIAM
DANIEL, JOSEPH
SEMMES, M. G.
JERNIGAN, JAMES
GILMORE, JOHN
FAULK, THOMAS
BEACHAMP, WILLIAM
RACHELS, GEORGE
RACHELS, BURRIL
DESHAZO, JOHN C.
PETTY, JOHN

Page 56
PETTY, J. B. F.
FURGUSON, ANGUS
MINCHEN, JOSEPH
JOHNSON, NICHOLAS
BOBBIT, THOMAS
COTTON, AVENT
GRANTHAM, WILLIAM
GLASS, LEVI
LEWIS, AMASA
ROACH, D. M.
BAKER, AUGUSTUS
HOLLMAN, WILLIAM
WHITTLE, MASTON
McCARTY, W. A.
CARGILE, JOHN
SUTTON, CHARLES
CUNNINGHAM, D.
RICHARDS, WILLIAM
REAVIS, ASHIN
BATTLE, CULLIN
McCULLOUGH, H. O.
RICHARDS, JAMES
McNIEL, SAMUEL
SMITH, JACOB
McGILVARY, JAMES

Page 57
KENADY, THOMAS
BROWN, MARK M
CAPERS, GABRIL
TREADWELL, B. F.
STRIPLING, AARON
HILL, A. L.
BELL, JOHN
LANDRUM, GEORGE
DAVIS, JOHN F.
PAULIN, W. L.
BRYANT, MOSES

SANFORD, JOHN A.
BROWN, JOHN M.
CONNER, FRANCIS
GLENN, JAMES E., SR.
HARRIS, S. M.
JACKSON, A. C.
FLAKE, WILLIAM
HOLT, WILLIAM
DANIEL, JAMES L.
McDONALD, J. M.
COOPER, JOSEPH L.
SANFORD, THOMAS J.
SAULS, JANE
SUTTON, DUNCAN
BERRY, MATHEW
CHANDLER, WILLIAM
HOWARD, JOHN J.
SIMPSON, WILLIAM
MOTES, JONATHAN

Page 58
URQUART, NEIL
FROST, ELI
SHEPHERD, J. H.
THARP, BENJAMIN A.
JOHNSON, W. K.
BATES, JOSHUA
ELLIS, JOHN M.
WELLBORN, JOHNSON
CARSON, ADAM
THOMAS, WILLIAM
MARTIN, ROBERT
SEALS, JAMES
CRADOC, JOSEPH P.
WILLIAMS, B. C.
KENT, THEOPHILUS
ALLEN, BENJAMIN
SINQUEFIELD, ASA
McKENZIE, DANNEL
ROBINSON, THOMAS
BARFIELD, MILES
WATSON, GEORGE
DECKER, WILLIAM
DUBOSE, WADE H.
HAYS, ELIJAH
FLOURNOY, THOMAS
MARTIN, MARTIN D.
BOSWICK, J. J.
CABINESS, JESSE M.
GRAVES, JOSEPH D.
JOHNSON, PHILIP

Page 59
THOMAS, T. H.
TRAYWICK, JAMES
KEARNES, GAINS B.
DENT, J. H.
CALDWELL, MILES
STRICKLAND, A.
WADKINS, L.C.
BENNETT, LUKE
McMILLAN, EDWARD
ROUSE, BARNABAS
JOHNSON, JESSE
DILL, ROBERT
GRAY, THOMAS
SHANKS, W. T.
GUNN, ALLIN
BOYD, GIBSON
WILEY, J. McCALEB
WILLIAMS, C. B.
McMURRAY, S. F.
BABB, Z. J.
BALDY, P.H.
SELARS, B. D.
McCRARY, JAMES
BURLISON, S. W.
WHEELER, G. B.
POWELL, GEORGE
JOHNSON, ALLIN
LONG, B. B.
ODOM, H. L.
WALLY, T. J.

Page 60
COWART, WILLIAM
TUCKER, JAMES
BRUNSON, M. A.
DANIEL, MOSES
McGILVARY, DUNCAN
KINER (?)LAWSON J.
KILLINGWORTH, THOMAS
WILLIAMS, WESLEY
HARRISON, WILLIAM
HARRISON, JOHN
FOREHAND, STEPHEN
DUBOSE, JOEL
PHILIPS, COUNCIL
DUBOSE, SARAH (?)
McRAE, A. D.
GRIMES, W. D.
ROE, J. R.
BLAKY, F. L.
FLORNOY, JOSIAH
GLOVER, THOMAS

BARBOUR COUNTY

SLAUGHTER, DANIEL
TORRENCE, ALBERT
McDONALD, COLIN
LOCKLY, E.
WOOD, BILLY
BROOKS, JOHN
ELLIS, WILLIAM
TABOR, SEABORN
LOCKLY, JAMES F.
LOCKLAY, THOMAS
Page 61
McBRYDE, SAMUEL
WORLICK, A.
POPE, R. B.
WILLIAMS, R. W.
WILLIAMS, G.
IVY, ORAN
ELYOT, WILLIAM
AVERETT, MATHEW
WHITE, W. H.
SLAPPY, J. G.
McLENDON, JOHN
NOBLE, WASHINGTON
MOORE, BRYANT
JERNIGAN, H. W.
AVERETTE, WILLIAM
SCREWS, BENJAMIN
CROCKET, JAMES E.
CROSS, BENJAMIN
CARDIN, WILLIAM
RICHARDSON, W. N.
ATHWAY, E. C.
TYUS, J. C.
CUCHESS, W. T.
ALLEN, MARTHA
BOON, JESSE
DENSON. A. C.
MITCHELL. R.
DANIEL, SETH
CANNON, R. J.
GRANBURY, J. B.
Page 62
WILLIAMS, ALBERT
LEWIS, JOHN
COLLINS, A.
ROCKMAN, T. J.
WILKS, JAMES
JONES, SEABORN W.
CULLER, ANGUS
PYRUS, WHEATON
DESHAZO, ROBERT

SARGENT, WILLIAM
MCLEAN, HECTOR
McLEAN, L.
VINCENT, WILEY
WORLD, ELISHA
BARFIELD, ARCHIBALD
SPURLOCK, JOHN
SWAILS, JAMES
MOORE, JACKSON
HAYS, ELIGAH
SPURLOCK, WILLIAM
THARP, WINDHAM
SHEPHERD, THOMAS
LEE, A.
TATE, WILLIAM
BAUGH, JEREMIAH
BLAYDES, ISRAEL
TAYLOR, REDIN
NOLIN, J. B.
WEATHERFORD, JAMES
DUBOSE, SEABORN
Page 63
JOHNSON, WILLIAM
BAKER, JAMES
HOUSTON, EDWARD
GIDDINS, JACOB
WOOD, YOUNG
READ, JOHN
LINDSEY, JAMES
TAYLOR, ISAM
CANNON, WILLIAM
BAKER, JAMES
BAKER, ROBERT
SMITH, D. J.
GIBBENS, STEPHEN
FEAN, MATTHEW
SEARCY, JOHN
LEE, STEPHEN
HENLY, JOHN
PACKER, MOSES
COOPER, A. D.
WALKER, GEORGE
BLAKY, JESSE
JONES, A. R.
WISE, EZEKIEL
BULLOCK, JOHN
FLOYD, THOMAS
JERNIGAN, S. L.
FLOYD, FRANCIS
MANN, PULASKI
PARIS, H. A.

STONE, JOHN
Page 64
VANN, EDWARD W.
PARMER, BENJAMIN
SMITH, JESSE C.
FURGASON, JAMES
BOWDEN, WILLIAM
STEWART, JOHN
GURLISON, A. D.
COTTINGHAM, U.
SEARCY, WILLY
JOINER, NATHAN
ATWELL, JAMES
MANN, W. B.
CRUISE, ARTHUR
WIMBERLY, DAVID
PARRAMORE, JOHN
McMILLAN, ALEXANDER
CAUSY, WILLY
NORTON, JOHN R.
McGILVARY, JOHN
CLEMENT, JAMES
MURPHY, JOHN
GILLINWATER, T.
FOUCH, F. G.
WILLIAMS, JARROD
DESHAZO, R. H.
COUCH, W. C.
SHEPHARD, M. A.
VINCENT, WILY
BURCH, MILTON
CATOSO, JOHN D.
Page 65
JACKSON, JOHN
JACKSON, MARK
TRUMAN, ANDERSON
(or FURMAN)
COOK, WILLIAM
CURRINGTON, R., SR.
CURRINGTON, R.
GRIFFIS, HENRY
FLUMERS, THOMAS
BAKER, SAMUEL
McPHURSON, ARCHIBALD
WHITTEMORE, JAMES
TRUMAN, ROBERT
RAWLS, JOHN
FOLSOM, ELISHA
BARKSDALE, B. R.
SEALS, ARCHIBALD
ELMO, JAMES

BARBOUR COUNTY

BROWDER, J. C.
McINNIS, JOHN
MARTIN, JOHN
BYNUM, JOHN
McDONALD, N.
OLIVER, WILEY
CLACK, JAMES
WARREN, THOMAS, SR.
BALL, HARTWELL
SPENCE, A. T.
JOHNSON, MARTIN
WARREN, BURRIS
WARREN, T. J.
Page 66
McMURRY, W. M.
HAWKINS, JOSHUA
COOK, BENJAMIN R.
WILLIAMS, JOHN L.
HAYS, ROBERT
WILLIAMS, WILLIAM
JUSTICE, BLAKE
GEORGE, EBIN
KINER, T. B.
WHISTELLE, GEORGE
ALLEN, MICAGAH
SPEARS, DAVID
McCALL, ALEXANDER
ANDERSON, JOHN
McRAE, WILLIAM
HERRING, IVY
FRASER, MALCOM
HUTSON, JOSHUA
EDGE, JOHN W.
HERRING, WEST
ELMOR, ALFORD
WILLIAMS, BUCKNOR
DESHAZO, JOHN
NIECE, L. W.
WILLIAMS, FURNEY
STREET, R. H.
NORTON, JAMES R.
FARRIOR, WILLIAM M.
HARPER, A.
CAMPBELL, DANIEL
Page 67
WHEELER, NOAH
COX, JESSE
LOVELACE, S.
BLACK, JAMES
BOGGS, JOHN M.
DANIEL, ROBERT
LOVELESS, WILLIAM

WILLIAMS, ALICE
WHITE, ROBERT
JACKSON, JOHN
LOVELACE, B. J.
COLE, JAMES
PETEY, BENJAMIN F.
McCARREL, JOHN
DUNN, JOHN M.
LEWIS, SEABORN
ARMSTRONG, W. L.
GAUGHT, W. H.
LOCKE, JESSE
FAULK, JAMES
EVANS, WILLIAMS
KENNINGTON, C. W.
HUTSON, ELIGAH
HALL, SAMUEL
GIBSON, JOSEPH
SMITH, LEWIS
HERRING, EDWARD
ARMSTRONG, L.
KILPATRICK, WILLIAM
RUMPH JAMES
Page 68
TOMPKINS, H. M.
HENRY, WILLIAM
VENTERS, NANCY
WALLIS, DILILAH
LIGHTNER, MICHAEL
COTTON, RICHARD
SIMMES, A. J.
DESHAZO, NANCY
CASSY, JAMES
LEWIS, BENJAMIN
JERNIGAN, MILLEY
CRUTCHFIELD, E.
COSTON, OWIN
MONTCRIEF, GUILFORD
WADKINS, JONAS
FRANCHAM, GEORGE W.
HOLLAND, JOHN
PULLIN, ROBIN
PULLIN, LEWIS
JACOBS, RICHARD
ROBINSON, A. J.
CULPEPPER, NATHAN
PARMER, GEORGE
GIBHART, SARAH
McKENZIE, J. G.
BROOKS, ESAU
ELLIS, GEORGE W.
FORT, ISAAC

DANIEL, JAMES
FLAKE, SEABORN
Page 69
GLENN, JOHN B.
MICHELL, JULIUS
ALLEN, JAMES, JR.
STANFORD, E.
ALLEN, JOHN W.
SLATTER, JOHN J.
DENARD, JARED
TREUTLEN, G. E.
FORTSON, T. W.
JACKSON, ROBERT
JACKSON, ANDREW
PITTS, A. W.
RAIFORD, J. M.
CADE, GUILFORD
DYKES, ISAIH
HOLT, THOMAS L.
MORRISON, R. T.
LEALAND, H.
BENNETTE, R.
DANIEL, WILLIAM
BATILE, ANDREW
JACKSON, TOM (?)
RIEVIS, T. H. B.
SEYMORE, JOHN R.
UPSHAW, L.
CRAIG, R.
CONUS, GEORGE
FRASER, ANDERSON
WILLIS, ROBERT
WRIGHT, MEREDITH
Page 70
GAULDELONG, WILLIAM
McDONALD, J. B.
THORNTON, WILLIAM
THORNTON, E.
BRYANT, OWIN
CARTER, SAMUEL
LAMAR, JOHN O.
SANFORD, A. M.
CUSICE (?), ISAIH
SANFORD, T. C.
HARDIN, HEZIKIAH
DAY, ROBERT
DAY, HENRY
MUNROE, JAMES
DELOACH, W. B.
McLEAN, DANIEL
GILCHRAST, GILBERT
DUBOSE, E. E.

BARBOUR COUNTY

MILLS, C. C.
LANG, JAMES M.
LEE, FERDINANT
HILL, B. M.
DUBOSE, W. M.
RAGAN, E. J.
SMITH, C.
ASKEW, BENJAMIN
TOMPKINS, DR.
SCOTT, B. C.
McCORKILE, SAMUEL
PICKET, L. B.
Page 71
JENKINS, H. J.
HEFFLIN, WILLIAM
STATON/SLATON, PLEASANT
FASON, THOMAS
JERRING, JOHN
TRAMMEL, JAMES J.
CUACH, NOAH
MADDOX, JOHN F.
BROOM. B.
PERSON, TRUDINE
PERSON, AMOS J.
MICHELL, JOHN
NEWBURY, JAMES
BALDWIN, KINCHEN
FAISON, W.
BRADLEY, S. C.
HARPER, WILLIAM
ECHOLS, CLARKE
HAMILTON, JOEL
BALDY, MARTIN
ALSTON, JOSHUA
BROWN, ELIZABETH
TRUMAN, JOHN
STREETER, S. W.
LONG, C. P.
STREETER, R.
CONNER, M. C.
SAUNDERS, N.
COBB, JOSEPH
BOWERS, JOHN
Page 72
McINTOSH, W.
KING, WILLIAM
McKASKEL, JOHN
MARTIN, GIBSON
McINTOSH, W.M.
WATSON, G.
BALLARD, WILLIAM

McGILVARY, JOHN
McINTOSH, DANIEL
GRIGGS, ROBERT
KENADY, JESSE
GACHET, NICHOLAS
GAY, LEWIS
HAYS, SEABORN
STREETMAN, W.
JOHNSON, JAMES F.
GREENWOOD, SAMUEL
VICARS, JAMES R.
McGEHEE, SAMUEL
MARTIN, WILLIAM
PEEBLES, HOWELL
NEWMAN, SAMUEL
JETIE, CHARLES
FEAGAN, S.
McLEAN, J. D.
STRIPLAND, WILLIAM
STRIPLAND, G. W.
BEVERLY, JOHN
HARDIN, F.
CAMERON, LAUCHLIN
Page 73
FILE, W. B.
GIBSON, WILLIAM C.
CASWELL, JOSHUA
WATSON, TOM
WATSON, ELIZABETH
BULLARD, JOHN W.
FORD, GARDNER
FORD, WILLIAM
BARON, HENRY
PICKET, THOMAS
DORMAN, MASON
BABB, WILLIAM
HOLSTIN, HIRAM
RAINS, F.
STRIPLAND, JAMES
CALLOWAY, DANIEL
SMITH, NEIL
SMITH, JOHN
McNEIL, NEIL
VINCENT, C. W.
BOYD, JAMES
MEDLEY, J. H.
McMILLAN, DANIEL
MALLOY, DUNCAN
FAULK, LEVIN
DANSBY, DANIEL M.
HILLE, NATHANUEL

Page 74
COLEMAN, WILLIAM
COOK, S.
COOK. B.
McMILLAN, JOHN
GORE, SIMPSON
SAUNDERS, JAMES
BYRAN, J. L.
WILLIS, A.
KENADY, T.
LINDSEY, D.
BOYER, HENRY
KIRKPATRICK, E.
SHARP, WILLIAM
KENDADY, THOMAS
FAULK, LORENZO
RAUSE, LOUIS
BIGFORD, SAMUEL
MEDLEY, E.
STUBBS, S.
LEWIS, E.
HAYS, WILLIAM
BOYETT, JESSE
URY, JAMES
POLLARD, ELIAS
WIRGHT, J.
PIPKIN, JESSE
PIPKIN, HAYWOOD
ROGERS, P.
COOK, ARCHIBALD
POTTS, J.
CARTER, S.
CARTER, E.
PHILIPS, ISAM
Page 75
LEE, DURHAM
MIRAN, M
HAW, WILLIAM
SMITH, JOHN R.
BATES, WILSON M.
TURNER, N. W.
EFIRD, T. C.
LEWIS, NANCY
MANN, ULATES
BELL, JOHN
JEARN, JAMES
EMERSON, B. H.
SIMS, JOEL
EFIRT, LUCY
HERRING, JOHN
ROE, SIMPSON
WARD, SILICUS ?

BARBOUR COUNTY

LANCASTER, L.
NEWMAN, H.
CURRIN, M.
NEWMAN, WILLIAM
McPHERSON, J.
SHARP, WILLIAM
McLENDON, WILLIAM
McLAIN, J. M.
BALL, J. F.
GRUBBS, WILLIAM
JONES, JOHN
DOUGLAS, JOHN
McNEIL, NANCY
Page 76
SAMPLEY, JACOB
WILKES, ELIAS
AUSTIN, JOHN
STEVENSON, S.
CASSY, LEMUEL
FARRIOR, JOHN
LEE, NEEDHAM
McCLURE, T. C.
KUTS, M.
FAULK, H.
NISBET, THOMAS
MOTES, CARY
ROUNDTREE, CALVIN
KING, GARY
WATSON, D.
GRUBBS, ADAM
HANCOCK, WILLIAM
JOHNS, FRANCIS
DANSBY, JOSHUA
MINSHAW, JACOB
DANBY, WILLIAM
FAULK, N.
FAULK, G.
BIZZEL, HARRISON
FAULK, RIGHT
THOMPSON, RHODA
EVANS, JOHN
JOHNSON, WILLIAM
POWELL, D.
BIZZELL, BENNETT
Page 77
BYRD, EDWARD
SAULS, R.
BYRD, R.
BYRD, H.
CAIN, JOHN
GILMAN, J. H.
BLACK, WILLIAM

MINSHAW, JOHN
NICHOLS, GEORGE
MINSHAW, ISAAC
MINSHAW, JACOB
WIGGINS, E.
SMILLY, E.
GARNER, JOHN
DANOR, THOMAS M.
ANDREWS, ELIGH
COOLEY, J.
HUTCHINSON, WILLIAM
WINDHAM, A.
SAUCIE, JOHN
SAUCIE, L. D.
DANSBY, JOHN
SUTTON, JESSE
MINSHAW, NATHAN
PHILIPS, R. W.
THOMPSON, L.
FAULK, R.
WARD, M.
FAULK, H., SR.
WOODBY, W. L.
Page 78
BIZZELL, H.
CLACK, E.
STEPHENS, S. A.
GRANT, THOMAS W.
CAMPBELL, JOHN
THARP, R.
FARMER, R.
DICKSON, WILLIAM
MCKELLAR, NEIL
McINNIS, JOHN
RAMSEY, JOSEPH
CHAMBERS, JOHN H.
McDANIEL, D.
KETCHUM, DAVID
COPEY, L.
BANKS, ROBERT
McINNIS, MILES
HEARN, JOHN
McKAY, DANIEL
CAMPBELL, W. D.
TEAL, ALLEN
SAMPLEY, BENJAMIN
SHIPMAN, JAMES
MAYBERRY, NANCY
DANIEL, JOHN
McNAIR, ALEXANDER
McLEOD, HUGH
NILVELS, O.

CORMACK, WILLIAM
WARD, A.
Page 79
HALLMAN, A.
SIMPKINS, SAMUEL
LASTER, JAMES
FAULK, JAMES
BASS, JAMES
McLENDON, P.
SKIPPER, JOHN
SHAW, WILLIAM
PASSMAN, JOHN
CURRIE, DANIEL
JONES, SEABORN
DIGGINS, STEPHEN
HUNTER, M.
CHAMBERS, D.
CANNON, ALEXANDER
CAMPBELL, ABNER
CAMPBELL, JOSHUA
MORTON, T. B.
McLEAN, JOHN
UTSEY, JACOB
BRYAN, D. O.
SITROUT, W.
LANDRUM, R.
BURHAM, JOHN
OWINS, JOSEPH
TINDALL, JOHN
WILKINS, J.
GALBREATH, D.
MURRY, JOHN
HOLLINS, JAMES
Page 80
MITCHELL, JOHN
McKITHEN, R.
PINKERTON, DAVID
PINKERTON, ULEN
WOOD, JAMES
LEWIS, JOHN
BAUMAN, B.
BAUMAN, BENJAMIN
BALLARD, B.
BAUMAN, BRYANT
BAUMAN, JOSHUA
RICHARDS, ROBERT
CRAWFORD, ALEXANDER
HOLMES, WILLIAM
SEARCY, BENJAMIN
BROWNING, JESSE
AYER, SAMUEL
BAXLEY, JOHN B.

BARBOUR COUNTY

WILLIAMS, JOHN A.
PURCELL, G.
MURPHY, WILLIAM
BLACKWELDER, A.
LEE, TIMOTHY
DYKES, R.
THOMAS, ELLIOT
THOMAS, JAMES
PEOPLES, D. H.
BRELAND, SAMUEL
CONDRY, G. M.
AYERS, WILLIAM
Page 81
CONDRY, JOHN
VALENTINE, L.
SHUMAKE, E. H.
KING. H.
CREAL, THOMAS
THORNE, NICHOLAS
BAXLEY, SOLOMON
KELLY, LAZARUS
WILLIAMS, JOHN
FARMER, BENJAMIN
FARMER, ABEL
HOLMES, A.
THOMAS, JOHN
DUBOSE, J.
LAVENDER, B.
HOLMES, JOHN
READER, WILLIAM
READER, NATHAN
SMITH, SIMON
HOLLAND, JESSE
THOMAS, JOHN W.
THOMAS, WILLIAM
HAIGLER, THOMAS
THOMAS, JOEL
THOMAS, MORTON
DUNLAP, MARY
HOLMES, MOSES
HANEY, JOHN C.
Page 82
HOWELL, E.
FADYERS, D. M.
RIDER, D. R.
CHAMPION, W. J.
MILLER. F. H.
COX, EDWARD C.
HERRING, A.
HIND, RICHARD
FAIRCLOTH, R.
HEAD, RICHARD, SR.

CADENHEAD, JOHN
DEWITT (?), T.F.B.
LEWIS, H. W.
VIARS (?), WILLIAM R.
NORTON, WILLIAM D.
GILLIS, ALEX. C.
WILLIAMS, A. D.
HODGES, GEORGE C.
BUSBY, JOHN
NORTON, JOHN W.
CALLOWAY, JOSEPH
HOLMES, M. G.
MOORE, HENRY
GREEN, HENELY
BENNETT, R.
WARREN, ODIA C.
BAKER, L.
KEENER, T. F.
KILPATRICK, WILLIAM H.
Page 83
DAVIS, ELISHA
POWELL, R. B. T.
MORRISON, D.
HOBDY, R.
WADE, JAMES
BARROW, T. T.(or BREWER)
BRYANT, JOHN, SR.
MCDONALD H.
BRADLEY, ROBERT
FOLSOM, HENRY
COLLINS. W.
KING, HARRY
DONOHUE, ELLIS
SMITH, WILLIAM
HARPER, J. M.
BURLESON, AARON
THOMAS, JOHN
HOWELL, E. D.
KNIGHT, WILLIAM
LEE, NEEDHAM (the older.)
LEE, NEEDHAM (younger)
McCALL, R
HOLLIMAN, A.
FLURNOY, JONAH
LIPSCOMB, WILLIAM H.
PURRSELL, H.
DYKES, SETH
TALLY, SUSAN
WILKINS, WILLIAM
Page 84
WOOD, E.
BROOM, ELIZABETH

BAIRD, B. C.
BEVEL, THOMAS
MURPHY, JOHN
McLENDON, A.
McLEOD, A.
McLEOD, R.
GRISSEL, M.
GILLIS, M.
PEARSON, B. F.
HAMMOCK, T.
HOLLY, B.
DURHAM, N.
BROWN, DOLLY
SNIPS, W. H.
FRALEY, WILLIAM
PORTER, MAHALA

Total population:
11,797

-8-

BENTON COUNTY

formed 1832

Page 5
WALDRIP, A. D.
CUFNER, PETER
BANE, ROBERT
ROBERTSON, ZECHARIAH
DEARMAN, JOHN
DEARMAN, ISABELLA
DEARMAN, JONAS
DEARMAN, JAMES
YORK, RILEY
MILLER, BRIEN
GAINES, THOMAS
EDGE, THOMAS
HOWARD, JOHN
CRUMPTON, DAVID
MATHES, ESAKIEL
NEELY, VICTOR
FLOYD, ELSA
SANDERS, DENISY
PRUITT, PHILIP
BROWN, CHRISTOPHER
PERKINS, H. W.
RIGHT, B. M.
ELSTON, JOHN
GAINS, THOMAS
ELSTON, ALLERS
TRAYLOR, G. W.
BAKER, SOLOMON
PHIPS, SAMUEL
COUCH, MARTIN
WEIR, JOHN R.

Page 6
TEAGUE, ELIJAH
WILLIAMS, JAMES A.
MAYS, JAMES
SMITH, JOHN
PHIRY, HENRY
WILKERSON, WILLIAM
LANSDAL, AARON
LANSDEL, EZEKIAH
WILKERSON, M.
BUITT, HENRY
THOMPSON, THOMAS
PRUITT, HALE
MATTOX, AARON
SMITH, MARTHA
CARY, WILLIAM
PIKETON, PARMENUS
WILKERSON, LEMUEL
BURCH, ALLEN
PILKERTON, JOHN
TEAGUE, ELIJAH S.

BURGES, JOSEPH
TEAGUE, SAMUEL
PRESNELL, JOHN M.
POSEY, WILLIAM W.
CAHEL, AQUILLA
THOMPSON, ROBERT
PILKERTON JOHN
VERNONS, G. W.
WILLIAMS, HALL
BURCH, HIRAM

Page 7
BURCH, REUBEN
TEAGUE, JAMES P.
TURNER, ELIZABETH
BEDWELL, LREOY
ABERCROMBY, ISAAC
DOWDY, JOHN
PRUITT, SAMUEL
BUCHANAN, WILLIAM H.
PRUITT, JOHN
PRUITT, SAMUEL C.
BARKER, JOHN
BARKER, WILLIAM
ROPER, JOSEPH T.
PRUITT, RANSOM
HARRIS, WILLIAM
REID, SAMUEL
YORK, NATHAN
COFFY, ABNER
DEPRIEST, WILLIAM
HARRIS, W. R.
KIRKPATRICK, JOHN
RUTHERFORD, JAMES
DEPRIEST, JOSEPH
PEARCE, LIHON (?)
BARRETT, WILLIAM A.
PRUITT, JAMES W.
CURRY, WILLIAM M.
PRUITT, WILLIS
CHANDLER, HAMPTON
ROBERTS, STEP

Page 8
BURGES, WILLIAM
EDWARDS, WILLIAM
CLAYTON, LEMUEL
BURGES, JOHN
BARKER, JOHN C.
GRAHAM, JAMES
*POSEY, HEZEKIAH (R.S.)
RHODAM, FRANCIS
BLALOCK, S. J.

HANLEY, THEOPHILUS
BROWN, WILLIAM R.
KING, WILLIAM G.
NORMAN, CHARLES
ROPER, CHARLES
MOBLEY, WILLIAM
TURNIPSEED, W. B.
WORTHINGTON, THOMAS
MARABLE, MATTHEW
AMERINE, HENRY
MAYFIELD, JAMES
*PRESNELL, JOHN (R.S.)
DOWDY, MICHAEL
PRESNELL, WILLIAM C.
DENNY, NATHAN
McKORLEY, SAMUEL
DEFUR, JOHN
GADDIS, GEORGE
MALY, HENRY F.
MUSELWRITE, A.
BURCH, WILLIAM

Page 9
BENEFIELD, HIRAM
HENRY, GEORGE
WALKER, DAVID
CHALKER, RACHEL
KENEDY, MARY
WILLIAMSON, WILLIAM S.
McCAHRAN, H. M.
WHITE, WILLIAM
REID, HENRY T.
ARNOLD, JAMES
WILLIAMSON, WILLIAM
WILLIAMSON, MAT.
REID, ASA
MAYFIELD, GILES
MAYFIELD, BATTLE
GAINS, WILLIAM
GAINS, ELISABETH
LANTRON, THEOPHILUS
THRESHER, WILLIAM
LOT, ELLIS
THRESHER, JAMES
CLAK, ZECHARIAH
WILLIAMSON, WASH.
THRESHER, DELILA
DODSON, EDMUND
ELLISON, ALVA T.
HOSLEY, JOHN B.
BEARD, HIRAM
BEARD, JOHN

*military pensioner

BENTON COUNTY

OWENS, ELEANOR
HORTON, EPTHA
Page 10
ALBRIGHT, NICHOLAS
LITTLE, SILAS
BOLIN, MARTIN
COCHRAN, WILLIAM
HORTON, JOHN H.
BOWMAN, DRURY M.
TENNISON, MAT.
TENNISON, COOK M.
KEMP, JAMES
POUNDS, NEWMAN
BOWMAN, ROBERT
CHANDLER, RICHARD
BENTLY, JOHN
LOTT, MARK
LOTT, MARK, SR.
LOTT, CIRAM
HIRD, GEORGE
WALLACE, ALEX.
OWENS, DANIEL M.
PLATT, OSBURN
MCGEE, JAMES P.
OWENS, JAMES M.
HIRD, RICHARD
MOORE, JACOB
ALBRIGHT, JACOB
ALBRIGHT, WILLIAM
GIBSON, WILLIAM
ALBRIGHT, ELI
BENTLY, ISAAC
Page 11
WALLACE, PATSY
BENTLY, AMELIA
McCAHER, ROBERT
CHALER, ROBERT
DOBS, SILAS
SISMORE, WILLIAM
BARNET, AMOS
BARNET, ISAAC
BARNET, JOHN
WILLIAMSON, PORTER
BROWN, JOHN
ISELL, JOHN
KERR, ISAAC
SKINNER, HOWARD
PATRICK, WILLIAM
TAYLOR, ABNER T.
CLEMENTS, ANDREW
CLEMENTS, P.
LITTLE, ISAAC

LITTLE, JAMES M.
BOWMAN, WILLIAM H.
BOWMAN, EZEKIEL
HARRIS, RICHARD
GUTHERY, HENRY
INGRAM, MARTIN
BARKER, EPHRAIM
BROWN, WILLIAM
BARKER, EPHRAIM M.
BROWN, EDMUND
JACKSON, SOLOMON H.
Page 12
BROWN, LARKIN R.
JACKSON, JOHN M.
PERRY, JOSHUA
BROWN, JAMES
PERRY, DANIEL
DEASON, WILLIAM
HONEYCUTT, JOHN
HOOPER, REUBEN
EZELL, CATHARINE
BROWN, JOSEPH
DUNCAN, WILLIAM
GRAHAM, JESSE
KELLY, WILLIAM
GRAHAM, JESSE
KING, WILLIAM
MITCHEL, SEBORNE
HOOPER, OBADIAH
*WATKINS, JAMES
WATTS, JAMES
*TOLBERT, SAMUEL
WATKINS, MATTHEW
WALLACE, WILLIAM
WILLIAMS, WILLIAM
GESHER, WILLIAM
DUAHOW, MARY
COATS, LEMUEL
COATS, DAVID
COATS, WILLIAM A.
SALTER, JOHNSTON
VINES, BUTLER
Page 13
CLAYTON, STEPHEN
LACKEY, SARAH
AMELINE, WILLIAM P.
MABRY/MALORY, WILLIAM
SMITH, JOHN B.
POPE, JOHN P.
TATUM, JOHN W.
TATUM, WILLIAM
LAMBERT, THOMAS

COWAN, DAVID
WALDEN, PETER
RICHARDSON, ALFRED
STEWART, REDMOND
PRISOCK, ADAM
BEAN, MARGARET
BEAN, LEMUEL
WOODS, WILLIAM
SCOTT, AMOS
RYAN, JOHN M.
POSEY, WILLIAM
PUTNAM, JOHN
WILLINGHAM, WM.
CUMLY, PLEASANT
McMICHAELS, RICHARD
LANDERS, ABRAHAM
LANDERS, JOHN
Page 14
PATY, JOHN
BEECHAM, LEVI
HENSON, WILLIAM
DOSS, WILLIAM B.
McCALUM, J.
McCALUM, ANSEL
DUNN, WILLIAM
JOHNSTON, COLIER
DAVIS, WILLIAM W.
CAMP, THOMAS
DUNN, JOHN
DUNN, SILAS
WALKER, GARLAND
GRIFFITH, WM. V.
MISELL, LEEK
LANE, JESSE
MULLINS, SALISBURY
MILLER, D.M.
MULLINS, WILLIAM
BRADFORD, SAMUEL
ANDREWS, DAVID
DUNN, JOHN, SR.
DUNN, BANEY
WALL, JESSE
TATUM, JOSEPH
McBEE, ISAM
LANE, WILLIAM M.
LEEK, JOHN B.
MOORE, WILLIAM
BEASLEY, WILLIAM
Page 15
CROWNOVER, JOSEPH
VINTNERS ?, SOLOMAN
McKAY, REUBEN

*military pensioner

BENTON COUNTY

JONES, JAMES W.
TOMASON, JOHN
CROWNOVER, ME--ble
WALKER, WILLIAM B.
LEATH, JOSIAH
LEATH, HARRISON
LEATH, JAMES P.
BOYD, WILLIAM
LEWIS, JOCK
HAMBRIGHT, ANNY
HORTON, BENJAMIN
MORAGNER, JOHN S.
SAMS, JOHN A.
BASLY, DAVIS
BOLIN, A.
BROWN, RICHARD
REID, WILLIAM P.
ADAMS, GREEN
HESTER, G. B.
LOGAN, THOMAS
HESTER, MARY
CUNNINGHAM, MARK
GREENLEE, SHARECK
HORNER, MARY
TILTON, ELISABETH
MELTON, PHILIP
Page 16
BEASLY, JOHN
SMITH, MATTHEW
BRADFORD, RANDOLPH
BLACK, JOHN
HANDY, JOHN
PERRY, THOMAS S.
ALFRED, BALLY
HALL, EDMOND
BLACK. N. D.
NIGHT, JOSEPH
LEATHERWOOD, AQUILLA
JONES, WILEY W.
LILLE, JAMES
PERRY, A. G.
SMITH, JOHN J.
SMITH, JOHN
TEDWELL, JOHN
CHADWELL, A. H.
ODUM, HEZEKIAH
FROST, SNOWING
CADWELL, JOHN G.
BREEDEN, GEORGE
BAKER, HENRY
BAKER, PETER

McRIGHT, WILLIAM
JOHNSTON, JOHN
HINES, SIMEON
HINES, NANCY
HINES, LUCINDA
Page 17
ROBINSON, ADAM
BURCH, WILLIAM C.
HOLLINS, JANE
BAKER, MICHAEL
BAKER, DAVID
JOHNSTON, LUCINDA
JOHNSTON, SAMUEL
GOODLETT, LAHON
LAWSON, JAMES
SHEHERD, THOMAS T.
PROCTOR, SAMUEL
HINES, DONAVIN
BLEDSOE, JOHN B.
CAROTHERS, WILLIAM
STANSEL, THOMAS
BROWN, WILLIAM
WATTS, BARTON
TEAGUE, JOSHUA
WILLIAMS, RICHARD
HARRIS, ROBERT
PEARSE, EDMUND
LETT, LEASH
CASELBARY, WILLIAM
CURRIER, RICHARD
HENRY, WILLIAM
LOGAN, WILLIAM
EUBANKS, ELIJAH
EUBANKS, WILLIAM
HOLLY, MITCHEL
Page 18
RAKER, GILBERT
DIFFY, WILLIAM
HARRISTON, M.M.
STEPES, GEORGE
ROBINSON A. C.
BANCROFT, D. C.
ADAMS, ANDREW
ADAMS, JAMES
ANDERHOLE, JACOB
SUTTON, L. U.
PREVETT, JAMES
TAYLOR, ABSALOM
MATTHES, GEORGE W.
ESTELL, WILLIAM H.
HAYNES, AARON

RUSH, THOMAS
RECINE, B.
BLACK, JAMES
WILLIS, WILOLIAM W.
SPENCER, JOHN
FORNEY, JACOB
LEWIS, CHARLES
ARNOLD, L. N.
SMITH, E. L.
WHITE, JOHN H.
JONES, E. G.
WILKINS, ANDERSON
HINDMAN, THOMAS C.
HOKE, JOHN D.
WILSON, WILLIAM
GRANT, I. F.
SAMSON, JOHN
Page 19
HOLLINGSWORTH, W. B.
HARRIS, JESSE
KELLY, WILLIAM C.
LAIRD, WILLIAM
HERNDON, EDWARD
FOSTER, EDWARD
FOSTER, JOHN
WOODWARD, E. L.
FLEMMING, GEORGE
MARTIN, WILLIAM B.
GREENE, C. A.
WALKER, THOMAS A.
BROWN, MORDICA
FRANCIS, JAMES C.
STONE, MICHAEL
MORRIS, WADE
SUBLETTE, CALDWELL
LUSTRE, STERLING R.
LUSTRE, CHAPPEL N.
WILSON, JOSIAH
FLEMMING, WILLIAM H.
THARD ?, GILLUM
STINER, JOSEPH
HADEN, JAMES N.
HOOPER, ELIAS A.
McADAMS, R. E. W.
McADAMS, J. T.
STINER, JACOB
NISBETT, JOHN
LINDLEY, ELIZABETH
Page 20
MORGAN, GEORGE
LAYSE, DANIEL

BENTON COUNTY

SNOW, FIELDING
MAHONY, STEPHEN M.
McCALPIN, ROBERT
BURRUS, RUSSELL
BULLSIDGE? HENRY
McGLINNIS, LAWSON
FLEMMING, ROBERT
DOUTHAL, H. V.
SMITH, GIDEON
CUNNINGHAM, E.
BLACK, MITCHEL
RINEHART, MARY
BRYANT, SAMUEL
NORRIS, NANCY
CANTRELL, AARON
LENNAHAN, PETER
MARION, HENRY W.
OREAR, WILLIAM
GRANT, G. R.
PERRY, AARON
SORELLS, W. I.
HOLLINGSWORTH, BENJAMIN
DALE, GEORGE
MORELAND, WOOD
GANSS, JSOEPH
YOUNG, PLEASANT
Page 21
GREENE, THOMAS
HAFFORD, W. C.
NELSON, SAMUEL
CHILDRISS, HENRY
MARSH, KAEMAN
SCOTT, WILLIAM
SHAMBLIN, J.
PRATER, JOHN B.
BORDEN? JOHN H.
WEAVER, LEVI
GREEN, WILLIAM
HARRIS, WASSON
JOHNSON, BENJAMIN
GREENE, SAMUEL
WELLS, ROSAGILE
COBLER, SAMUEL
EPPS, RICHARD
DAVIS, MICAJAH
BOYD, JOHN
PALMORE, ELIZABETH
SHIPPEN, JAMES V.
MILLER, WILLIAM B.
BROOKS, CATHARINE
MILLER, ROBERT

MILLER, RUTH
CHAMBERS, SARAH
NELSON, WILLIAM
McLELLAN, JOHN
McLELLAN, DAVID
Page 22
BUTLER, JAMES
ASHLEY, JOSHUA
MORRISON, ARCHIBALD
THACKERSON, RICHARD
ABLES, MOSES
McQUAIG, MACON
HENDERSON, WILLIAM
CHAMBERS, JOHN
HOLCOMBE, MOSES
HUNT, HANSEL
SIMMONS, JAMES
PIKE, JOHN
MAYFIELD, FANNY
ALLSUP, THOMAS
GARRETT, MARY T.
ALLSUP, THOMAS
DERKINS, JOHN
ELLIOTT, CHARLES
ELLIOTT, GEORGE
HOWELL, ELI
CASSON, JOHN T.
WILLIAMS, THOMAS R.
SHAMBLIN J.
LARRISON, PETER
LINLEY, SAMUEL
ALLSUP, HENRY
DARKINS, SAMUEL
STUART, THOMAS
JONES, JOHN W.
Page 23
ACKEN, WILLIAM L.
MORRISON, MARY
JOHNSON, MARY
DONALDSON, RACHEL
ACKIN, AMOS
WEBB, MICAJAH
TURNER, THOMAS
HARBOW, JOHN
ELLIOTT, MOSES
ELLIOTT, WILLIAM
GORE, WILLIS
WILLIAMS, ISAAC
BOLE, JOHN
DOBB, PETER
RAY, ANDREW

VAN MOSBY, FOUNTAIN
LECROSS, SARAH
OWENS, ELI B.
VARDENA, LANFORD
WISMAN, JOSHUA
PARKER, THOMAS
THORP, JAMES
SHEARER, JOSEPH
GRAHAM, WILLIAM R.
SHEARER, ISAM
SHEARD, WILLIAM
GRAHAM, GEORGE W.
GRAHAM, ALEXANDER
PINCKET, WILEY
Page 24
LIVLY, ROBERT
WELLS, THOMAS
PUCKET, ALEXANDER
GRIFFITH, BENJAMIN
LAIN, WILLIAM
BURRUS, ANTHONY
NABORS, BENJAMIN N.
NABORS, THOMAS
SIMMONS, WILLIAM
NIGHT, JOHN
DOWDLE, ROBERT J.
RENFRO, WILLIAM
PRATER, JAMES
MOORE, JAMES
PARISH, ISAAC
ALLEN, EDWARD
JORDAN, HEZEKIAH
TREADWELL, STEPHEN
SCOTT, DUNLOP
BOOSER, ADAM
BOOSER, JOHN
BOOSER, HENRY
MUCKLEROY, ELIJAH
MUCKLEROY, ANTHONY
McBEE, JESSE
MUCKLEROY, JAMES
NABORS, THOMAS
MOORE, JOHN
Page 25
ROBERTS, RICHARD
ROWLAND, R. D.
TAYLOR, JOHN
ALLEN, ISAAC
GAINING, MICAJAH
REMLEY, JOHN H.
SMITH, JAMES

BENTON COUNTY

McINTOSH, LAUGHLIN
KEMBLE, PETER W.
BECKUM, JESSE
CARPENTER, WYLY
HILL, JOHN
RUAKS, WILLIAM.
RENFRO, WILLIAM A.
TITTLE, HIRAM
GLOVER, WYLY
CANNON, THEOPOLUS
CANNON, JAMES
HOLLINSWORTH, JOHN
GRADY, JONATHAN
MARTIN, HENRY L.
WOOD, JAMES
OLIVER, JOHN W.
ABERNATHY, MILES W.
DALE, JOSEPH
WADKINS, HENRY
ONEAL, GRAY
POE, JAMES W.
POE, JOHN J.
Page 26
POE, STEPHEN
GEORGE, JAMES
GEORGE, DAVID
HONEY, JOHN
HONEY, WILLIAM
ANDREWS, JESSE
BROOKS, ABEL with TOBIAS
    HONEY, R.S. in household
NUNNALLY, DANIEL
TALLEY, SAMUEL
ALEXANDER, A.
TREDWELL, DAVID
TREDWELL, JAMES
SMITH, FRANCIS B.
NELSON, STOCKLEY
McDOW, DAVID
BAILEY, HIXON
THOMPSON, JAMES N.
WOODLEY, CALEB
WOODLEY, TEMPERANCE
PEARCE, MARY
SANDERS, JOHN
CROSS, HEZEKIAH
CROSS, W. D.
REYNOLDS, ANSIL
GAINEY, PENDLETON
GAINEY, DORMAN
MEAD, THORNTON

ROBERTS, ELIZABETH
LEBIN?, COURTNEY
Page 27
LEBIN?, F.
ROBERTS, JOHN
BROWNING, YOUNG H.
HARRIS, THOMAS J.
BLACK, JOHN E.
CHANDLER, LITTLEBERRY
ROBINSON, MARY
HATTON, E.
ALEDANDER, THOMAS
SUMMEY?, GEORGE
YOUNG, JOHN J.
JOHNSON, HUGH
HOKE, DANIEL
HOKE, ALFRED
FRENCH, GIDEON
BLAKE, JAMES
REEVES, RANSOM
SMPLES, JEREMIAH
TANKERLEY, BASIL
WYLY, B. C.
CHANDLER, JOHN
REEVES, RICHMOND
HUEY, SEABORNE J.
WALLS, GEORGE J.
DOUTHARD, JAMES
YOUNG, JOHN N.
PINSON, JOSEPH
RAELY, AXUM
REEVES, EDMOND
Page 28
BROWNING, W. L.
OWENS, JOHN
FORD, BAILY
CHANDLER, JOEL
ADERHOLD, AB.
*CHANDLER JOHN (R.S.)
BINT, HUDSON
ALLEN, CHARLES
MORRIS, GEORGE L.
DOZIER, DENNIS
VESTAL, ISAAC
DALE, DAVID,
GLOVER, GOERGE
GLOVER, JAMES
SULLIVAN, JOEL
BONDS, VARDY
BONDS, MOSES
WILLIAMS, NATH.

COLLIAR. V.
BLAKE, WILLIAM
McKORKLE, JAMES
SAMPLES, LEAH
HOLYFIELD, JOHN
McMAHAN, BENJAMIN
FARRAR, JAMES
TINGLE, SOLOMON
REAVES, NATHAN
BLACK, CARLISLE
VINES, BENJAMIN
Page 29
SIDES, CHARLES
HENLEY, JAMES
McLEMORE, DANIEL
COLE, JAMES
SHARP, FRANCIS
WHITES, JAMES T.
DAVIS, JEREMIAH C.
JOHNSTON, WILLIAM
SIMMONS JAMES L.
KELLY, RICHARD B.
MORRISON, ROBERT
WILLIAMS, JOSEPH
PRUIT, HATTON
JOHNSON. M. P.
PORTER, JOHN H.
WILSON, JOSEPH H.
ANDERSON, DANIEL
DODSON, WILLIAM
KIER, ELIJAH
MATTOX, HOPE H.
KELLY, CHRISTOPHER
CROZIER, ARTHUR
WALKER, WILLIAM
BRITTAIN, WILLIAM P.
PRUIT, ASENATH
THOMPSON, JOHN L.
WILLIAMSON, WILLIAM
FAUGHSEND?, SAMUEL
MORRING, EDWARD
Page 30
ANSEL, HEZEKIAH
HANK, ENOCH
WHITESIDES, JONATHON
HARRIS, FRANCIS M.
GIVENS, WILLIAM
YOUNG, FRANCIS L.
ALEXANDER, SAMUEL B.
ARNOLD, ALBERT
REEVES, WILLIAM

*military pensioner

BENTON COUNTY
Page 31

RENFRO, THOMAS P.	SPRUEL, ZEBULON	VARNUM, JAMES
WILLINGHAM, WILLIAM L.	LLOYD, ELIJAH	TOWNS, ELISHA
BOX, SALINA	HAGAN, WILLIAM	TEAGUE, JOS. A.
TURNER, BENJAMIN D. with	ONEAL, WILLIAM	SIMMONS, ELAM
*SAMUEL RODEN, R.S. in	FULLINGAME, WILLIAM	TUNNEL, ENOCH
household as military	McBRIDE, SHADRACK	*Page 33*
pensioner	TIDEWELL, MAJOR	CHANDLER, WILLIAM A.
BONDS, WILLIAM	FULLINGAME, HENRY	BYNUM, ELY
RIDNER, JOSEPH	LLOYD, GREENE	FOREMAN, BENJAMIN
SUMTER, JOHN	LILMAN, BENJAMIN	SELF, JOHN
TURNER, SARAH	MONTGOMERY, JOHN V.	MILLER, WILLIAM
NABORS, JOHN M.	WEAVER, INDSEY	BAGLY, JOHN M.
DAVIS, ABIJAH	WEATHERLY, JOSEPH	SELF, FRANK
RENFRO, BARTLETT	WEATHERLY, FRANCIS A.	McKASHLER, MARGARET
WEIR, ELIZABETH	WOMACK, ASA	GARROTT, WILLIAM
STUART, JAMES	LEATHERWOOD, ZACHERIAH	STEPHENS, JOHN R.
HOWELL, LEVI	WORMACK, LEVI	ANDREWS, ALLEN
FINLEY, JOHN A.	LILMAN, WILLIS	TEAGUE, ELIAS
MOFFIT, WILLIAM	McAGEE, WILLIAM	VATILLA, GEORGE C.
GRIFFIN, CLARK	STOKES, SYLVANUA	OWENS, JOHN
HAMLIN, DANIEL	SMITH, EUSAH	HALL, JAMES
BURT, CATHARINE	BOYD, JAMES	PORTER, RO. L.
WIGHTLE, MARTHA	BURROW, NOAH	PORTER, HENRY H.
Page 30	KILGORE, WILLIAM H.	RODEN, THOMAS
RIGGS, JAMES	VICE, JOHN	DIFFY, JOHN
OLIVER, JOSEPH	MADDOX, JESSE W.	NAPPIER, THOMAS
CAMPBELL, JAMES A. M.	CRANE, P. J.	PITTS, MARK
MOFFITT, SAMUEL	TEAGUE, JAMES	JOHNSON, HUDSON
OLIVER, JAMES	TIDEWELL, AUSTIN	McCURRY, JOSEPH
ROBINSON, JAMES	*Page 32*	McCURRY, JONATHAN
HUGHS, JOHN T. A.	COBB, ROBERT	SIMMS, WILLIAM
WEIR, DANIEL	COBB, SAMUEL P..	WINN, GENUBATH
HUBBARD, JOHN	GLENN, HENRY	YOUNG, DAVID
WARNOCK, JOHN	VINES, DANIEL	YOUNG, JOSEPH
ALLEN, JONES	JOHNSON, THOMAS	POLLOCK, JOSEPH
TANKERLY, CARTER	SKINNER, SIMPSON	*Page 34*
CURL, WILLIAM	CLARKE, ELIZABETH	YOUNG, ISAAC
RENFRO, JOHN B.	MAY, JAMES	BLACK, THOMAS H.
RENFRO, JOHN	PALEY, WILLIAM B.	GOSA, FREDERICK S.
PARKS, NATHANIEL	TEAGUE, WILLIAM	BADGET, WILLIAM C.
ALLEN, MATTHEW	EASLY, BENJAMIN	SAVAGE, JOSEPH
WOODRUFF, MOSES	ALLEN, SAMUEL	MARTILLA, N. D.
PACE, URIAH	MADDON, JOHN J.	RANEY, PARIS
MONTGOMERY, WILLIAM	MURPHEY, SOLOMON	HINTON, SAMUEL
PACE, V. H.	MURPHEY, M.	STEGALL, WILLIAM
SHADDEX, JAMES	MALLORY, R.	SCOTT, JEREMIAH R.
PELHAM, ATKISON	TUNNELL, JAMES	THRADER, HENRY
NEAL, JESSE A. M.	TUNNELL, ELISHA	EDMISTON, DAVID M.
MOODY, V. H.	BERRY, R. W.	HELM, GEORGE
LOYD, JOSEPH	BASS, WILLIAM	DAVIS, LARKIN
SMITH, JAMES D.	MADDOX, JOHN	ACUFF, WILLIAM
BATES, JOHN V.	MADDOX, WILLIAM	YOUNG, WILLIAM N.
SMITH, WILLIAM D.	TOWNES, ABRAM	PRUIT, ROBERT

* military pensioner

Benton County

SNYDER, GEORGE
PORTER, WILLIAM C.
COBB, EDMOND
HARRIS, JAMES H.
WILLIAMS, W.
McROBERTS, JOSEPH
BOWDON, REDDING
MOTES, ELIZABETH
PASWELL, MOSES
CURLEW, WILLIAM F.
HAMILTON, JAMES C.
SIMPSON, ARCH

Page 35
INGRAM, JAMES C.
WATES, JOSEPH M.
WRIGHT, JAMES L.
NAPPER, HUGH
LOYD, JAMES V.
HANNA, JOHN
HANNA, WOODFORD R.
BICE, VALENTINE
SIMMONS, ELISHA
KENNEDY, WILLIAM J.
RIDDLE, TERRY
MITCHELL, WILLIAM W.
BAKER, WILLIAM
McDONALD, F. G.
CLOUD, JASON
NAYMAN, JOHN
LACKEY, WILLIAM I.
CARTHEY, ARGH. C.
EDMISTON, JOHN T.
SIPSEY, REDDING
CHADWICK, JESSE
CALDWELL, GEORGE
CALDWELL, SAMUEL
RUSSELL, ROBERT
SIPSEY, HIRAM
NORMAN, GEORGE W.
HINES, MATHIAS
McMAHAN, WASH C.
RAYSON, WILLIS

Page 36
VAUGHT, ANDREW
COATES, WILLIAM
PARNEL, A. I.
HINES, MATTHIAS, JR.
BOWMAN, JOHN L.
WORTHINGTON, DAVID
McCURRY, GEORGE
PORTER, JANE
PORTER, ROBERT W.

PETERS, BENTON
WALLIS, JOHN
SNYDER, JACOB
RAINS, THOMAS
CURRIER, JAMES
COOK, JAMES M.
FOWLER, PHILO
KENNEDY, WILLIAM
CARTER, AARON
WORMACK, DOBSON
MORRIS, JAMES
BAKER, RANKIN J.
HARDIN, JOHN L.
SEGANS, ALFRED
REAGAN, BENJAMIN
RAGAN, NATH'L
VINES, JOHN
CARTER, MARY
MATTON, EARLY J.
DAVIS, NATHAN

Page 37
TEMPLETON, SAMUEL P.
SIMMONS, LEVI
MALLORY, HENRY H.
*MALLORY, JOHN
WILLIAMS, JOHN W.
ANDREWS, JAMES
HAMBRIGHT, WILLIAM
BOLLINGER, PETER
WILLIAMS, JOHN B.
SMITH, JOHN
MULLINS, NATH'L
JONES, JAMES R.
PORTER, WILLIAM, SR.
SMITH, WILLIAM
BORDERS, JOHN
KELLY, STEPHEN
TURNIPSEED, ANDREW
MORRIS, JOHN
GRAHAM, WILLIAM
GILL, LEONARD
MOORE, JAMES C.
BROWDER, DAVID
HOLLAND, NOAH/NEAL
BUSH, JOHN
PRUIT, PHILLIP
YEATMAN, JOHN
CARMICHEL, HUGH
CUNNINGHAM, WILLIAM
CUNNINGHAM, WILLIAM N.
*CUNNINGHAM, W.
TURNIPSEED, GEORGE

Page 38
BOGGS, KINCHEN
HARRIS, GEORGE W.
SAWYER, R. H.
COATS, DANIEL
HASNER, JONATHAN
BUTTS, WILLIAM
CUMMINGS, ELIZABETH
CUMMINGS, SARAH JANE
HESTER, JOHN
YEATMAN, JOHN
CUMMINGS, WILLIAM
LEWIS, DUDLEY
MITCHEL, WILLIAM J.
HARRISON, WILLIAM
MADISON, BENJAMIN
YEATMAN, WILLIAM T.
MADISON, WILLIAM T.
MASSEY, WILLIAM
MARTIN, JOHN
PICKENS, REESE
LOVE, FIELDING
CAMERON, WILLIAM
HUGHS, CHESLEY
ELLARD, JEPTHA
SELLARS, JACOB
THOMPSON, SAMUEL
TOWNS, WILLIAM G.
ANDERSON, ANDREW
JOHNSON, NOBLE

Page 39
JONAS, REUBEN
FINN, MIDDLETON
CLARK, BENJAMIN
HEATON, JAMES B.
HEATON, DAVID
NICKLES, WILLIAM G.
SELF, AMON
SELF, ISSAC
VARNEEM, WILLIAM
TAYLOR, HARRIS
SELF, ISAAC, JR.
ELLISON, ASAPH
KENNEDY, WILLIAM
BROCK, JOHN
COLEMAN, ALFRED
VAUGHN, JOHN
SKELTON, ASA
BROWN, RUFUS
WILSON, ROBERT H.
WILSON, BENJAMIN
RICHEY, JOSEPH
HOGE, JAMES

*Military pensioner

Benton County

SELF, PRESLEY
DODSON, JOEL
DICKENSON, WILLIAM A.
DOBBINS, NATH'L
SKELTON, RHOSA ?
VARNUM, DAVID
Page 40
TURNER, HENRY B.
DULANY, URIAH
VARNUM, JOHN
O'BANION, GREEN H.
CARDEN, JOHN
BATTLE, L. B.
NAGER, WOFFERD
CHAMBLESS, JOHN
LAMBERT, ISAAC
WATSON, COMFORT
MARTIN, JOHN
ROBINSON, GEORGE W.
WISNER, JEREMIAH
ASBELL, JAMES
CHAMBLESS, WILLIAM
LEWIS, DAVID
FIELDS, ISAAC
LANTRIP, REBECCA
ISBELL, SARAH
CALDWELL, POLLY
LANTSIS, JOHN
PRICE, G. B.
ENGLAND, JAMES
WHITE, EDNA
BLAIR, GEORGE
DRIVER, WILLIAM
CLAY, JOHN
CRAMP, SAMUEL
DAVENPORT, JOHN
Page 41
LOVE, WYLY
ARMSTRONG, JASON
BULER, GEORGE
PHILLIPS, JACOB
BISHOP, JOHN
McDANIEL, ANDREW
CARLSON, SAMUEL W.
CHAPMAN, ENOS
SULLIVAN, FELIX
SULLIVAN, JOHN
MCCALL, ROBERT
WESTON, BOOKER
AcACKER, HENRY
WASHINGTON, DARLINGTON
CHILTON, ASA

PHILLIPS, WILLIAM
PHILLIPS, THOMAS
GREENE, AARON
ACKER, PETER
LEWIS, J. B.
BROWN, MARTIN R.
BROWN, JOHN
BROWN, JOHN JR.
INGRAM, JOHN B.
MOORE, WOODS
CHILTON, PELATISH
PHILLIPS, ZACHARIAH
VOYLE, JOHN R.
VOYLE, JACOB
Page 42
COLEMAN, HEZEKIAH
PHILLIPS, FRANCES
MOORE, ALEX. M.
MOORE, JAMES
DOYLE, JOHN
CASTRAL, L. C. (teacher)
EUSN, JOHN
JONES, LEWIS D.
BASH, DANIEL
COCKRAN, JAMES
WAKEFIELD, JAMES M.
WILLIAMS, WILLIAMSON
WADE, ARCHIBALD
STOCKDALE, JAMES L.
GIVENS, WILLIAM L.
McCLELLAN, ELISHA
CROW, DAVID
KELLY, WILLIS
KEITH, M. H.
COBB, JESSE G.
McCALLY, BASAEL
DEVINORE, ROBERT
GALLAHER, JAMES
CAMPION, WILLIS
CARROLL, ASA
McCALLINS, DAVID
HERD, GEORGE
WARE, HENRY S.
BULLOCK, DAVIS
Page 43
RAY, MARY
CROW, FARRINGTON
KELLY, WILLIAM D.
POE, AUGUSTINE
RAIFORD, WILLIAM
HENLEY, MARY
YOUNGBLOOD, THOMAS

BROTHERS, PATTON
CROOK, JOHN M.
GLADDEN, JOSEPH
CLARK, JOHN R.
HAMPTON, JAMES
HARGROVE, JAKE P.
ROGERS, REBECCA
WEATHERLY, JAMES A.
SPARKS, MATTHIAS
BURR, MOSES L.
FINCHER, WILLIAM J.
NEVENS, JAMES B.
OSSINGTON, CHARLES
SPENCER, JAMES
McCIBBIN, JOHN
CHAMBLESS, ASBON
CUNNINGHAM, JOHN
CUNNINGHAM, JAMES(tea
PRICE, STERLING
COUNSEL, WILLIAM B.
BUTLER, JESSE
LOVE, WILLIAM
Page 44
BAGLEY, ELIZABETH
NICHOLS, JAMES B.
WILKINSON, JONATHAN
DOWNING, THOMAS J.
PRICE, GEORGE W.
PRICE, BENJAMIN
WARHAM, THOMAS
AUTRY, GEORGE
CRUMPTON, JESSE
COKER, LARKIN
WILDMAN, JOHN
BENNET, JAMES P.
MOUNT, JULIUS
SAMUELS, ELISHA
GRIFFIN, BENJAMIN
MOODY, BENJAMIN E.
CRISWELL, JOHN
HARRIS, R. B.
DARTHEL, NANCY
YOUNGBLOOD, LUCIAN/S
PUTMAN, REUBEN
CAST, ISAAC
DEATON, WILLIAM
COPELAND, JESSE
RICHEY, GEORGE W.
DANSBURY, ELBERT
DIAL, SHADRACK
WILLIS, JOHN
BROWN, JOHN

Benton County

Page 45
WILLIS, BENJAMIN J.
JOHNSON, GREENE
SLACK, DANIEL
CROOK, JAMES
CROOK, JAMES M.
WHATLEY, L. J. T.
DRUMMOND, JOHN
COMPTON, WILLIAM
WILKINSON, STEPHEN
BOYD, SAMUEL
WADDILL, ELISHA
POWERS, JASPER G.
SIMS, STERLING
GRIST, WILLIS
MORGAN, JAMES
BOYD, SAMUEL, JR.
WOODRUFF, FRANKLIN
WESTON, BENJAMIN
MOORE, ROBERT H.
CASE, THOMAS
GREENE, JACOB R.
NOAH/NASH, ABRAM
CANTRILL, DAVID
WEAVER, SAMSON H.
DENSON, COLLEY
POR, WILLIAM
HAMBY, EZEKIEL
ARTENBURG, MILLY
RICHEY, JOHN

Page 46
DODD, JOHN
WEEMS, ROBERT
HOUSTON, JOSIAH
PHILLIPS, MARK
JORDAN, SION
PETTIT, JOHN P.
PETTIT, NATHAN
LEE, INGRAM
SHUFFIELD, PLEASANT
MELTON, JAMES
PETTIT, JOSHUA
BRITTIAN, THOMAS
McBRAYER, JOSEPH T.
GILBERT, WILLIAM R.
CHANEY, PETER C.
HALL, MEREDITH
BAKER, MARTIN
GORE, WILLIAM
DAVIS, NATH'L
KESLING, ABNER W.
PAGE, WILLIAM

GUEST, JOHN M.
SAPATER, ARCHIE
ELLISON, JONATHON
BRAKEBILL, HENRY
METCALF, SAMUEL
SMITH, BENJAMIN
SHEFFIELD, ADAM
BRADBERRY, NATH'L

Page 47
WILLS, ARCH.
RICHEY, ISAAC
WHITE, AARON
PHILLIPS, JOHN
SAPATER, SAMUEL
McKARNEY, JOHN
MOODY, EPPS
BLACK, ALIN
COPPORD, MARK
ALLANS, JAMES
McKARNEY, ALFRED
RICHEY, W. M.
PHILLIPS, GEO.
LEE, ELIJAH
LITTLE, WILLIAM
LITTLE, JOHN
CALVIN, A. H.
PETTIT, HENRY
MORRIS, WILLIAM
RICHEY, JAMES
HAGOOD, E.N.C.
ALLEN, JOSEPH
BROYLES, JOHN C.
BROYLES, GEORGE
HARPER, MARGARET
WALKER, JOSHUA R.
BROWN, ALEXANDER
HARRIS, STEPHEN
COUCH, GEORGE

Page 48
SAMPLE, JOSEPH R.
SHEPPARD, JOHN
HARDY, GEORGE W.
KELLY, SIMS
HUGHES, WILLIAM J.
SIMS, EDWARD J.
POSEY, WASHINGTON E.
McCLUNEY, THOMAS
DUNCAN, JOHN
WALKER, JOHN
SCHERCK, JOHN
McCONNEL, SAMUEL C.

PRICE, JAMES
REYNOLDS, LEVI
BOYD, ISABELLA
JEFFRIES, NATH'L
YOUNG, ROBERT
PAGE, NELSON
BROWNING, JAMES L.
LOVE, JOHN M.
NOAH, JOSEPH
BRUTON, LECIL
HAMPTON, JOHN M.
PRICE, L. R.
WEBSTER, MATTHEW
LLOYD, THOMAS (teache
POOL, WILLIAM (teache
PARTON, RICHMOND
RICH, WILLIAM

Page 49
POWELL, FRANCES L.
THOMASON, WILLIAM
RUSSELL, GEORGE
ASHLEY, HIRAM
GRIFFIN, ELIHU
POWELL, WARREN
HAMPTON, WADE
WYATT, JESSE C.
WYATT, WYLY
WYATT, MOSES
LITTLEFIELD, HAZARD
CANNON, WILLIAM
CANNON, ALSIA B.
CANNON, CORNELIUS
CANNON, DAVID
LEE, WILLIAM C.
WESTON, JAMES
WESTON, JOHN
WESTON, WILLIAM (teach
BARTON, LEWIS
JACKSON, JOHN
FULKS, PHILLIP
GALLATIN, OBEDIAH
LITTLEFIELD, WILLIAM
GIBSON, FLEMON
HALL, MARTIN
GIBSON, JOL.
BARTON, JOHN
GILBERT, WILLIAM

Page 50
LAWSON, REUBEN
MILTON, SARAH
BLAIR, MARY

Benton County

MILTON, JOHN
ROBINSON, JOHN W.
MASON, JAMES
RICHEY, JOSEPH
WARE, ROBERT
STEPHENS, SHADRACK
ALDRIDGE, JOHN
BARNET, DANIEL
GRIFFIN, WILLIAM
GRIFFIN, BARNET
RICHEY, WILLIAM
HARPER, THOMAS
BRITTIAN, BERRY
REED, ANDERSON
HALL, SAMUEL
HODGES, THOMPSON
WOOD, JAMES
POSEY, DAVID P.
DICKENSON, ANTHONY
McMICHAEL, WILLIAM
BORDEN, SARAH
LEE, JOHN W.
COBB, NATH'L
ELLIS, JESSE
SMALL, NATHAN
COOK, THOMAS K.
Page 51
WILL, NATH'L
STATON/SLATON, JOHN
WALKER, B.
BRIDGES, BENJAMIN
PELHAM, RICHARD
JENKINS, MEREDITH
ANDREWS, JESSIE, JR.
WHITE, JOHN M. SR.
WRIGHT, GEORGE
HOWELL, WILSON
PORTER, WILLIAM L.
HARDWICK, H.
REED, BERRY
SICILY, JOHN
WILSON, BENJAMIN
THOMPSON, JAMES
GRIFFIN, OSWALL
BRADLEY, REESE
MEADERS, JOHN
WATSON, JOHN H.
WILLIS, ARCH.
PHILLIPS, ELY
NABORS, E.L.
JENKINS, REUBEN
NASH, ABNER

FOSTER, JOHN F. C.
MABRY, RUSSELL
NAPPIR, JOHN
CLAY, JOHN G.
Page 52
GRAHAM, GEORGE
JENKINS, OWEN
ANDREWS, RASSELL, JR.
ARNOLD, LEWIS
MORILAND, GREENE
THOMPSON, SAMPSON
CHAMPION, WILLIAM
JENNINGS, JOHN B.
GRUBBS, JOHN
TAYLOR, HIRAM
LEACH, JOSEPH
WRIGHT, DAVID
SMYTHE, JOHN
SIMS, JOHN L.
JENKINS, JAMISON
McCARTNEY, BARRY
WILLIAMS, JAMES J.R
WASHINGTON, JOHN
BURNS, ISABELLA
BURNS, JAMES F.
THOMPSON, WILLIAM D.
PARKISON, RICHARD
GAINES, HENRY
ANDERSON, JOHN
TEAGUE, ELIJAH
GREGG, NATHAN
BURDEN, JOAB
HILTON, WILLIAM
CLEMENS, SOLOTHEAL?
Page 53
BRADWELL, AUGUSTIN
HATCHER, NANCY
WILT, SILA
SEWALLER, WYLY
WRIGHT, ELIZABETH
HOYLE, JOHN
BENTLEY, TURNER
NOLEN, JOSEPH
ODELL, WILLIAM
SINGLETON, THOMAS
WRIGHT, JOHN
SCROGGINS, VICY
CHAMBERS, JAMES L.
CHAMBERS, SAMUEL
MOORE, JOHN
BOX, CORNELIUS
GRIFFIN, HORATIO

MITCHEL, ELIJAH
NABORS, CHARLES
WILLIAMS, JOHN
SHIPPEN, JOHN W.
SIMMS, WILLIAM
BATES, HENRY
HAYNES, ISAAC
MAGELL, JOHN D.
HALL, THOMAS
MORGAN, CHARLES
MORGAN, THOMAS
Page 54
BERKET, FREDERICK
BARAHAN, E. B.
AMBERSON, WILLIAM
MONTGOMERY, J. N.
LEWIS, JAMES L.
CAMERON, JAMES
SCROGGINS, CHATT.
HUGHES, GIBSON
PILGRIM, JOHN
DUKE, GEORGE W.
HUDSON, THOMAS W.
DODD, WILLIAMSON
MORGAN, WASHINGTON
AMBERSON, MATTHEW
MORGAN, SAMUEL
MORGAN, THOMAS
WILLIAMS, SEABORN
McLUSKEY, ALEX. L.
SWAN, SAMUEL F. D.
THACHASON, WILLIAM
HILL, HENRY
SHIPPEN, JOHN
ANDERSON, WILLIAM
MORGAN, SPENCER
THACKERSON, RICHAR
BOLES, RICHARD R.
MORGAN, JOHN
MORGAN, CALEB
STUART, ARCH.
Page 55
BAIRD, ANDREW N.
LITTLE, WILLIAM
PRICHARD, BERRY
STUART, JOHN
STUART, WILLIAM
HAGLER, WILLIAM T.
HUTSON, ROBERT
WRIGHT, CATHARINE
TAYLOR, WILLIAM
SMITH, JOHN

-18-

Benton County
Page 57

TAYLOR, SAMUEL
MILAM, WILLIAM
JONES, WILLIAM R.
JONES, JOHN
PATERSON, WILLIAM A.
MILAM, RICHARD E.
MOLEY, WILLIAM P.
WHITE, THOMAS
TATE, COOPER B.
WHITE, GEORGE W.
WHITE, WILLIAM C.
PEARCE, DANIEL
DONALDSON, ANREW
SAVAGE, THOMAS D.
DANKLER, JONATHAN
ROONEY, ELIZABETH
WHITE, JOHN G.
CASEY, BARNABAS
CASEY, WYLY

Page 56

McTHRASH, JOSEPH
SHARP, RICHARD
WILLIAMS, WILLIAM
HUTSON, WILLIAM B.
REED, BAILEY
STROTHER, ANDERSON
COVINGTON, WILLIAM
CASEY, P.P.
PEA, JAMES
ENNIS, GEORGE
AKINS, JOHN T.
BURNES, ANDREW
GILKISON, ROBERT
SAVAGE, JOSIA L.
CALLAWAY, WILLIAM
COLEMAN, R. R.
CALLOWAY, ISAAC
MOTE, WILLIAM
HOYATE, JAMES
PALMER, SEABORN
MARTIN, JOHN
WHITE, LECIL
PHILLIPS, JOSEPH
WHITE, HENRY
CAMERON, JOHN
JACKSON, RALPH
FORTENBERRY, JOHN
BLACKWELL, D. R.
SIMS, R. B.

CASEY, JOHN A.
ENNIS, JAMES
BEVIL, McNEIL
CLEMENS, LORICK
SPARKS, MALINDA
BROWN, SPENCER
MAHAFFY, MARTIN
COCKERSON, THOMAS
FLANIGAN, JAMES
ANGLE, JOHN
WOODSON, THOMAS
WOODSON, ROBERT
LEWIS, JOHN
ROBINSON, ELIHU
HYATT, JESSE
HYATT, DAVID
GRAHAM, CHILIOM
PALMER, MARTHA
GRAHAM, JOHN, JR.
GRAHAM, JOHN R.
ROBERTS, JOHN
BUCK, ZACHERIAH
LEWIS, ENOS
BILLINGSLEY, WALTER
MEDLOCK, L. H.
MINTER, SYLVANUS
HENDESIN, JAMES JR.
HENDSAN, WILLIAM
MINTER, REUBIN

Page 58

WEBB, ASA
SPARKS, JESSE
HENDRIC, JAMES
McGAGE, JAMES
LAMBERT, JOHN
FERGUSON, AQUILLA
HENDRIC, JOHN P.
CHITWOOD, PLEASANT
CLARKE, GEORGE
McGUIST, EVAN
HARDIN, JOHN
SWORDS, J. M.
WOLF, LEWIS
KENADY, THOMAS
MAXWELL, JAMES
MOORE, JOHN
ALEXANDER, ARTHUR, JR.
WHEELER, BENJAMIN
CHANDLER, HEMINWAY

MORRIS, J.A.
ROYSTER, JAMES W.
ROYSTER, JOHN
LOGAN, RIAL
HORTON, NIMROD
BURDENS, GEORGE H.
WILSON, JOHN
WILSON, WARD
CARNES, DAVID

Page 59

ARRINGTON, WILLIAM
HENDERSON, NATH"L
KENUM, LEWIS
GAY, GRANVILLE
MCCANDLISH, JAMES
WHEELER, JOHN
ALEXANDER, MATHEW
HAYES, ROBERT
HATFIELD, HANSFORD
DAVIS, ANDREW P.
WATSON, WILLIS
ALEXANDER, ARTHUR, JR.
MAXWELL, JOHN
BURDEN, JOHN
MANNING, JOHN M.
LEDBETTER, WILLIAM
LEWIS, ISUM
WOLF, CARLTON
WHITESIDE, JOHN W.
PENLAND, SAMUEL
PAGE, DAVID
RALSTON, ELIZABETH
PARKS, BENJAMIN
STRIPLIN, WILLIAM
BARNETT, RILEY
ELLIOTT, JESSE
HEATON, THOMAS
WALKER, ROBERT W.
HENDERSON, J.W.

Page 60

KEMP, SHERAFF
KEMP, J. B.
KEMP, LARKIN
WILSON, CRAVINS
COE, WILLIAM A.
SCARBOROUGH, SAMUEL
CARTER, CAMPBELL
MURRY, JOHN
WELLS, SAMUEL

Benton County
Page 62

CHITWOOD, R. B.	RAGSDALE, JOHN W.	OWENS, PLEASANT
MORELAND, F. T.	ALEXANDER, CHARLES T.	HOWELL, WILLIAM
BURTON, JOHN H.	BERRY, EDMUND	CLARK, HENRY P.
THOMPSON, LEONARD	ALEXANDER, ALBERT	ROPER, STEPHAN
HART, ANDREW	BROCK, LEONARD	BROWN, JAMES
ROBINSON, JAMES	RIGGS, WILLIAM D.	STEAD, SALLY
PERRYMAN, WILLIAM J.	WALSTON, B.B.	HERD, FREDERICK
GRIFFIN, JOHN	SMITH, WESTON	NALLY, JOSEPH
HILL, JOHN C.	PAULMER, ELLENDER K.	Page 64
HILL, WILLIAM	SATTEMORE, JOHN	*ROPER, JOHN
NELSON, JAMES C.	BROCK, JACKSON	ROBERTS, JOSHUA
PACE, ISAAC	EVANS, WILLIAM	DEAN, JOHN
KELLY, ELIJAH	SIMMONS, JOHN W.	BAILY, CHARLES
KELLY, ALBERT	WILLIAMS, MARY	DEAN, CHARLES
LINDSAY, JOHN	POWERS, JOHN	KING, HENRY R.
SADLER, THOMAS	STUART, ALEX.	KING, JAMES
MARTIN, CHARLES	CLARK, THOMAS B.	BAILY, JAMES
HARRIS, JOHN C.	AKINS, WILLIAM	HOWELL, JOHN
REESE, WILLIAM	WELSH, SAMUEL	GRUBBS, ALLEN
REESE, FRANCIS	SPARKS, DAVID	BURDEN, JOSEPH D.
Page 61	POWERS, KESLING	RAGSDALE, ALLEN
HOLLINGSWORTH, HENRY	RANEY, JOHN	KENNEDY, SAMUEL
NEWTON, ISAAC	HOLCOMBE, BENJAMIN	LEACH, GEORGE
JOHNSON, MARGARET	ROBINSON, CHARITY	GRIMES, WILLIAM K.
JOHNSON, HENDERSON	STUART, JACKSON	GRIMES, JOHN
SIMS, WILLIAM	MURPHY, JOSEPH D.	LAUGHLIN, WILLIAM
NIPPER, ABSOLOM	WILLIAMS, BENJAH	TAYLOR, ISAAC
VRITCH, JESSE	STEWART, ARCH. O.	CHADWICK, JOHN
WILSON, JOSEPH	Page 63	KENNEDY, JOHN
MATHIS, LEWIS	SESSION, MOSES	NOBLETT, SAMUEL
McQUAIG, NEILLY	NEWTON, JAMES	KENNEDY, WILLIAM
ELLIOTT, THOMAS	WHITE, BENJAMIN	CHANDLER, SAYRE
NABORS, LEWIS	ST. CLAIR, WILLIAM	LAUGHLIN, MARCUS
NABORS, NATHAN	JORDAN, RUBEN	ELMORE, FRANKLIN
WHITLOCK, LOTT	JORDAN, ALAN	KESS, HUGH
SMITH, SINGLETON	FAGANS, WILLIAM	WILSON, JOSEPH, JR.
SMITH, HARPY	ROBINSON, JAMES	MEASELY, DANIEL
SCARBROUGH, JAMES	COX, ZACHERIAH	ELLASON, JOHN
REYNOLDS, LINDSEY	HATON, WILLIAM	GRUBBS, WYLY
BLAIR, JOHN	CONN, WILLIAM	Page 65
SMITH, JACKSON	CONN, ISAAC S.	HOWELL, ELIAS
SMITH, HEZEKIAH	FINLEY, M. W.	FOSTER, ROBERT
WHITESIDE, MOSES	HOPSON, WILLIAM P.	EDWARDS, SAMUEL
BENSON, ENOCH	STRATTON, AARON	EDWARDS, PETER
SMITH, MASSIE	FINLEY, WILLIAM	WEAR, SAMUEL, JR.
LASAGE, SAMUEL	DANIEL, JAMES M.	BROWN, JAMES M.
BLAIR, MARGARET	WILLSON, JOHN	DUNCAN, WILLIAM B.
GREGORY, JOHN	CARMICHEAL, WILLIAM	BURNET, MARK
WOLF, REBECCA	REYNOLDS, JONATHAN	HOOPER, JOHN C.
LEDBETTER, J.W.(teacher)	BURDEN, ELI	EAST, DANIEL

*military pensioner

Benton County
Page 67

BAKER, JAMES
DAVIS, MARTIN
HUGHS, FRANKLIN
OWENS, THADDEUS
LACKEY, JOHN P.
KELLER, JOHN
THOMPSON, SAMUEL
VINEYARD, WILLIAM
MATHEWS, JOHN G.
MOORE, RICHARD W.
BOSWELL, DAVID
*WARDEN, SAMUEL
BARNETT, URIAH
BARNWELL, ROBERT
DANIEL, ALFRED
BARNET, CALVIN
ELLASON, JAMES
ROBERTS, JOHN J.
TOLBERT, FRANCIS
HOGAN, ELIJAH

Page 66

DOROUGH, JOSEPH J.
VINEYARD, JOSEPH
BENTLEY, SOLOMON
PERRY, EDMUND
BROWN, AMBROSE
EZZELL, MASON
STATON/SLATON, SAMUEL
WADE, ELIJAH
VINES, DAVID
VINES, JAMES
BASSETT, FREEMAN
WASSON, WILLIAM
RUTHERFORD, JOHN
CLAYTON, JOHN
WALLACE, HUGH B.
OWENS, BARTLEY
WATTS, JOHN
THOMPSON, SAMUEL D.
BROWN, WILLIAM
WORTHINGTON, LEVI
CONGER, J. S. V.
SMITH, P J.
HENK, HENRY
NEYMAN, JACOB
McLEOD, ALEX.
RHODES, WILLIAM
BOLTON, JAMES
REEVES, THOMAS
ESTES, JOAB

RIPLEY, JAMES
EATON, JAMES
OWENS, WILLIAM
COOK, JAMES
ALLEN, HUDSON
HAMET, JAMES
RAGAN, MICHAEL
MILLER, JAMES
BURCH, THOMAS
WARREN, WILLIAM
CAREY, JOHN
EKINGTON, DAVID N.
CRISTIE, SAMSON
ROSS, FRED.
BLACK, J. R.
HAMET, JOHN
EVANS, WILLIAM P.
HAMET, DAVID
DAVIS, THOMAS
PRESTON, JACK
WILLIAMS, J. R.
TEAGUE, BENJAMIN
BROGDEN, DAVID
ROBINSON, JOHN
THOMPSON, JOHN W.
CHRISTIAN, WILLIAM L.
LANSDEL, MOSES
VINEYARD, JESSE
WILLIAMS, JAMES

Page 68

GRAHAM, JOEL
POUNDER, NATH'L
WATSON, DAVID
WHITESIDE, JACKSON
NEAL, REBECCA
FREEMAN, FLEMMING
DOWDY, ROBERT
POOL, DICY
GIPSON, ALLEN
GOSSET, WILLIAM B.
BASS, MARY
GOBER, JAMES
VINES, J. B.
CHANDLER, EMORY
BONDS, ANDREW
AYRES, SUSANNA
CURRIER, WILLIAM

Chambers County

formed 1832

Page 169
WALLY, WALTON W.
LAMBERT, JAMES
STROZIER, WILLIAM
CALAWAY, WILLIAM
MEADOWS, JASON W.
GILBERT, JOHN R.
AIKEN, JAMES
PENN, THOMAS L.
RUFF, JOHN
PEARSON, SAMUEL
THOMAS, DAVID S.
OATES, JAMES
HARTY, CHARLES C.
VICKERS, MARTIN
FLOYD, CORNELIUS
GARRETT, BLUNT T.
BRIDGES, JOHN
ALEXANDER, JAMES M.
PARISH, SPEVEY
SWAFFORD, WILLIAM
GRANT, DAVID
BROOKS, WILEY M.
SUMMER, JOHN
SHEPPARD, LEWIS A.
ROSE, HENRY
WATTS, TEMPY
BYRD, HENRY C.
GRIFFIN, DANIEL
MCKAY, HUGH

Page 170
JONES, URIAH
MADUX, JAMES
HODGES, JOHN
WHEAT, MOSES
CUNNINGHAM, ANDREW
WALLACE, HENRY
WALLACE, ROBERT
THOMPSON, SAMUEL
THOMPSON, JAMES
JONES, HARRISON
REESE, RICHARD
WELSH, WILLIAM
LEE, CHARLES H.
WEBSTER, JOHN
BROOKS, GEORGE
JAMISON, JOHN
BOZEMAN, FED
JOHNS, OBEDIAH

MOORE, ELEANOR
RIEVES, ISSAC
MCCULLOUGH, WILLIAM
MANSFIELD, ALEXANDER
McCULLOUGH, THOMAS
McCULLOUGH, JOHN
McCLELLAND, JAMES
CAR, JOHN
CAMACK, WILLIAM
MARTIN, JOHN
ALLEN, WILLIAM
Page 171
COLEMAN, RICHARD B.
COE, GEORGE W.
ANDERSON, JAMES
THOMAS, GEORGE E.
PURSEY, ALFRED
LEE, KENNADA P.
FLECTCHER, JOHN
BARBERREE, ELLIS
WELCH, ROBERT
McCATS, ROBERT J. P.
KENADY, ALEXANDER B.
THOMAS, EBENEZOR A.
PENDERGRASS, SIMSON
LYLE, THOMAS G.
SANDERS, LUKE
WINBUSH, WILLIAM
CLAYTON, NELSON
STALLINGS, JEPTHA
ROSS, ISSAC
MATHEWS, JOHN J.
ANDREWS, MARK
CLAYTON, SUSAN
CLAYTON, JAMES
HORTON, MARTHA
RAWLS, JAMES
CALDWELL, JOHNSON
HEART, DERRYL
BIRD, WILEY M.
BARROW, JOSIAH
Page 172
ROBINSON, DANIEL
McCULLOUGH, JOHN
RAMAGE, BENJAMIN
FINCH, JOHN
ASKEW, JAMES
STAMPS, JOHNATHON

MEADOWS, WARNER W.
SCOTT, JAMES
BOZEMAN, BAMBRIDGE
BARROW, WILLIAM
JARVIS, PATRICK F.
JOHNS, ROBERT
ALFORD, JOHN R.
AUTRY, GEORGE
LUSTER, HENRY
BARROW, JOHN
WILLIAMS, DANIEL
LEE, BOYAKIN
LEE, SAMUEL
CLAY, EDMUND
GARRET, JESSE
MATHEWS, ABNER
WOOD, LEWIS
BOND, JESSE
BOND, RICHARD
ALLEN, JOEL
GARRET, JOHN
KENDRIE, ALEXANDER F
McHENRY, ROBERT W.
Page 173
HALE, LUCIOUS
GAN, ARCHIBALD
HODGE, FRANCIS T.
PRICE, JOHN B.
LANG, CHARLES
HILL, JAMES M.
ALLEN, SAMUEL
NORRIS, JOHN M.
HIGHTOWER, AARON
BANKSTON, JOHN
CHAFIN, BLUFORD
DAVIDSON, JAMES
VESSELS, JOHN F.
TUCKER, EATHON
HODGE, TULLISON R.
MARTINDALE, MARY
HODGE, JOHN N.
BENTON, REBECCA
HODGE, JAMES R.
HODGE, GEORGE E.
ADDAMS, JOHN
ADDAMS, ANDREW I.
HOPKINS, WILLIAM B.
WHALEY, ISSAC

-22-

CHAMBERS COUNTY

HODGE, JAMES F.
BUTLER, NATHAN
CLAYTON, JOHN B.
HIGHTOWER, DANIEL P.
McCURDY, EDWARD L.
Page 174
SWITZER, PETER P.
TUCKER, ROBERT
FRETWELL, LENARD
TUCKER, ETHEL
TUCKER, DANIEL
TUCKER, EPPES
TUCKER, FLETCHER
FREEMAN, JESSE
COLLINS, RILEY
TIMERMAN, FREDRICH W.
KELLY, DICEY
BURTON, JOHN
GILES, WILLIAM
BAUGH, ELIZABETH
BALLARD, JAMES
BRAGAN, RICHARD P.
CREED, MESHICK
McGREGOR, HAM R.
STAPS, BRITTON
DORSET, JOHN
BURTON, JACOB
ALFORD, ASENATH
BELL, THADIUS
McLEROY, JOSIAH
FLANAGAN, JOHN M.
FREDERICK, DIANA M.
BANE, WILLIAM F.
PRATT, THOMAS A.
STANLEY, FELIX
Page 175
BECK, JEDEDIAH J.
McLEMORE, CHARLES
DUNN, URIAH
FINDLEY, ATCHESON
CRAYTON, WILLIAM L.
McKEONS, SPECSER J.
GOODMAN, BENJAMIN L.
CHISLOM, JOHN
McKINLEY, ROBERT
DRIVER, GOODRIDGE
GUNN, GEORGE W.
HOLOFIELD, ALSIA
SHELMAN, THOMAS P.C.
MUSE, ELLIOT H.
MASTERS, ROBERT
RICHARDS, EVAN G.

TOWNS, HAWKS, L.
HUDSON, CUTHBERT G.
HURD, THOMAS R.
BRANTLEY, GUIN G.
PITS, GILES
ADDAMS, JACKSON
SMITH, CLARASA
KEY, ANN B.
HOOPER, GEORGE D.
STEWART, THOMAS J.
CALAHAN, WILLIAM
HERRON, BENJAMIN
SMITH, JOSHUA
Page 176
PRATHER, JOHN L.
SHEPARD, PHILLIP M.
WHITTEN, JAMES
BACHELOR, JOSIAH W.
REED, ELIZABETH
RICHARDSON, PETERSON T.
BLACK, PERRYMAN
McCOY, NELLY
SIMMONS, ACY C. A.
MITCHEL, MARY H.
GRISHAM, LEMUAL
FOREMAN, JAMES H.
BOSTWIC, JOHN
BLAND, JAMES E.
WALKER, AUGUSTA
ANDERSON, DAVID
FLOURNOY, MARKUS A
TAYLOR, RICHARD
HARRIS, JAMES W.
LAWHON, ARCHY
PHILIPS, MATHEW
BAUGH, EDWARD
McCOY, NEILY, JR.
O'CONNER, JOHN
COOPER, LOYD T.
WILLIAMS, JOHN J.
LOYD, JAMES H.
SMITH, THOMAS K.
Page 177
BROADFOOT, WILLIAM
APLEBY, JOHN
FURGASON, WILLIAM
PARKER, LITTLEBURY
PATTON, WILLIAM K.
HARRIS, JESSE D.
NORRIS, THOMAS
McNIELY, RICHARD
THORNTON, DOZIER

KENEDY, WILLIAM
MOORE, THORNTON
RICKS, GIDEON
HARRIS, MINOR W.
WILSON, GILBERT
MERCER, WILLIAM
KIDD, WEBB
THORNTON, NATH'L M
SPARKS, GILES P.
NORTON, ISSAC
ROBINSON LIGGET
MORRICE, GARROT
ANDREWS, ROBERT J.
OWENS, ROBERT
GOLDSMITH, WM. H.
EASON, ISSAC P.
CADENHEAD, JAMES
FATHEMS, WILLIAM
MENAFEE, TATUM
KENSEY, JESSE
Page 178
HARRIS, JAMES
HOWARD, JOHN
HANCOCK, JOSIAH
HORTON, JOHN R.
DAVIS, JOHN
BLOUNT, WILLIAM
FREEMAN, GRIFFIN
HOOKER, MOSES
TICKNOR, URBAN C.
SLAYTON, WILLIAM A.
COMBS, WILLIAM
HARDEN, RALPH
PENN, MOSES
ADDAMS, JAMES M.
WINSLETT, SAMUEL
WINSLETT, JOHN
TAYLOR, EZEKIEL
HOWLE, THOMAS
WILEY, THOMAS
BAGGET, ANDREW B.
BELL, SUSANNAH
JOHNSON, STEDMAN
JOHNSON, LINDSAY
HARPER, WILLIAM W.
DANIEL, JAMES L.
OSBOURNE, BRITTON S.
JONES, SAMUEL G.
DENSON, EDMUND
CALDWELL, NEWELL S.
Page 179
HILLER, JOHN

Chambers County

GRYMES, GEORGE W.
OSBOURNE, WILLIAM R.
OSBOURNE, THOMAS B.
GLOVER, SANDERS
BARROW, HENRY
COOK, JOSEPH
BURK, ASBURY
BURK, JESSEE
BLANKENSHIP, JOHN T.
THORNTON, SANORD
McCOY, BAILEY G.
HAWKINS, THOMAS
CALHOUN, ARCHIBALD
STEWART, MARY
COLLIER, THOMAS W.
PARKS, JOHN
DUNN, JOHN
LANGLY, ISHAM
DENNIS, ERVIN
DENNIS, SAMUEL P.
LIGON, DAVID G.
MILLER, LEMUEL
LAWSON, DAVID
LYLE, GEORGE W.
ROGERS, THOMAS
CULPEPPER, FRANCIS
LANGLY, JARVIS
SANFORD, DANIEL

Page 180

CROWDER, THOMAS T.
DAVIS, MADDISON
LOGAN, JOHN
MERRIL, LEMUEL
HOLTZCLAW, ELIJAH
HARREL, SEABOURN
THOMPSON, JAMES
CRITTENDEN, JOHN
RUSSELL, JOHN
GOODWIN, ZACHARIAH
GOODWIN, CHARLES
GREGORY, CHARLES
GILDER, FRANCES
GIBSON, CHURCHILL
NELSON, NOAH
OBION, BESSEE
FLETCHER, THOMAS
RICKS, ANDREW
CULBERSON, DAVID
THOMAS, JOHN
THOMAS, WILLIAM
HALL, JOHN

FREEMAN, JAMES
GANDY, ALFRED
SHARPE, WILLIAM
BIGERSTAFF, JEFFERSON
BIGERSTAFF, ANDREW
WRIGHT, JAMES T.
LANGLY, ZACHERIAH
BAILEY, ALLEN L.

Page 181

STAPLES, ELIZA
LANGLY, WILLIAM
WILSON, MANASA
SOWELL, THOMAS L.
PYLANT, HENRY
RUSSELL, THOMAS R.
GARRETT, JESSE
CULBERSON, BIRD
AUTRY, WILLIAM
SMITH, WILLIAM W.
CADE, JAMES H.
KEMP, SIMEON
STORY, SUSANNAH
CROFT, GEORGE
EADY, JOHN R.
RUNNELS, THOMAS
RIDDLE, JOHN
ROBINSON, OBEDIENCE
HARABLE, ERASONUS G.
PARKER, JAMES
THAXTON, WILEY
STANFORD, OLIVER H.P.
ELMORE, THOMAS
ANDERSON, DAVID R.
LUMPKIN, MARCUS T.C.
LEBAN, JAMES M.
SMITH, GREEN
CHAPPEL, HENRY

Page 182

THOMAS, WILLIAM C.
JETER, SAMUEL G.
BOYD, JOHN
FITTEN, JOHN
NORWOOD, JAMES M.
NORWOOD, WILLIAM
TAYLOR, JOHN
MARK, GEORGE W.
GUNIGHAM, JOSEPH H.
EVANS, JOSHUA
MORRIS, JOSEPH
BARROW, ROBERT
HAWKINS, JOHN B.

KENNEDY, LORENSO G.
BIRDSONG, JAMES
HARREL, WILLIAM
THOMPSON, ASAT
SMITH, BIRD
DEAN, THOMAS C.
STONE, THOMAS
WALDROP, WILLIAM
COZENS, GREEN
JOHNSON, JOHN G.
HOUSE, ISHAM F.
WHITEHEAD, HENRY M.
TAYLOR, JAMES
FURGASON, DANIEL
LEVERET, WILLIAM
BUFFORD, JOHN B.

Page 183

WILEY, THOMAS P.
PENNY, JOHN
MOONEY, ISSAC
HORTON, HENRY W.
BARKER, HILLIARD
BARNET, WILLIAM
WRIGHT, WILLIAM
ROBINSON, JEPTHA
DAWSON, LEMUEL G.
CAMPBELL, DANIEL
GRIER, JOSEPH
HYTOWER, JOSHUA
CONNER, EDWARD
PARKER, WILLIAM
BARKER, ELDRIDGE
THORNTON, WILLIAM S
RICHARDS, JAMES W.
GOLDSMITH, GEORGE M.
BRUMMIT, WILLIAM
KING, JOSIAH
HUTCHISON, ABNER
BILLINGSLEY, LYNIS
KINGKADE, JOHN
SHAW, ROBERT
MULLICAN, CARY
FULLER, STEPHEN
CULBERTSON, GREEN
WRIGHT, JAMES N.
TAYLOR, BRYANT

Page 184

STROUD, JAMES
WHITINGTON, WINDER
PASS, WILLIAM H.
WILAFORD, BRITTON

Chambers County

TURNER, ELIJAH M.
JONES, JAMES K.
PRESLEY, CALVIN
FURGASON, NORMAN
McDANIEL, WILLIAM
RIEVES, WILLIAM
BLACKBURN, SERENA
MOORE, BARTHOLOMEW B.
HOLOWAY, CALEB
MITCHEL, THOMAS M.
CHAPIN, STEPHEN
BOID, RICHARD
WALL, EZEKIEL
ALLEN, THOMAS
CONE, ASA R.
FIELD, LUIS
HUBBARD, JAMES
WINBUSH, JOHN
DAWSON, JOSEPH W.
WHITE, JAMES
MOORE, HORTON
MASON, ARCHIBALD
CHANDLER, WILLIAM
TRICE, ELIZA
WILKINSON, HENRY L.
Page 185
MAY, SAMUEL
TELLIS, CHARLOTTE
CALTON, JOHN
MATTOX, ANTHONY W.
PATRICK, BENJAMIN P.
THORN, NICHOLAS
RAMAGE, GEORGE W.
TURNER, BARTHOLOMEW
STARR, JAMES
GINN, SHEARWOOD H.
TULLUS, JOHN
ANDREWS, JOHN M.
STARR, HENRY
GILMORE, JOHN
MURABLE, CHAMPION
GILMORE, HENRY
LINDSEY, JACOB A.
MOORE, HUEY
MATTOX, WILLIAM
JACKSON, EPAPHRODITUS
MUSSEL, WILLIAM
PAGE, JOHN R.
MULIGAN, ISSAC
WALKER, WILLIAM
SHAW, ROBERT
CAMPBELL, JOHN

CAMPBELL, JOHN D.
GUTHRIE, JOHN
HUNTER, JOHN
Page 186
SWENY, WILLIAM
HUNTER, MATHUS G.
BARROT, JOHN
WILLIAMSON, HENRY
FORBES, CHARLES
ROBINSON, GEORGE W.
BENNET, RUBEN
SMITH, JAMES
FORMBY, JOHN
WOOD, SAMUEL
RIDGEWAY, DRURY
SHANNON, THOMAS
HOLSTON, WILLIAM
WILLIAMS, DAVID
HUFFMAN, HENRY
HAGOOD, JAMES
HAGOOD, ELIZABETH
SIMMONS, JOHN
PAGE, ALFRED G.
FULLER, ELIJAH
TAYLOR, DAVID
MCINTIRE, ARCHIBALD
DOUGLAS, ROBERT
McKINSY, ALEXANDER
GIST, NATHANIEL
SMITH, JAMES L.
McBRIDE, MALCOM
GOLDSMITH, JOHN T.
Page 187
SIMS, JOSEPH
BARKER, EDMUND A.
CALDWELL, DANIEL
SMITH, JOHN W.
MARTIN, GILES
PAGE, JOHN L.
McLEAN, JOHN
THORNTON, MEMORY W.
STEWART, ROBERT
EADY, HENRY
STANLEY, ISHAM
McKINLEY, JAMES
FORGASON, THOMAS
BOOTH, WILLIAM N.
STEPHENS, HYRAM
WEBB, ABNER
FITZPATRICK, JESSE
NOLEN, WILLIAM
SWINT, FREDERICK

NOLEN, THOMAS F.
JOHNSON, WILLIAM
CRECY, THOMAS
MOBLEY, JOSEPH
HAMBLEN, NATHAN
SWEENEY, MARCUS B.
SMITH, LEVI
BROWN, CHARLES
Page 188
MULINAX, JOHN
MULINAX, MATHEW
DUNCAN, ARNOLD
HAUGH, NEEDHAM
SIMPSON, HENRY M.
SIMPSON, CHARLES
FLOYD, ELIZABETH
WALLACE, ALLEN
ELLIS, LANGDON C.
REESE, GEORGE
REESE, EDWIN
REESE, THOMAS S.
STANLEY, JESSE
MYZE, JAMES
BORDERS, MARY
GAULMAN, JAMES
FREEMAN, WILLIAM
HARREL, ALFRED
GENNEL, FIELDING
HILL, JAMES M.
EDWARDS, THOMAS
JACKSON, LEMUEL
STRAYHORN, SAMUEL
TODD, HENRY W.
FIELD, CALEB
HANCOCK, HARDY
PRUIT, BAILY W.
NIEL, DAVID
McGUIRE, THOMAS
Page 189
DUNLAP, DAVID
ROBESON, J.T.J.
JOURDAN, JAMES D.
JOURDAN, WILLIAM R.
PATTERSON, ABNER
HARRELL, SAMUEL
BORDERS, LEWIS
WHITAKER, ORIN D.
GAMMELL, STEPHEN P.
FORGASON, BURRELL
GAMMELS, WILLIAM
RUNNELS, JOHN J.
WALLIS, ALBERT F.

CHambers County

STORRS, WILLIAM
TANKERSLEY, WILLIAM
MASON, DAVID D.
ROBESON, ANDREW
CROFT, SAMUEL
ROTCH, SAMUEL
PRUET, ADAM
LOFTON, GEORGE
HUDMAN, DANIEL
LIVINSTON, JAMES T.
TUTT, JAMES
TAYLOR, WYAT A.
McGARROW, NANCY
McKEY, DAVID W.
CABELL, JAMES
COLLERN, NANCY

Page 190
NORRIS, WILLIAM
MOORE, LEVEN
CHERRY, JAMES A.
WATTERS, WILLIAM
CLEMENS, GABRIEL
HANCOCK, HERROD
WELCH, WILLIAM
SEGLER, MATILDA
FERRILL, ELIZABETH
BROWN, D. F.
McGINTIE, WASHINGTON
TAYLOR, SIMEON
BOLEY, JAMES W.
HARRINGTON, JEPTHY
SMITH, HENRY
HEDSPETH, MARK
ARANT, DAVID
ARANT, ELIZABETH
CHAMBERS, JAMES E.
FORGUSON, MALCOLM H.
McREA, MARGARET
STARNES, FREDERICK
WATSON, JACOB
STOREY, JOHN
WELCH, ROBERT
JOHNSON, WILLIAM
CARLILE, EDWARD W.
BREWSTER, JOHN
GUNN, MOSES

Page 191
BURSON, HAZEL G.
ROBESON, GREEN B.
WATSON, DAVID

JOSEPH HOLT
MIMMS, HAMPTON
REEVES, PRIOR
DOWNS, JAMES
WILLIAMS, WILLIAM B.
STEPHENS, THEOPHILUS
DARDEN, MOSES
STEPHENS, FLEET
MEADOWS, ISHAM
BELCHER, COLLIN H.
McCULLOUGH, BRIANT
McCANE, WILLIAM L.
THOMAS, ETHELDER
GANT, THOMAS
SHERROR, BENJAMIN
ABNEY, JACOB
GANT, THOMAS
SHERROR, BENJAMIN
REESE, THOMAS
YARBROUGH, JEPTHA
LANEY, GEORGE
McLENDON, JOEL
NICHOLS, JOEL
McKISICK, JOHN
NETTLES, SAMUEL
WILLIAMS, AARON
WILLIAMS, WILLIAM
OWENS, MARTHA

Page 192
HORTON, ALFRED
RAMMAGE, ROBERT
FANNING, WILLIAM
ERVIN, THOMAS B.
WALKER, JOHN
WILSON, JOHN
JONES, JAMES
KELLERSON, HENRY
KENNADA, JOHN D.
McWHORTER, WILLIAM H.
CORLEY, McCRELESS
GRAY, T. A.
JOHNSON, WILLIAM A.
BLACKMAN, WILLIAM B.
BROWN, CHARLES
MURRELL, THOMAS
BURSON, JOHN
WILSON, WILLIAM
JOHNSON, LEVI
STEWART, JOSHUA
BARR, THOMAS D.

JONES, WARRINGTON
YARBOROUGH, WILLIAM
HOLT, JOSEPH
PEARSON, PENELOPE
RIEVES, JOHN
STARKIE, DANIEL
MEADOW, BENJAMIN
HINDMAN, THOMAS M.

Page 193
SLAUGHTER, ALFRED T.
LANGSTON, JAMES
ROBESON, NOREVELL
PITTS, WILLIAM
DISMUKES, EDMUND
WILLIAMS, AARON
WALDEN, ALFRED
BUCKHALTER, JOHN
EVENS, RANSOM P.
HOLT, WILLIAM
HOLT, JOHN
HOLT, HARRISON
RAMBO, JAMES
REEVES, JOSEPH A.
McCLENDEN, JACK
GOLDSMITH, ALLEN
TAYLOR, WILLIAM
AMIES, WILLIAM
STINSON, ANDREW
JONES, WILLIAM
BLACKMAN, JOHN
BLACKMAN, JAMES
STOKES, REBECCA
STOKES, GILLIAM
HOWARD, JOHN
STEPHENS, DAVID
DAVIS, WILEY
GOLDSMITH, JOHN

Page 194
GRIFFITH, WILLIAM
HANCOCK, THOMAS
HANCOCK, HERMAN
HANCOCK, JOEL
MEADOWS, DANIEL
LOFTEN, JAMES
DENORES ?,GRAY
WARE, HENRY
WILLIAMS, ISSAC
NASH, JOHN
GOLDEN, MARK
HAY, HENRY

Chambers County

MOBLEY, WARREN
STEWART, JAMES
HOWELTON, WILLIAM C.
WYATT, MOSES
ELLISON, JOSEPH
GEORGE, WILLIAM
BOULDING, WILLIAM
SHELTON, SMITH A.
LEE, ELIJAH
JONES, WILLIS
DAY, DOLLISON
BRADBERRY, SPENCER E.
SELMAH, LARKIN
Page 195
YARBOROUGH, NIMROD B.
GERMANY, WILLIAM C.
ANDREWS, MILTON
ALLEN, WOODROW P.
YARBOROUGH, JACKSON
COOK, JAMES
WILKISON, HAMMOND J.
GARDNER, HARRIET
SUTTON, SEABORN
McDONALD, WILLIAM
WOODYARD, FELIX D.
ROSS, WISEMAN
DUCK, ROLAND A.
BURNET, HARDY
RUTLEDGE, SAMUEL
HAMBRICK, ELIZABETH
RIDGEWAY, ELIZABETH
BOLING, QUINCEY R.
SHERLY, HEZEKIAH
WILLIS, PAUL T., JR.
HARMON, JOSEPH
THOMPSON, LORENZO
Page 196
ECHOLS, JOHN W.
BURDETT, SAMUEL M.
CARTER, JOHN
WILSON, CLARK
BOWLING, SMITH
MILTON, WILLIAM
HUDAMAN, HEZEKIAH
BRYANT, WILLIAM
JACKSON, JOHN
PETERS, MATHEW
WYNN, ROBERT B.
HUNTER, ALSA
GRAGG, WILLIAM
JOHNSON, JAMES
THIELA, GEORGE

COBB, WILLIS
WINSLETT, EDMUND
NOBLE, LUKE
CHRISTIAN, CAROLINE
PASCALL, BENJAMIN
CLAY, MARTIN
CALLWAY, FRANCIS
VERNON, EBENEZER B.
VENTERS, STEVEN
SPERLING, JAMES
BAKER, LITTLEBERRY
HOOKS, JOHN
GAINES, STROTHER
Page 197
DAY, ISHAM F.
SALLEY, WILLIAM
SHELTON, CHARLES T.
COLLEY, JOHN H.
COOPER, ALSEY
JETER, BARRET
DAVIS, WILLIAM
PATTEN, SOLOMAN
HAGOOD, MARCUS
NICHOLS, HENRY
WILKERSON, JESSEE P.
NORRIS, JOSHUA M.
COLWELL, MARCUS
WILKISON, JARED
HEATH, TINSLEY
TURMAN, THOMAS J.
PHILLIPS, JESSE B.
CHAMBERLAIN, WILLIAM
FARLEY, JOHN
TOLBERT, GREEN
McCOWAN, GREENBERRY
IVEY, ANTONEY
GARDNER, WILLIAM A.
BRAWNER, TILMAN
EASTERWOOD, MATHEW
BARTON, JOEL
GOODWIN, JESSEE
RUTLIDGE, CHARLES
Page 198
McCLENDON, SAMUEL
McCLENDON, JAMES
KENDRICK, HESEKIAH
WESTER, BENJAMIN
SANDERS, JOURDAN
GIDEON, WILLIAM
HOWARD, WILLIAM
OLIVER, JAMES O.
FARMER, JESSE

OLIVER, McCARTY
OLIVER, FRANCES M.
FORTUNE, WALTHOR
WISE, JACKSON
SMITH, WILLIAM
WALTHOL, WILLIAM
SMITH, HUGH
MARS, GILBERT
JACKSON, STEVEN
GILMORE, ROBERT
FORSHEE, JOSEPH
GRAVY, WILLIAM
BRIGGS, JACOB
PATRIDGE, THOMAS
JARVIS, JOHN W.
JARVIS, THOMAS T.
EDGE, RICHARD
BLACKSTON, JOHN
HARRELSTON, ABNER
CLIETT, THOMAS
Page 199
MATTHEWS, ANNA
CARTER, THOMAS
CARTER, JAMES
TURNER, GEORGE
JOHNSON, JOSIAH
CAUSEY, WRIGHT
BIBBY, NATHANIEL
WARDLAW, WILLIAM
ELKINS, ELI
GILLELAND, HUGH
BIBBY, MOSES
PERRYMAN, JOHN A.
TOLBERT, GEORGE W.
WILLOBY, THOMAS
TEACH, NIPPER
McDONALD, JOSHUA
GOGGINS, SOLOMON,
OTWELL, BERRY
BECK, JACOB
RODGERS, ELI M.
IVEY, WILLIAM
STROTHER, AARON
GAY, GILBERT
GAY, JOHN
DUKE, JOHN M.
ABERHEART, JAMES
EAST, STEPHEN
WOOD, JOHN
TRAILOR, WILLIAM
Page 200
HENRY, JACOB F.

-27-

Chambers County

McDONALD, THOMAS J.
CHAMPION, MARTIN
HUDMAN, JOHN
LANEY, DAVID
HOUSE, WILLIE
BELLAMY, WILLIAM W.
HENRY, WOODSON D.
OTWELL, RICHARD Y.
HENRY, EZEKIEL
PEARSON, FRANCES
STUDHAM, ZACHERIAH
CAUSEY, CHRISTOPHER
STUDHAM, GEORGE
CROSS, JOSEPH
CAUSEY, WILLIAM
HAYS, BENJAMIN W.
WELLS, LAMUEL
COTTON, LEONARD
BIBBY, ELI
McCLANE, SELHEEL J.
WELCH, JOHN
BENTLEY, JESSE
FIELDS, JOSHUA
WILLIAMS, WILSON
BIBBY, JOHN L.
BENTLEY, JOHN
HOTNEY, WILLIAM
Page 201
LOTT, WYAT C.
SORRELL, GEORGE W.
McKNIGHT, ANDREW M.
HARDY, JAMES
LOTT, HUGH
LOOSER, JOHN C.
PHILLIPS, MATHEW
QUATTLEBAUM, GEORGE
BAILEY, JACOB
SORRELL, GREEN
BISHOP, IRA
FINLEY, THOMAS P.
SORREL, JOHN L.
McKNIGHT, JOHN
FINNEY, WILLIAM H.
QUATTLEBAUM, GEORGE
TURNER, HENRY G.
SIMMS, CLAIBORN
TREADWELL, DAVID
BENTLEY, HIRAM
SIMMS, HIRAM
SPRAGGINS, ARSINUS
TEAL, HENRY

HARRISON, JOHN
DOSTER, LEMUEL
McCLENDEN, THOMAS M.
KNIGHT, MOSES
WILSON, ROBERT
Page 202
SHAW, DANIEL
LYMAN, JULIUS H.
CHILDERS, BRURY
STILO, ABNER
ADDAMS, WILLIAM
PATRIDGE, HENRY R.
HUSSEY, JOHN T.
KELLY, LUIS
VANN, EDWARD F.
GERMAN, HENRY W.
LOCKLER, JOHN
HUSSEY, JAMES S.
HUGINS, DAVID
McKNIGHT, ROBERT
HEATH, CICERO
CLIFTON, LORINZO
THOMPSON, JOHN
LINDSAY, JAMES
BAKER, WILLIAM
SIMS, ANDERSON
JONES, JAMES
LACY, WILLIAM
BEATY, JOHN
WILLIAMS, WILLIAM S.
McCOY, HENRY
BLAKELY, JAMES
CHILDERS, EDWARD
DUNNINGTON, RICHARD
PHELPS, WILLIAM W.
Page 203
GREEN, MOSES W.
ATKINS, WILLIAM
CARLISLE, ROBERT W.
PALMORE, WILLIAM W.
CARLISLE, MICHAEL
DOWNS, ISAAC
GOOD, WILLIAM
THOMPSON, GEORGE W.
GRAVES, ROBERT C
GERMANY, EMORY
DURHAM, JAMES C.
LAWSON, BOOCKER
WILLIAMS, WILLIAM W.
BIBB, WALTHALL
BAKER, SAMUEL

PATTERSON, ROBERT H.
RUSK, THOMAS
WADE, THOMAS B.
DORMAN, WILEY
WILKERSON, GREENBERRY
EDGE, JAMES
BLAIR, ROBERT K.
BUTTS, HENRY
NORRIS, HARRY F.
McKNEELY, WILLIAM
KNOX, CHARLES
BLEDSON, PEACHY
MARSHALL, JESSE L.
BLACKBURN, WILLIAM
Page 204
SATTERWHITE, OBEDIAH
WILSON, JOHN W.
LYLE, RANDOLPH
ATKINSON, WILLIAM
NEWTEN, ISAAC
STRAYHORN, HUEY
REEVES, STEPHEN
HOLSTON, ELBERT A.
STEPHINS, JONES
JOURDIN, GENNET
HOLSTON, STEPHEN
LITLE, ACEY
JONES, WILLIAM
JONES, RICHARD
MITCHUM, JOHN
BARTON, ENOCH
GANTT, JOHN
HOLSTON, TALMAN M.
EDGE, WILLIAM B.
HOLSTON, SEABORN J.
WILLIAMS, TILMIN
MARTIN, WILLIAM C.
SPIKES, THOMAS
STEPHENS, ISAAC
STEPHENS, JOHN
STEPHENS, FRANCIS
AWTRY, GREENBERRY
WEBB, WILLIAM
TAYLOR, TILMON
Page 205
PATTERSON, JOHN
BENTON, WILLIS
DUNN, JOHN V.
GERMANY, JAMES
BLASINGAME, BENJAMIN
MUSIC, JONATHON

Chambers County

*TAYLOR, THOMAS
GRAY, SEABOURN B.
CRAFT, EDWARD
WARSON, SAMUEL
PATTERSON, ANDREW
PATTERSON, JOSHUA
RAINEY, THOMAS
CARTER, DANIEL E.
HEAD, RICHARD B.
HOWELL, WILEY
HOWELL, ISAAC
HARREL, THOMAS J.
McKEE, JAMES
YOUNGBLOOD, JACOB
JOHNSON, ROBERT
HALSEY, WILLIAM
MILLAGAN, HUIE
SHEPARD, JOHN T.
CARGIL, WILLIAM H.
COGGINS, ACEY
VICKERS, FREDINAND
HUCKNEY, JAMES B.
JONES, WILLIS
STALNAKER, BENJAMIN
Page 206
McKINLEY, DAVID
HUMPHRIES, AMOS
SMITH, THOMAS
BABER, NATHANIEL
MERRIL, JAMES A.
GOOS, BENAJAH
McCRIMMONER, JOHN
WILDER, JARRET
JOHNSON, JOHN P.
PROTHRO, ANNA
TAYLOR, FRANKLIN
THOMASTON, THOMAS
GREGORY, JOHN W.
CRAWFORD, FARR
PARKER, JOHN
SLOAN, GEORGE
SMITH, WILLIAM B.
ANDERSON, JAMES W.
CLANAHAN, ROBBERT
WILLIAMSON, MACAGER
STROTHER, PERRY
STROTHER, AARON, JR.
DURHAM, JOSIAH
HUDMAN, GERRET
JOHNSON, MARTIN
WARDLAW, ROBERT H.

COOK, THOMAS S.
WEBB, JAMES
ROUNDTREE, CADER
Page 207
PATTERSON, DAVID
BLAIR, JOHN
COBB, CHRISTIANA
FENN, ANDREW J.
THOMPSON, WILLIAM P.
SWEENEY, JETHAM
STROTHER, MARTEN
CAPEHEART, JOHN
COHRAN, JOHN
SMITH, THOMAS J.
LEES, WILLIAM L.
LEE, WILLIAM
ABNEY, JAMES
NEIGHBORS, WILLIAM
ASLEY, JOHN Y.
TRAMMELL, JOHN
WALTON, HAMMERING
HOLSTON, STANMORE
CARR, BURREL L.
CASON, EDWARD J.
BARBER, JAMES
BROWN, SAMUEL E.
BROWN, WILLIAM
McKERLEY, WILLIAM
MANGNUM, JOHN
NOLEN, WILLIAM
NOLEN, HIRAM
Page 208
GARRETSON, COLOMAN H.
MILLER, WILLIAM R.
*LANGLEY, JAMES
PRUETT, HENRY
TAYLOR, JESSE
NOLEN, STEPHEN
TAPLEY, WINSFORD
JACKSON, HEDEN
SATTERWHITE, DAVID
HOOD, GREEN
HOOD, BRYANT
WILLINGHAM, THOMAS
REA, WILLIAM
TATE, HARRISON
RAMSY, HENRY
ROBESON, THOMAS
ROBESON, JESSE B.
RODGERS, ROBERT
THORNTON, JOURDAN

THORNTON, WILLIAM A.
WARD, PASCAL E
MITCHELL, JOEL
PUPNAM, JAMES M.
SATTERWHITE, ANDERSON
ANSLEY, GILBERT D.
CHISOLM, WILLIAM A.
MCKERLEY, DAVID
SHERRARD, JAMES
LAWRENCE, SHERWOOD
Page 209
BOHANNON, AGNES
RICE, JAMES
GRADY, ALFRED T.
HOLLAND, ERASTUS
SAXON, ARCHELAUS
JOHNSON, BUTLER C.
WARD, SOLOMAN
McDONALD, SMITH
WEED, JABES
KEMP, RICHARD
LAW, JAMES R.
TAYLOR, BENJAMIN
SHAW, WILLIAM
PORTER, PETER B.
FINLEY, ELIZABETH
FINLEY, AUGUSTUS H.
BLEDSOE, WILLIAM
WARD, JAMES L.
STAPLES, WILLIAM N.
BREESON, BENJAMIN
COX, WILLIAM E.
TRAMMELL, JOHN Y.
HOLLIDAY, FAGUE B.
MCPHERSON, WILLIAM
GRAY, MARGARET
SAMUEL, WILLIAM A.
GRADY, NATHANIEL
GRADY, WILLIAM J.
BROWN, LEROY
Page 210
RUTLAND, WATSON
NUNN, GEORGE
JETER, RICHARD C.
ATKESON, WILLIAM
O'HARA, ALLEN
JETER, ARCHLAUS
TRAXLEY, HENRY
JETER, RICHARD
HOLSEY, BENJAMIN
BRANDON, JAMES

*military pensioner

Chambers County

FARRIS, STEPHEN D.
FAUKNER, WILSON
SHORT, REUBEN
FULLER, WILLIAM
SMITH, CHARLES
O'HARA, FREDERICK
SMITH, WILLIAM
BROMELOW, EMANUEL J.
SHORT, JESSE
EAVES, JESSE
REEVES, JESSE
CARMICAEL, HARRIET
GARRETT, MILES
NORBIS, SPOTTELOW M.
HAND, SEABORN
HARRIST, TOMAS M.
HARRIST, WESLEY
Page 211
HOOD, JARED
CULPEPER, JOHN J.
RAMSEY, JACOB
WILKENS, JAMES
HICKS, AMOS
BOWEN, JOHN
BARBER, JOHN
GORDON, RICHMOND
HALL, CALEB
BERRY, THOMAS
WILLIAMSON, ANDREW
SMART, GEORGE W.
MITCHELL, JOEL
ANSLEY, GILBERT, SR.
CHISOLM, FORT.
ROBESON, JESSE
HARRIS, LITTLEBERRY
FRANKLIN, WILLIAM
TURNER, SAMUEL
SPIKES, WILLIAM
TURNER, CLAIBORN A.
DUNN, DRURY
JOHNSON, WILLIS
JOHNSON, FRANCES
REA, SUSANNA
WRIGHT, DAVID
DEESE, ALEXANDER
HOLLIS, ISAAC K.
BORING, DAVID
Page 212
HILL, WADE
KINSEY, JESSE
TOWLES, JOHN C.
McDANIEL, MATILDA
GRISHAM, YOUNG Q.

JAMES, JOHN
TRAMMELL, PULASKI
NOLEN, ISAAC
LINDSEY, ROBERT
GOLDSMAN, WILLIAM
JOURDAN, JOHN L.
TRAMMELL, MARY
McKEY, JOHN A.
SCOTT, JAMES
HARRY, MICAJAH
CARDWELL, ANSEL
WELDEN, ANDREW
WILLINGHAM, ALBION
WARD, ABNER
ROUNDTREE, JOHN
HOWEARD, HENRY
McCOY, TERRY
HOWARD, JOHN
NEWELL, WILLIAM P.
GREGORY, DAVID W.
RUTLAND, JAMES
Page 213
ROUNDTREE, FRANCES
HAGOOD, JAMES
ADAMS, CALEB
HOLSTUN, WILLIAM
MOORE, SANDFORD W.
SAMPSON, WILSON
ROBERSON, THOMAS
CANDLER, JOHN K.
HARWELL, JACKSON W.
HOLSTEN, LORENZO
UPSON, MALACIAH
NOLEN, JAMES
COOK, WILLIAM B.
TAYLOR, WILLIAM L.
McCOY, DALIEL H.
DUPOISTER, LEVY
CLEMENT, WILEY
LYLE, WILLIAM A.
AMOS, CASPER M.
HARWELL, SAMUEL B.
POWERS, EDMUND
BIRD, BURREL
BROWN, TARLETON
NOLEN, STEPHEN, SR.
NIGHT, JOHN F.
EWEING, JOHN
BOON, JOSEPH W.
PATTERSON, JAMES, JR.
PATTERSON, JAMES, SR.
Page 214
TOWLES, LABAN

COOK, THOMAS A.
HOLMAN, MATILDA
MOMAN, SILAS
ROBERSON, JAMES
MORAN, STEPHEN
DICKSON, JOSIAH
LEE, EDWIN
COTTON, JAMES
WATLEY, ELIZABETH
SMITH, JACKSON
JOHNSTON, THOMAS
SIMENGTON, FELIX
SMITH, MOSES A.
BROOKS, WILLIAM
BURNES, DARIOUS
WHEELER, BOOLING
TODD, WILLIAM
GATES, FREDERICK
FENDLEY, ROBERT
MOODY, ALBION
HOLLIDAY, WILLIAM H.
MARONY, WILLIAM
BONNER, JONAH M.
ARGO, HILLERY H.
SMITH, JOHN W.
YOUNGBLOOD, WILLIAM
HOLLEDAY, DANIEL
FINDLEY, GEORGE
Page 215
POWERS, LARKIN H.
STEPHENS, ISAAC
SMITH, WILLIAM
COLEMAN, NANCY
MUSICK, AUSTEN
McWHORTER, ISAAC
LEE, DIONSIOUS
MEDLEY, MADISON
ADAMS, JAMES
BASS, THOMAS
*STEPHENS, REUBEN
STEPHENS, JOHN C.
JONES, THOMAS
McCAIN, THOMAS M.T.
POWELL, CHRISTOPHER
SHACKLEFORD, COLLEN
WARD, RICHARD W.
McKINNEY, ELI
ANDREWS, ALICE
BENNET, WILLIAM
ALLEN, ROBERT
GUNN, JESSE
JOHNSTON, WILLIS T.
DUGGAN, EDMUND

*military pensioner

Chambers County

McCLAIN, JOHN
BILBRO, MARY
BILBRO, CHARLES D.
GRADY, JOHN
HAMMOND, JOEL
Page 216
ADAMS, FRANKLIN
SHARP, JOHN F.
DAVIS, ABSOLUM T.
HAMMOND, ROBERT
THURMAN, PHILLIP
ESTES, REUBEN C.
HARRIS, CHARLES
THORNTON, EDWIN G.
THORNTON, THOMAS A.
BLEDSOE, BLED
INGHAM, JANE
GAMBRELL, MARGARET
PARKER, JOHN C.
WARD, WILLIAM
JACOBS, BENJAMIN
HOLLIS, NATHANIEL
DICKSON, HAMPTON
McCOY, DANIEL
NICHOLS, WILLIAM
CROWDER, GARROT
CROWDER, MARY
CROWDER, DANIEL G.
COFIELD, THOMAS
LAWRENCE, WILLIAM
HOLLIDAY, LATIERA
BONNER, BENJAMIN
NEWMAN, LEMUEL
DOGGEN, JOHN
GREEN, JOSEPH H.
Page 217
GRAY, WILLIAM A.
BROADNAX, CATHARINE
MILAM, DUDLEY
ROBERSON, NIPPER
WEBB, ELIJAH
CORPREW, JAMES
SLAUGHTER, LAWSON C.
LUMPKIN, PITMAN M.
JACKS, YOUNG
HOTZLAW, SILAS
BUCKHANNON, RICHARD
SIKES, JACOB
MURPHEY, JOHN
MEADOWS, WASHINGTON
KNOX, WILLIAM B.
RICHARDS, WILLIAM

ADAMS, JOHN
FLURNOY, THOMAS G.
WARD, JAMES D. G.
STRODER, AARON
THOMPSON, SAMUEL
JOHNSON, WILLIAM
GRISHAM, FELIX
MORGAN, WILLIAM C.
MOBLEY, ELDRIDGE H.
BOSTICK, CHARLEY H.
TRAMMELL, FARR H.
MOORE, GEORGE
JONES, PLESANT S.
Page 218
SPEARS, WILLIS
FOSTER, WILLIAM
REA, ELISHA
BOLEHER, MATHEW
ROBERSON, ISAAC N.
ADAMS, JOSHUA
JOHNSON, WILLIAM
WESTMORELAND, HARRISON
MARTIN, SAMUEL
FOSTER, JOHN
BARROW, THOMAS
*HENDERSON, RICHARD
CARLILE, ELIZABETH
DOWNESS, EMMON
WILLIS, NAHAM
WOOD, STEPHEN W.
GOGGINS, ISAAC
REED, ROBERT M.
SIMINGTON, THOMAS
FANNINGTON, JOHN
McKINLEY, HANDY
HARRIS, CHARLES
NORRIS, NEEDHAM
DAUTFORD, JAMES
HANSON, GEORGE W.
DARDEN, JAMES H.
WINBURK, CHARLES E.
FIELDER, JAMES H.
BOLING, JARRET
Page 219
MARSHALL, JOHN
AVERY, ELIAS H.
THRASH, VALUNTIAN
THOMPSON, JAMES
BARROW, JOSEPHEN
CHRISTIAN, THOMAS
THOMAS, KINCHEN
MAXEY, EDWARD R.

FEMELE, WILLIAM
QUATTLEBUM, JAMES
McCLELLAN, FOGGY
HUGHEY, EPHRAIGAN
HANCOCK, JOE
GRAY, THOMPSON P.
COPELAND, SAMSON
FEENEY, JOHN M.
THAXTON, WILLIAM
WARREN, REUBEN
SMITH, NANCY
WILLIAMS, STEPHEN
SMITH, WILLIAM H.
COPELAND, THOMAS
STOKES, ALLEN
HANEY, BRITTIAN
WEATHERS, CLAIBORNE
DEAN, SARAH
BARTLEY, FANNY
TYSON, HINCHER P.
Page 220
HARRIS, TABITHA
FEARS, SAMUEL
GRIFFITH, JOEL
WATSON, JOHN
COGGINS, MILLEY
TOLLESON, DAVID
HAMMOCK, THOMAS
HAMMOCK, WILLIAM
HAMMOCK, JOHN
BUTTS, CATHARINE
STELE, ELIZABETH
HOUZE, ADHAM T.
HOUZE, JAMES
GREEG, ROBERSON
LEE, CHARLES S.
MARTEN, DAVID
ROBERSON, JAMES
STRONG, DAVID E.
CURRY, ROBERT M.
TAYLOR, THOMAS
JONES, HARDY
WICKES, JOHN A.
CARLILE, JAMES W.
DRIVER, LEROY
CARLILE, GREEN W.
KELLUM, WILLIS
BANKS JOSEPH
VINCENT, JOHN
WALKER, BEVERLY

*military pensioner

CHEROKEE COUNTY, ALA., 1840 CENSUS

Formed 1835

Page 111

ROBERTS, Z.
BELL, E. G.
WILKINSON, JOHN
CONNER, A.
WEAVER, JACOB
BEAZLEY, R.
WEAVER, DAVID
SMITH, JOHN
WILDER, N.
WEAVER, H.
PENNEGER, JOHN
TOLBERT W.
WEAR, WILLIAM
DYKE, R.
BELL, WILLIAM
TILLMAN, D. G.
REED, JOSEPH
HALL. J. M.
COLLINS, G. A.
BIGGER, J. M.
FRAZIER, T.
WELCH, T.
BARKLEY, A.
JOHNSON, WILLIAM
BARKLEY, WILLIAM
BARKLEY, J. B.
BARKLEY, JEFF.
RAYBURN, DAVID
COOK, WILLIAM C.
COPELAND, A. H.
MULLIGAN, S.

Page 112

BARRY, JOHN
SMITH, JOHN
SMITH, WILLIAM
MILLER. C.
DOBBINS, J. B.
PARKER, D. A.
SIMMONS, JOHN
LEWIS, J. C.
BENSON, J. J.
ROPER, H.
KENNEDY, JOHN
HUGHES, JAMES E.
ROSS, J. T.
SMITH, MOSES
McGUGAN, A.
SMITH, MARY
KENNEDY, JAMES J.

WADDELL, E.
STRICKLAND, JAMES
HUGHES, WILLIAM
CANNON, R. G.
HUGHS, WILLIAM D.
O'NEAL, G.
SHORT, W. W.
POWELL, THOMAS
HUDGINS, G.L.
SANDEFER, J. P.
WOODWARD, J.
McKINNISH, G.
GRAHAM, THOMAS
HARLTON, ALEXANDER

Page 113

SHERRELL, HUGH
SHELTON, HENRY
HOLOWAY, SAMUEL
CUNNINGHAM, J.
HAMPTON, R. B.
SANLIN, JOHN
McDANIEL, Z.
McCOY, HENRY
HUGHES, SINGLETON
WEBB, A. B.
CLIFTON, HYRAM
WESTER, S. W.
KING. F.
FINCH, WILLIAM
MILLER. R.
CLIFTON, A.
LEATH, JOHN
WADDLE, N.
BRODDEN, J. B.
BRODDEN, WILLIAM F.
HURLEY, THOMAS
STALLING, WILLIAM
ABERNATHY, SETH
CULPEPPER, JOEL
BAKER, ANDREW
KEITH, A.
CARR, S. J.
DRAKE, E.
DRAKE, JOHN C.
BOOKER, R. M.
BARRY, JOHN

Page 114

NEAL, ADAM
BANKSON, JAMES N.

DAVEAST C. T.
HERRIN, SQUIRE
FOWLER, R. T.
POTTS, JOSIAH
WILSON, JOSEPH
EDWARDS, THOMAS
EDWARDS, H. P.
ENGLAND, JOSEPH
LEE, WILLIAM
BARRUM, E. B.
HARRIS, A. F.
CLARKE, JOEL
TINER, WILLIAM
HANES, EPHRAM
TRIPP, JAMES J.
WHARTON, WILLIAM
WHARTON, JOHN
LEGG, LEWIS
HEAD, ALLEN
NELSON. A.
BRAUER, JAMES
JONES, H. C.
AIKEN, H.
PINE, JOHN
CROW, GEORGE
CROW, GEORGE, JR.
DOBSON, JOSEPH
OLIVER, S. K.
GARRETT, PLEASANT

Page 115

LEATH, JOHN
CHAPALEER, B. F.
PHILIPS, B.
SPEARMAN, THOMAS
RAY, HENDERSON
BROTHERS, E.
BROTHERS, WILLIAM
BURNS, WILLIAM A.
GARRETT, JOSEPH
HALL. H.
MACKIN, THOMAS
PAYNE, JOHN
MACKEN, F. B.
MACKEN, JOHN
MILLER, WILLIAM
SMITH, N.
BENTLEY, B.
WILSON, WILLIAM A.
SUTTLEMEN, J. L.

Cherokee County

MACKEN, H.W.
GARRETT, THOMAS
HENDERSON, C.
HAMMONDS, JOHN
ADAMS, WILLIAM
HONEYCUTT, JOHN
BATES, J. F.
MACKIN, N. B.
Page 116
MILLER, ROBERT
FAULKNER, LUKE H.
BURGESS, SAMUEL
KENNEDY, WILLIAM
GANT, JOHN J.
EMERSON. S. H.
RUSSELL, S.K.
GRIFFITH, J. D.
COLLIER, GEORGE
MITCHELL, ALEXANDER
SCOTT, JOHN S.
ROSS, ROBERT
REVILL, DAVID
ECHOLS, SARAH C.
HILL, JOHN W.
BATTLES, WILLIAM
ASHBY, JAMES
CRAWFORD, LEWIS
GRAVES, WILLIAM
GREEN, JOHNATHON
BRILEY, J. C.
BURGGES, JACOB
BARKER, JOSEPH
HUGGINS, ROBERT
COATES, SARAH
LEATHERWOOD, AQUILLA
MIDDLETON, WILLIAM
McDUFFEY, ALEXANDER
OWENS, JOHN
WATSON, JESSE
GRIFFIN, L. D.
Page 117
UNDERWOOD, WILLIAM H.
GAYLOR, JOHN
LOWRY, JOHN
CROZIER, G. W.
ROSS, J.
McMAHAN, JOHN
*MOSS. E.
LOWRY, S. L.
SMITH, JAMES G.
CONNER, JOHN
GILBERT, DANIEL

*military pensioer

RAINES, HUGH
RUSSELL, JOSEPH P.
RUSSELL, JOHN F.
COLLINS, JAMES A.
FLEMING, WILLIAM
COLLINNS, JAMES A.
HAREMAN, JOHN B.
PARKER, JOHN
McBRIDE, J. H.
LOVE, BAIRD
DICKSON, THOMAS
HAWKINS, A.
CLARKE, JAMES
UNDERWOOD, WILLIAM P.
COWAN, J.
HERRIN, S.
ROSS, WILLIAM P.
LOWRY, A. J.
HENDERSON, J.B.D.
GILLIAM, L. D.
LAURIE, R. E.
Page 118
HUSKERSON, WILLIAM
DUMANE, B. A.
SHED. C.
DANDY, JOEL
FOSTER, WILEY
BIRD, JACOB
MARTIN, SAMUEL
COOK. B. D.
ADAMS, WILSON
MADDOCKS, WILLIAM
GAMBLE, J.A.B.
BARNETT, WILLIAM
TENNESON, NANCY
PATY, E.
PATY, JOHN
MCCULLOUGH, CELL.
McCULLOUGH, WILLIAM
BRYANT, A. B.
SHARPE. E.
SHIDY, JOHN
OSBORNE, ALEXANDER
CASE, J.L.
MILLER, STEPHEN
CANNON, A.
HOWELL, G. W.
HILL, JOSEPH
CULPEPPER, J.T.
McCLUNEY, THOMAS
MACKEY, G.H.
BONDLEE, A.R.
McGEHEE, N.

Page 119
CHISHOLM. A. C.
TURNLEY, JAMES A.
WEAKLEY, JOSIAH
WILSON, JOHN S.
GARRETT, JOHN B.
COOPER, THOMAS B.
LEE, R.R.F.
HALE, E. P.
SMITH, H. L.
FAGAN, S.
HADEN, SILAS
BURKE, WILLIAM
SANDLIN, WILLIAM
HOGG, JAMES V.
TURNLEY, M.G.
VARNER, CHARLES
MARTIN, WILLIAM
GLOVER, WILLIAMSON
BULLARD, HENRY
CLANTON, NANCY
SANDERS, HANNAH
GILLMAN, JESSE
BROWN, J.B.
JOHNSON, BURREL
GLOVER, RICHARD
MARTIN, WILLIAM
WITZELL, E.G.
BLACK, JAMES
DOHERTY, G.M.
GRIFFIN, L.D.
McLAUGHAN, J.T.
Page 120
BURNETT, WILLIAM
SAXON, JOHN
McCRACKEN, CICERO
WHITT, A.G.
MICOSZOLZKI, PAULINE
THORPE, JOEL
GODDARD, WILLIAM
GILMORE, WILLIAM
TAILOR, WASHINGTON
CREWES, GIDEON
EVANS, JANE
RUDWELL, GEORGE
GILBERT, GEORGE
RANSOM, SAMPSON C.
EADS, JOHN
McDANIEL, WILLIAM
NEWBERRY, E.
BLASON, R.B.
THOMPSON, JOHN W.F.
BEAZON, E.F.
TURNER, ALICE H.

Cherokee County

*GRAVES, JOHN
DAVIS, JAMES
LEITH, JAMES
COBERN, J.
WEBB, JAMES
DAVIS, JOHN
FAULKNER, F.
HENDERSON, JOSEPH
COBERN, JESSE
GRIMMETT, WILLIAM
Page 121
ADAMS, ELIZABETH
COVINGTON, R.B.
ANTHONY. H.T.
FLUTING, J.
BOGGS, JOHN
LEWIS, R.
DANIEL. L.
TRIPP, H.W.
BARRINGTON, ISSAC
SULLIVAN. E.
STEPHENS, B.
CAMPBELL. L.
WATSON, N.
THOMPSON. B.
MOUNTAIN, THOMAS
BATES, J.S.
BLAIR, E.S.
TAYLOR. R.
ALEXANDER. R.S.
CASON, JOSEPH
TAYLOR, CHARLES
ANTHONY, J.B.
LEWIS, MOSES
LEWIS, SAM
FERRINGTON, ELIZABETH
SULLIVAN, JOHN
COWAN, WILLIAM W.
HURRAGE, MARY
LUSK, G.W.
ADAMS, J.J.
Page 122
MONK, G. H.
HENSLEE, J.J.
HENSLEE, MARY
VAUGHAN, J.B.
LONG, J.
CHAPELL. E.
POLLARD, BENJAMIN
POLLARD, JOHN W.
AWBERRY, BENJAMIN

* military pensioner

PERRY, H.
LAY, H. H.
GAGE, S.P.
McMAHAN, JAMES
NELSON, JOHN
McCARRELL, A.
DAVENPORT, J.B.
MATHEWS, JOHN J.
LANDRUM. E.
EVANS, JOSEPH
CHANDLER, J. M.
WAITES, W.
HALL, HENERY
MALONE, JAMES
McTEER, JAMES
HOLLEY, J. W.
HAMBRIGHT, B.H.
BARBER, S. B.
COATS, S.
CRANE, J. J.
PENN. R.
WILT, I.L.
Page 123
GARRETT, JOHN H.
BEAM, ALBERT
LEWIS, T.A.
HARVEL, JAMES
CAIN. A.B.
GILES, THOMAS
WESSON, A.
HEFNER, D.A.
DAY, WILEY
SANSOM, WILLIAM
FIELDER, WILLIAM
COLEMAN, JOHN
FIELDER, GEORGE
LOWRY, GILES M.
CRANE, JAMES
CHANEY, N.N.
SMITH, G. W.
McADAMS, H.G.
FARRIS, SAMUEL
TATE, JOHN
WOODLEY, WILLIAM
JACKSON, WILLIAM
WILLIAMSON, GEORGE
BROWN, C. W.
HOUSE, A.
FOSTA, ARTHUR
WHARTON, JAMES
DEBERRY, BENJAMIN
EATMAN, A.

REED, A.
BRILEY, JESSE
Page 124
GOLIGHTLY, WILLIAM H.
GOLIGHTLY, H.C.
RUTLEDGE, JAMES,SR.
RUTLEDGE, JAMES JR.
SMITH, JOSEPH
BELL. G.W.
KIMBELL. R.
LAMB. A.
WILCOX, H.
GRUBBS, D.
COLWELL, E.
GRADY, WILLIAM
HALE, WILLIAM C.
HODGES, WILLIAM
NELSON, D.
BEARD H.
TOWLES, JAMES
THOMPSON, WADDY
DOHERTY, JOHN
McDANIEL, THOMAS
BARRY, R. (son of R.)
DAVIS, G. M.
ARTHUR, WILLIAM
GROGAN, THOMAS
GROGAN, JAMES
HOLCOMBE, J. L.
SHOEMAKER, JOHN
PUCKETT, JOHN
RIDINGS, CHARLES C.
LITTLE, JOHN
DICKINSON, ANDREW
Page 125
VALENTINE, JAMES
TURNER, P.M.
TAYLOR, W.H.
COWAN, R.T.
HANNON, S.C.
DUNN, H.,SR.
MEANS, J.G.
REYNOLDS, GEORGE
WILLIAMSON, G.J.
BOOKER,ISSAC
WELLS, GOERGE
SMITH, S.
CAPSHAW, A.
CREWS. J.R.
VANDIVER, A.F.
SHOCKLEY, WILLIAM

Cherokee County

SNIDER, JOHN
PRICKETT, THOMAS
HUFF, WILLIAM H.
MATTHEWS, E.
RISEN, J.F.
LOFTIN, JOHN
McDANIEL, WILLIAM E.
BAILEY, WESLEY
MARTIN, G.A.
LEE, J.
BARNETT, WILLIAM
TIMMONS, R.
HENDERSON, JOHN C.
SLATTONGS, L.
HUFFAKER, G.L.

Page 126

WESTBROOKS, J.R.
COGGAN, JAMES
PRICKOLT, JOEL
CHRISLER, J.
McCOY, A.
DAVIS, THOMAS R.
SMITH, JONATHON
NELSON, JAMES
BARRY, J.G.
MOSELEY, JOEL
HARKIN, J.B.
LAWRENCE, HARRY
DOHERTY, J.M.
GANT, J.B.
JACK, G.G.
LEETH, EBENEEZER
BISHOP, JAMES
WILT, J.M.
MOORE, A. N.
CLAYTON, JOHN
ASH, NANCY
McCULLOCH, JAMES
NEWMAN, JOHN
CANNON, THOMAS
BAKER, T.A.
KEETON, MARY
TUFF, W.R.
COFFMAN, JACOB
REAVES, W.J.
BAKER, JOSEPH H.
BLACK, G.

Page 127

KRAFT, P.
HOWELL, JONAH
CAMPBELL, LAWSON
WEIR, GEORGE
HALE, MARTIN

PITTS, E.
HIGH, P.W.
WILLIAMSON, JOHN R.
TILLY, EDMUND
DAY, LOT
EDWARDS, THOMAS
WHITE, D.J.
MILLER, SAMUEL
ROBINSON, DAVID
SMITH, GEORGE
JOHNSON, JOHN J.
MATTHEWS, HENRY
BACKSTER, R. J.
RANDLE, N.
HIGH, E.
PATTON, DAVID
BURSON, L.L.
SMITH, JOHN
WILSON, R.J.
ROUSEAU, H.
BURNETT, J.S.
LOWRY, JOHN
LAYMAN, MARY
WALL, WILLIAM D.
MOORE, SAMUEL
HUGHES, M. H.

Page 128

GREEN, AMBROSE
JOHNSON, C.
SUMNER, NANCY
KELLY, ARTHUR
MARTIN, JOHN
SPANN, TOLIVER
BAILEY, JOHN
FULLER, BENJAMIN
FULLER, ABNER J.
NELSON, ABSLAOM
ROBINSON, ALLEN
COCKRAND, JOHN
COCKRAND, WILLIAM
BURROUGH, THOMAS
LAWSON, WILLIS
BURROUGH, A.
ODELL, THOMAS J.
HASKERSON, ELIAS
SAYMON, JACOB
MOORE, WILLIAM
NEWBERRY, JAMES
VANDYKE, JOHN J.
ISRAEL, JAMES
WEAVER, LUCINDA
STINSON, JOHN
WHITMORE, LARKIN

LYNES, FRANCIS
CLINAS, JAMES
COCKRAN, JOHN W.
PHILLIPS, JOHN
GREEN, JESSY

Page 129

WHITMIRE, STEPHEN
CROFT, WILLIAM B.
CROFT, JOHN W.
BENTLEY, HUGH
NEALE, THOMAS
RAY, JOHN
MONAGAN, SARAH
EDWARDS, GIDEON
QUINN, JAMES M.
JOY, J. H.
WATERS, ELIZABETH
YARBOROUGH, JOHN
RAY, ROBERT
ROWEN, B.T.
DUNN, HARRIS
IVY, Z.
MARTIN, JAMES
COOK, ARCHIBALD
GUTHRIE, HENRY
COX, TABITHA
GOODMAN, HENRY
NANTZ, TAPLEY W.
WILSON, EPHRAIM
MILLER, ORRIN
PARKER, JOHN
BROWN, ROBERT
PARKER, STEPHEN
PARKER, WILEY
ARNOLD, JAMES R.
JACKSON, JOHN
JACKSON, WILLIAM

Page 130

SPARM, JOHN
GARRETT, JAMES
LAWRENCE, JAMES
LAWRENCE, G. W.
SHOOK, W.T.
DEAN, A. L.
BURNETT, E. P.
BAKER, JOSEPH
MAPLES, JOSIAH
CLIFTON, GEORGE
CLIFTON, L.
PATEY, CHARLES
WHITE, W.
KENNEDY, G.
MATTOCKS. J.

Cherokee County

GRAY, E.
LAY, JOHN
MOONEY, S.
RAY, S.L.
BAKER, E.
GRAY, WILLIAM
ELDER, H.M.
HOLINSHEAD, GEORGE
LOVE, B.
PATTERSON, A.N.
GAMBLE. J.C.
WEAR, J. M.
LAWLER, I.L.
EWTON, E.P.
FOWLER, DAVID
McCONNELL, JOSEPH
Page 131
STANDEFER, L.J.
STANDEFER, F.H.
STANDEFER, WILLIAM H.
DANIEL. C.
COUPLAND, A.J.
BELL. J.G.
JOHNSON, E.W.
RISSELL. I.S.
DAVIS, JOHN
PARSONS, JOHN
CHILDRESS, R.L.
PRICE, J.T.
McGINNIS, I.S.
ADAMS, B.S.
THOMPSON. G.
McNEW, E.
McGEHEE, B.M.
BARRY, S.W.
SHARPE, JAMES
GILLIAM, WILLIAM N.
GARRETT, C.
FAULKNER, J.W.
TEAGUE, MOSES
ALEXANDER, E.O.
ORSON, F.C.
BORING. M.
GANT, M.
CLARKE, W.J.
STANDEFER, ISRAEL
MILLER, JAMES C.
TEAGUE, SILAS
Page 132
COOK, R.B.

ANDERSON, M.P.
MILLER, JAMES
DOHERTY, WILLIAM
PICKLE, DAVID
MOSELEY, J. M.
BEVIN, JOHN W.
VARNELL, JAMES, SR.
NELSON, DAVID
GRIGGS, JOHN
VARNELL, WILLIAM
MILLER, JOHN
SWAFFORD, ISSAC
HAYES, DAVID
PROVENCE, ELIZABETH
McGINNIS, JOHN
RYAS, ROBERT
CORNER, ROBERT
SMALLWOOD, M.
COLLINS, JOHN
BOWLES, JAMES M.
DUNNIGAN, JOSHUA
PRESLEY, CLINUS
COTTON, GEORGE
CEWSLY ?, P.T.
RUTLEDGE, WILSON
PITTS, WILLIAM S.
MILLER, JOHN
Page 133
BLACK, WILLIAM
THOMAS, JONATHON
HENDERSON, WILLIAM
COTTON, WILSON
THOMAS, JAMES
GRIFFIN, THOMAS
GARNETT, HIRAM
BURGESS, KING
SMITH, MARY
CAMPBELL, MURDOCK
BROOKS, JAMES
ENGLAND, POWELL
DICKSON, HUGH
STRICKLAND, S.
WATERS, CHARLES
TEAGUE, JACOB
GUPPIN, WILLIAM B.
WALDEN, ROBERT S.
CHISHOLM, P.J.
HUDGINS, WILLIAM
ANTHONY, HARRISON
BOOKER, J.

WELLS, GEORGE
MARTIN, J.
MACKAY, JOHN
HOFF, VALENTINE
WILHITE, CONSEY
READING, ISSAC
MILLER, JOHN
McIVER, ANDREW
TEAGUE, JOSHUA
Page 134
BULLARD, JOSEPH
BULLARD, TIMOTHY
SEWELL, DICEY
EARP, RICHMOND
CAMPBELL, JAMES N.
BULLARD, CHRISTOPHER
BUSE, BENJAMIN
BOLEN, JEREMIAH
BULLARD, JACOB
GOSSETT, JAMES
WHITE, JOHN A.
SMIDLEY, WILLIAM
WILLIAMSON, WILLIAM T
TAYLOR, WILLIAM N.
DOCKERY, E.
McELRATH, JAMES
McGEHEE, MARY
HAMMOND, JOSEPH J.
McMAHON, WILLIAM
CHAPMAN, SOLOMON
SHOCKLEY, ARCHIBALD
PATY, J.
ALLEN, MARK
RENDLEY, JESSE
ROWE, P.
HELMS, E.
HELMS, A.
STORY, SAMUEL
NICHOLS, WILLIAM I.
WESTMORELAND, ALEX.
WEBB, E. B.
Page 135
HARPER, J. T.
HUFF, A.
DUNMAN, ELY
CRANE, GEORGE, SR.
LAY, WILLIAM
SANDERS, N.
HALL, SAMUEL
HARPER, E. E.

Cherokee County

MATTHEWS, E.
GUTHRIE, D.
HOOPER, C.
MACKIN, E.
HOUSE, P.
WHEELER, JACOB
FELLOWS, WILLIAM
COURTLYNNE, J.F.
WHISNANT, N.
FRY, F.S.
PENN, WILLIAM
DURRER, C.
HOLLY, S.
DUNN, S.
TURNER, THOMAS F.
DUNN, F.
DUNN, D.
COATES, G.
BRYANT, WILLIAM S.
BRYANT, W.
BRYANT, SARAH
EDWARDS, JOHN
HUGHES, JAMES
Page 136
JOHNSON, A.
STREET, J.C.
COFFMAN, J.
TUCKER, JESSE
McRATH, WILLIAM
HARRIS, H.
WOOD, J.R.
TINSLEY, J.P.
ANDRES, GEORGE
HADLEY, A.
MASON, WILLIAM S.
McGRAGAN, D.
COBB, D. G.
HEFFNER, A.J.
ROGERS, GEORGE
NICHOLS, A.J.
AIKINS, I.
NICHOLS, JOHN B.
HUGHES, J. A.
HAILEY, DAVID
McDOUGLE, R.
SMITH, MICHAEL
HARDWICKE, WILLIAM
BEARD, E.O.
COCKRAN, E.
SCOTT, I.
PERRY, WILEY
HARDWICKE, F.M.

HARDWICKE, V.
BAKER, JOSEPH
RAWLINGS, JOHN
Page 137
WOOD, LUCILLA
COLLIER, J.N.
RAY, R.
HARWELL, H.
COLEMAN, R.
CASON, FM.
EDWARDS, S.
BRACEWELL, W.
EDWARDS, JAMES
EDWARDS, JOHN
VANN. H.
VANN, A.
WATT, MARY
McADAMS, S.
McADAMS, G.
REEVES, ISSAC
WILDER, J.
TUCKER, I.R.
ROWE, JAMES
ROWE, WILLIAM
DEAN, WILLIAM
CHESNUTT, WINEY
VINCENT, WILLIAM
CASTLEBERRY, JOHN
RAE, JOHN
WHITTEN, C.
HINTEN, SAMUEL S.
PEARSON, C.
BROWN, R.C.
SMITH, H.
Page 138
ALSOP, RANDOLPH
HAMILTON, DAVID H.
COTTEN, MOSES
ARNOTT, LEWIS
CAMBELL, TERRELL
CAMBELL, MOSES JR.
CARLTON, R.M.
WILSON, SAMUEL M.
HAMILTON, WILLIAM
GLOVER, H.
ROGERS, MARGARET
WALKER, RILEY
BEVERLEY, WILLIAM
ALSOP, W.
BRANDON, H.H.
REDWELL, SQUIRE
JOHNSON, JAMES M.

JACKSON, CHECKWELL
HENDERSON, JOHN R.
SMITH, JOHN
MUSKETT, CHARLOTTER
PERSON, WILLIAM
COOLEY, JAMES R.
SPENCE, JOHN
CARRELL, JOHN
KENT, RAWFORD
VEVERETT, LANCELOT
WILLIAMS, A.J.
WHARTON, JACOB
HUGHES, JOHN
HICKMAN, JOSIAH
Page 139
DOZIER, TULLY
CAMON, JONATHON
MATLOCK, JOHN R.
SMITH, RUSSELL
CURDEN JOHN
DEMPSEY, HEMPY
HALLMAN, CORALEE
JENNINGS, ROBERT
RANDOLPH, PEYTON
DENT, ROBERT
SOWELL, WILEY T.
SPAIN, S.H.
HUMPHRIES, BENJAMIN
GOODMAN, JOHN E.
DUNCAN, THOMAS
ODELL, THOMAS J.
FROST, J.D.
ODELL, JOHN M.
McGEHEE, SOLOMAN
FENNER, NATHANIEL
ROBESON, DANIEL
ROBESON, THOMAS
ANTHONY, WHITFIELD
ANTHONY, LEWIS
SPAIN, ALLEN
GREEN, SAXON
GREEN, HENRY
ANTHONY, JOHN
SHARPE, WILLIAM
MILLER, JESSE C.
WARB, SARAH
Page 140
HONEY, C.
HENSLEE, WILLIAM
HENSLEE, C.P.
PAYNE, MARY
MACKAY, J.J.

Cherokee County

RAINES, J.W.
RAINES, D.
MATHEWS, JOHN
DEJARNETT, ISRAEL
DAY, AMOS
HIGGINS, JOHN
POLLARD, WILEY G.
POLLARD, WILLIAM B.
DUPREE, WILLIAM S.
POLLARD, B.G.
NELSON, THOMAS
GRIZZELL, W.
SUTTLEMEYER, J.S.
LEGG, J. M.
WILSON, R.E.
NELSON, RAYMOND
CARLTON, JAMES
BREWER, A.S.
FARISH, MARAGERT
HALL, ALDEN
KELLY, CHARLES
POLLAIC ?, JAMES
DENMAN, THOMAS
LEE, NATHAN
BREWER, C.
SUTTLEMEYER, JOHN
Page 141
CARRELL, E.
MILLER. A.
PEEDEN, B.
GRIFFON, JESSE
DEARING, L.
MILLER, J.P.
HAMBRICK, C.
PEARSON, WILLIAM
STALLINGS, JOHN
ELAM, JAMES E.
CAMPBELL, ANDREW
DEAN, F.
WILKON, JOHN
RUSH, JOHN F.
DEAN, JACKSON
READ, JAMES M.
WILTEN, JEREMIAH
DOGAN, JOHN L.
NICHOLS, T.C.
NICHOLS, ARCHIBALD
STEPHENS, C..G.
SAMMONS, JERE
DOCKREY, E.
OWSLEY, RICHARD
GRIGGS, JAMES
ARNOLD, JAMES

GILMER, WILLIAM
ANTHONY, REBECCA
SEWELL, ISSAC
STANDIFER, JESSE
Page 142
DAVIDSON, R.
HODGES, THOMAS
DAVIDSON, JAMES
SHEEZOG, RICHARD
AKRIDGE, C.P.
CARRINGTON, D.
DOLLAR, WILLIAM C.
CREWES, WILLIAM
CREWES, J. H.
QUARLES, JESSE
CIRON, J.A.
BARRY, H.W.
CASH, LUCY
GILBREATH, A.
CAVIN, A.
HENDERSON, WILLIAM R.
TOPP, L.
SPAIN, A.
CAVIN, JOHN
STANDIFER, J.S.
PERKINS, JANE
HARTLINE, GEORGE
SHACKLEFORD, WILLIAM A.
JACKSON, ASA
HEFFNER, E.
CRAWFORD, L.
THOMPSON, AL.
HULL, M.
WALTERS, SARAH
Page 143
COMBS, WILLIAM
WOODWARD, SAMUEL
WESTER, JOHN
FIRESTONE, WILLIAM
HUDSON, JOHN N.
RIORDEN, A.W.
WILSON, S.W.
MORRISON, JOHN D.
DAVIS, JESSE
STRAND, ELIZABETH
TAPP, CURTIS
CRAIG, GILBERT C.
GRIFFETT, WILLIAM
WESTBROOK, BARNEY
POWERS, JOHN R.
WEEMS, JOEL
OSBORNE, JESSE
CLARKE, GEORGE

CLARKE, SAMUEL
ROBERTS, MARMADUKE
McDOUGAL, A.R.
McCABRON, JOHN
LEWIS, WILLIAM
RAINWATER, R.
THORNTON, JAMES
KING, GEORGE W.
DAVIS, VANN
DAVIS, JOHN
KENNEDAY, GEORGS
STEPHENS, WILLIAM
COMBS, WILLIAM, SR.
Page 144
JETT, A.
TATE, HANNAH
SMITH, STEPHEN
WESTER, JAMES
JOHNSON, JESSE
JACKSON, W.W.
ATES, WILLIAM
TATE, Q.
JONES, BENJAMIN
OWENS, JAMES
ROPER, MARTIN
RAINES, JOHN
WOODARD, JONATHON
RICHARDSON, IVY
PRICE, J.G.
HOUSE, A.
JOHNSON, S.
JOHNSON, L.
WOODLAND, CADOR
HORTON, BENJAMIN
BLACKSTOCK, JOHN
DOWNEY, JOSEPH
COTHERN, DANIEL
BLACK, DAVID
BLACK, J.R.
MURRELL, D.J.
CATHORN, DAVID
WOODSON, JAMES P.
MILLER, THOMAS
DACEY, JOHN A.
TRAYACK, W.
Page 145
GIFFETT, E.
MURPHY, R.
JACK, JERI
HOPE, JOHN
BURNETT, THOMAS M.
DAY, NICHOLAS
ST. CLAIR, JOHN
WILSON, ENOCH

Cherokee County

page 147

GOLDEN, F.
WILSON, STEPHEN
HALE, R.M.
HALE, G.W.
WILMOTH, P.D.
SKINNER, L.
HUGHES, ISSAC
PULLEN, THOMAS
HENSLEY, D.S.
HINSON, J.L.
SYCLAY?, JOHN
DARNELL, S.
LATHAM, S.G.
PATRICK. H.
CRUMPTON, W.T.
LEA, GEORGE
SMITH, A.W.
SMITH, BENJAMIN
MEADOWS, THOMAS
HAMPTON, J.H.
HELMES, D.

Page 146

GASKIN, J.P.
EARP, M.
MILLIGAN, JONATHON
RENTON, R.F.
CAMPBELL, M.
MURE, JOSEPH
MEDLOAK, JOHN
WELCH, JOSIAH
ROBINSON, JOHN
POTTER, HENRY
AMOS, MARGARET
BLACKWOOD, THOMAS
FARMER, Z.
CAGLE, G.
CHAMPION, WILLIAM
WADDLE, SETH
GANN, A.
McGEHEE, SARAH
BRAZELL. J.
PATTEN, SILAS
SHOCKLEY, JEPTHY
WHISTLE, A.C.
WILLIS, JACOB
ROBESON, JOHN
WARE, J.R.
WARE, JACOB
CASTLE, JAMES
SLATON, Z.
SHOCKLEY, MARGARET
RIGGS, THOMAS
LANDON, WILLIAM

WESTMORELAND, GEORGE
DOSSON, WILLIAM
LILLY, R.J.
COKER, SARAH
REED, SAMUEL
LACY, MARK
WOODLEY, JONATHON
WESTON, GEORGE
SMITH, WILLIAM
SMITH, JOHN
GREEN, P.
WESTON, JOHN
SMITH, JAMES
ANGLE, JOHN
WESTEN, P.
ALLEN, JOSEPH
REED, WILLIAM P.
OWEN, A.R.
OWEN, A.
MOORE, MARGARET
MOORE, JAMES
McLANE, ANDREW
PULLEN, PETER M.
BURNETT, ISABELLA
BURNETT, MADISON
ROBERTS, RACHAEL
MARTIN, WILLIAM
NOKERN, JAMES
DEAN, ELISHA
JACKSON, JAMES
WESTERN, EXOM

Page 148

WATKINS, G.B.
TIDMORE, H.
CALWELL, THOMAS
MERRITT, WILLIAM C.
LOOPER, SAMUEL
LOOPER, SAMUEL JR.
SPEARMAN, L.
WATTS, J.S.
TURNER, L.P.
LAMEASTER, JAMES
WASHINGTON, WARNER
KAY, JAMES
TRILMAN, JOHN
GARRETT, WILLIAM
HARRIS, G.
HARRIS, C.J.
HUGGINS, J.
CHRISTIAN, JOHN
ANDREWS, THOMAS
PATTERSON, WILLIAM
SMITH, WILLIAM W.

PARKER, GEORGE
WAGNON, P.
PARKER, P.H.
DAVIS, J. M.
HIPP LUCINDA
ADAMS, WILLIAM
WEST, WILLIAM H.
LEGGITT, C.S.
COVINGTON, J.B.
TIDMORE, A.

Page 149

FERGUSON, ELIZABETH G.
WILLIAMS, M.G.
CASTLE, WILLIAM
COBB, WILLIAM H.
HILL, JOHN
HOOPER, C.B.
CALDWELL, A.
ODEN, E.
SMITH, JAMES
FAVOR, JOEL
GIBSON, ELIZABETH
WISDOM, JOHN
DUNN, HENRY
DUNCAN, L.
HAMBRIGHT, M.A.
SPEARMAN, ROBERT
PALMER, W.
ODEN, MALACHI
SPEARMAN, EDWARD
GREEN, ISSAC
TILLESON, L.
WATERS, J.C.
McMAHON, JOHN
WINTERS, J. H.
HUGHES, G.
HOGE, MILDRED
*GARNER, JOSEPH
SPRING, WILLIAM
PAGE, R.
JONES, JOHN

Page 150

SMITH, JOHN J.
GOODSON, J.F.
ROBINSON, JOHN
FITZER, JOHN H.
HURLEY, S.
BOOKER, JANET
SMITH, R.W.
COFFMAN, D.
HOLLOWAY, J.
HURLEY, E.
HURLEY, H.

*military pensioner

Cherokee County

BLACKWELL, D.
WILLIAMS, S.J.
WATSON, JAMES
BLACKWELL, F.G.
BLACKWELL, THOMAS
ALTERS, D.
DEAN, A.T.
FINLEY, JOHN
LANKFORD, JOHN
LANKFORD, WILLIAM
FENLEY, R.
ELLIOTT, J.J.
SWANSEY, WILLIAM
MOSS, J.D.
FIELDER, THOMAS P.
CHILDRESS, THOMAS
MOSS, MARSHA
HARLIN, JOHN
MURPHY, JAMES
RAGAN, A.
  Page 151
WHARTON, A.J.
ELLIOTT, JOHN
MARTIN, A.
SMITH, R.
KIRKENDALL, JOHN
BELL, JOHN N.
BELL, JAMES H.
BELL, WILLIAM
HUSKERSON, R.
HAMILTON, H.E.
HUSKERSON, JOHN
GREEN, GEORGE
CHAPMAN, JOHN
KINCAID, WILLIAM D.
PRICE, THOMAS
STEPHENS, R.
DREW, N.
ROBERTS, L.
NICHOLS, A.
SIMMONS, A.
McRIGHT, M.
JONES, J.
ELLIOTT, P.B.
EVANS, ISSAC
ALLSOP, J.R.
WHITE, A.
JOHNSON, J.A.
VARNER, J.A.
JOHNSON, JABEZ
WILSON, SAMUEL

THOMASON, V.
  Page 152
VANDERVERT, ROBERT
CROUCH, G.M.
TAYLOR, DAVID
TAYLOR, DANIEL
CANNON, J.T.
THOMPSON, JAMES
CANNON, R.
McELRATH, THOMAS
THOMPSON, R.R.
RAWLINGS, J.
WHITSON, C.
MORRY, B.
LEE, J.D.
FLANAGAN, J.C.
HODGES, THOMAS
MONAHAN, D.A.
HARRISON, HENRY
COLBERN, JAMES
WATSON, L.

COOSA COUNTY

Formed 1832

Page 284
WINSLETT, WILLIAM
CALDWELL, WILLIAM S.
BURGESS, BRICE M.
STAMPS, WILLIAM G.
CALHOUN, E. A.
SMITH, THOMAS
AULD, JOHN A.
HENRY, WILLIAM
LAUDERDALE, DAVID
LAUDERDALE, ROBERT S.
McKINNEY, HARRIS
McKINNEY, PATRICK
DOLLAR, ELIZA
SOCKE, FRANCIS
SPEAKS, RICHARD
ETHERIDGE, JOHN
SMITH, JOSIAH
SPIVEY, AARON
SPIVEY, EPHRAIM
JORDAN, REUBEN
MARBURY, LEONARD
WHITSTONE, WILLIAM C.
THOMAS, E. W.
MITCHELL, JOHN
MITCHELL, MRS.
GADDIS, JOHN
HAYNES, HENRY
HAYNES, WILLIAM
OGLETREE, EDMUND
BRADFORD, JOSEPH H.
DRISKILL, JOHN

Page 185
HAGAN, CHARLES
WATKINS, AGNES
HARRIS, WILLIAM B.
NIX, ABSOLUM
NIX, WILLIAM
NIX, CHARLES
LEA, FREDERICK
VAUGHAN, ROBERT
WEEMS, THOMAS
VAUGHAN, GUILFORD
PATE, CHARLES
LEA, JOHN T.
FOWLER, NATH"L
FOWLER, ZEPHANIAH P.
FOWLER, WILEY
LEOPARD, LUKE
BALLARD, TOLIVER

KELLY, DR. JAMES A.
LAUDERDALE, JOSEPH
LAUDERDALE, J. C.
HUGHES, STEPHEN T.
NABORS, LEWIS
ADAIR, JOSEPH
WILKES, BENAJAH
GRAY, GEORGE
GRAY, J. M.
GREENWOOD, WILLIAM K.
TERRY, WILLIAM S.
PASCHAL, JAMES M.
CAMPBELL, JAMES C.
ULAN, BURREL

Page 186
DRIVER, DAVID
GRAHAM, SAMUEL S.
CHAPMAN, SIMEON
McKENZIE, JOHN
CHAPMAN, JOHN A.
McNAIR, JAPHETH
McLEOD, WILLIAM
CHAPMAN, WILLIAM
MITCHELL, DAVID
NABORS, PRYOR
WHITE, DAVID
VANN, JORDAN
MUNDAY, UPTON
DOWNING, JAMES
MORRIS, MARY
SHELTON, MRS.
EMBREE, JOHN M.
TULLIS, NEWEL
MORRIS, S. B.
CHILDERS, THOMAS
CLONCH, HARVEY
FORD, TIMOTHY
LEWIS, ABIJAH
LEWIS, JOHN B.
LEWIS, BENJAMIN
HARRIS, C. B.
LEWIS, THOMAS J.
PEARSON, JOHN
MILLER, WILLIAM, SR.
MILLER, WILLIAM, JR.

Page 287
MURRAY, CHARLES
MURRAY, CATLETT
LAMB, ISAAC

MARTIN, JOHN
SHAW, WILLIAM
MARTIN, JOHN R.
LEWIS, JOHN W.
GOODGAME, JAMES
MIZZLE, GLISTEN
HAMILTON, WILLIAM
McELRATH, JOHN P.
ULARD, WILLIAM
McMILLAN, H.G.
McMILLAN, JOHN C.
MOSS, WILLIAM T.
BATTOR, JOEL
BALLARD, THOMAS
WHITLEY, COKER
BULLARD, JAMES
BARNETTE, JOHN
CAMPBELL, MRS.
HAMILTON, G. W.
CUMMINGS, THOMAS
ROBERTSON, JOHN
THOMAS, JOHN
GOODGAME, ROBERT C.
ROLLIN, WILLIAM
PRICE, WILLIAM
STIDHAM, WILLIAM A.
PHILIPS, JAMES B.

Page 288
GREEN, HARMON
ABBOTT, ABRAM
PHILIPS, JOEL
WHITE, RICHARD
PHILIPS, HAWKINS
DAWSON, JONAS B.
BOYT, CHATTEN
PODY, ANDREW
MAHAN, ALFORD C.
MYERS, WILLIAM P.
PETERSON, THOMAS
PETERSON, SAMUEL
GOGGINS, JAMES
MAHAN, AMEY
PRATER, JAMES
RADFORD, SAMUEL
TUCK, JOSEPH
BOZEMAN, NATHAN
SMITH, JOHN
ADAIR, BENJAMIN
BOWMAN, JOHN

Coosa County

HUEY, EPHRAIM
HUEY, ALEXANDER
GRIMES, JOHN
HAGAN, DANIEL
RYLANT, BENJAMIN
LIVINGSTON, JOHN
ATKINS, WILLIAM
BISHOP, MARY ANN
DEASON, WILLIAM

Page 289

CHILDERS, WILLIAM
BAILEY, SAMUEL E.
COLIN, PATRICK
PHILIPS, JAMES C.
CAUSEY, JOHN
QUINN, E. W.
CAUSEY, EZEKIEL
CAUSEY, THOMAS
ROBERTSON, THOMAS
ROBERTSON, HENRY
BROWN, JOHN
VARDEMAN, THOMAS
HOWELL, JOHN D.
SAMS, STEPHEN
MEASLES, MARK
HACKER, SARAH
PATE, THOMAS
McGOUGH, WILLIAM M.
BUTLER, CHRISTOPHER
BARNETTE, RIAL
CHILDERS, DOUGLAS
UNDERWOOD, JOHN
PHILIPS, JAMES
PHILIPS, HIRAM, SR.
PHILIPS, REUBIN
CAMPBELL, DAVIS
COOPER, URIAH
MAHAN, DAVID
BARNETT, GLENN
PINSON, JOEL

Page 290

CRANFORD, RICHARD
GOODGAME, WILLIAM A.
WATKINS, THORNTON P.
WOOTEN, BENJAMIN
CONNER, DAVID

Page 291

POWELL, ZACCHEUS
HICKMAN, JESSE
ROBBINS, SOLOMAN
ROBBINS, DANIEL
BONNER, B.B.
ALLEN, GEORGE

BRANAN, CALEB J.
CLEAVELAND, LARKIN
CRUMPLER, ALMOND
CORBIT, JOHN
NASH, GEORGE B.
HOBDAY, STARK
HALL, BOLLING
HALL, THOMAS
ROBINSON, DR. PETER P.
BULGES, JOHN C.
WILSON, ISAIAH
SWAIN, JAMES
RICHARDS, WILLIAM
HILL, ADAM
SWAIN, WILLIAM
WHATELEY, JAMES
BILLIPS, JOSEPH
GOODMAN, JAMES N.
PLUNKET, RICHARD
GRAVES, JOHN R.
WITTON, JAMES
GRAHAM, JOHN G.
REYNOLDS, HENRY
MARTIN, ROBERT S.
HARDY, ROBERT

Page 292

SPEARS, RUFUS
LITTLE, ROBERT
JOHNSON, GEORGE
PEACOCK, JOHN
COTTON, CHARLES K.
GULLEDGE, JOEL
RALSTON, E. S.
EDEN, REV. JAMES
CULLEN, MRS.
SUTER, OBLAN
YORK, JOHN A.
MacLEMON, MRS.
SIKES, J. D.
WILLIAMS, WARNER
POE, JOHN
WEAVER, WILLIAM SR.
HOGAN, DANIEL
RAY, M.
ROBERTSON, ELISHA
WEST, REV. B.S.
TOWNSEND, PASCHAL
JONES, GABRIEL
JOHNSON, HOWELL
CRUMPLER, ALBERT
HOWARD, WILLIAM
GRAHAM, JOHN P.
GRAHAM, ALEX., JR.

GRAHAM, JAMES P.
GRAHAM, GEORGE

Page 293

SMITH, ALEX.
FINLAYSON, DANIEL
SUTTLE, WILLIAM
BYRD, PETER
McDANIEL, JOHN
SMITH, S J.
HARRELL, JESSE
THOMPSON, DICKSON
RUSHING, ABRAM
SALTER, SAMUEL
MARTIN, ROBERT
SALTER, WILLIAM
SALTER, JOSEPH
WILKINSON, SIDNEY
BARTON, WASHINGTON
KINDRICK, ANDERSON H.
BENSON, ROBERT
BELIER, OBADIAH
WEAVER, W. N.
ROLLASON, NATHANIEL
LEE, HENRY
SHACKLEFORD, RICHARD
MURPHY, MADISON
RAY, WILLIAM M.
LEDBETTER, JAMES
WORREL, BRYANT
MOON, MARK E.
UBANKS, J. M.
WATSON, HENRY
OGLETREE, JOHN S.

Page 294

CARLTON, RICHARD
BULGER, WILLIAM C.
SUTTLES, ISAAC
JONES, GEORGE
LEA, WILLIAM C.
LEA, MILBURN
COKER, M.
THOMPSON, JACKSON
BENSON, J.
HARRELL, ELI
HAGERTY, MRS.
GRIFFIN, JOHN
RAY, STEPHEN
BRADLEY, W.W.
ROBERTSON, ELISHA, SR
DOBBINS, R.
CRUMPLER, J. P.
SMITH, DANIEL K.
SMITH, LAUCHLIN K.

Coosa County

McNEILL, JOHN
JONES, RUSSEL
ALLEN, ELIZA
POWELL, JEFFERSON
THORNELL, WILLIAM
TUNNELL, JOSIAH
TUNNELL, STEPHEN
GILLY, G. W.
CATO, WILLIAM
THOMPSON, IGANTIUS
ROBINSON, JOHN
Page 295
BENSON, WILLIAM
WALKER, DANIEL
WILLIS, REV. JAMES
THOMPSON, ZACHARIAH
AUSTIN, THOMAS
McCULLERS, WILLIAM
TEMPLE, URIAH A.
PHILIPS, HIRAM
PHILIPS, RUFUS
Page 296
WILLIAMS, JAMES
CLARK, L. B.
WILLIAMS, LAMBKIN
WILLIAMS, HILLARY
SMITH, HARDAWAY
SMITH, VINE
BENSON, GEORGE
JOHNSON, ALEX.
LEWIS, LAZARUS
JONES, LEWIS C.
Page 297
FOSCUE, BENJAMIN
COWARD, ZACHERIAH
CROWSON ?, DAVID
*BLANKENSHIP, REUBEN
STEWART, RICHARD
BRAZIER, RICHARD H.
PERRYMAN, G. W.
PYLANT, J. A.
LINDSEY, JAMES
CORBIN, THOMPSON
SHELTON, SEPHTEN
SHELTON, JAMES
FERGUSON, LEWIS
HARMON, WILLIAM
LIGHTFOOT, JOHN R.
LANCE, CHARLES H.
JOHNSON, JACOB
RUSSEL, JAMES

MOONEY, JOSEPH
ERWIN, ROBERT
BLANKENSHIP, MARK
COFFEY, NEVIN
SMITH, ELIJAH
SMITH, PATRICK
BLANKENSHIP, JAMES
KELLY, JOHN
BURGESS, RICHARD
COFFEY, SAMUEL
FORCUE, CALEB
PATTERSON, GREEN
KELLY, JAMES
Page 298
SMITH, SAMUEL
FOSCUE, WILLIAM
MORRIS, JOHN
MORRIS, BAYLIS
CROSS, EPHRIAM R.
BLANKENSHIP, HENRY
GENTRY, JAMES
WILSON, WILLIAM
HARWELL, JEREMIAH
McCANNON, ISAAC
GIFFIN, WILLIAM
BLANKENSHIP, JOHN
KELLY, SURRY
MORGAN, THOMAS
CONE, MATTHEW
FRANKLIN, P. J.
HARDY, JOEL
SMITH, JAMES
SMITH, GUY
McNEELY, J. J.
RICHARDS, JACOB J.
LEWIS, ABEL
WHITE, MAJOR
WHITE, RICHARD
STANLEY, WILLIAM
SCOTT, A.J.
MEADOWS, ARA
BRYAN, JOSIAH D.
CAMPBELL, JAMES
ESPY, WILLIAM
Page 299
POND, EBENEZER
CLEAVELAND, R.W.
POWELL, JAMES R.
McDONALD, JOHN S.
CHANCELLOR, ABRAM
WALL, THOMAS T.

HATCHETT, THOMAS W.
HATCHETT, WILLIAM E.
GRAHAM, WILLIAM
STUBBLEFIELD, JOHN
PATTERSON, SARAH
MELTON, GEORGE
MORRIS, CHESLEY
ROBERTSON, WILLIAM F.
RAY, WILLIAM H.
ROBINSON, WILLIAM
ECHOLS, ISAAC
LOGAN, SAMUEL
LOGAN, MRS.
WILSON, WILLIAM B.
HAMILTON, JOHN M.
WILLIAMS, REV. G. D.
STRINGFELLOW, WILLIAM
CAVENNESS, J.
RAY, JOSEPH
McGOUGH, JOHN
JONES, DAVID
LOGAN, ALEX
EDWARDS, ISHAM
CAMPBELL, WILLIAM
LOGAN, HENRY
Page 300
JONES, HENRY
MURCHISON, JOHN
HANNON, THOMAS
ALLEN, ETHELRED
HARRELL, ADAM
CARROL, ETHELRED
CHANCELLOR, WILLIAM
WILLIAMS, CHARLES
BAGGET, JOHN
HUGHES, R.R.
MANNING, ARCH'D
McREA, D. W.
MOORE, JAMES
McDONALD, DANIEL
MURCHISON, WILLIAM E.
HUGHES, GRIGBY
HICKS, JAMES
PETERS, WILLIAM
JONES, JACOB
ROBBINS, BENJAMIN
BOLES, JOSEPH
PUTTS, WILLIAM
ADKINSON, ARTHUR
MILLER, JOHN A. J.
ROLLASON, SILAS

* military pensioner

Coosa County

HAYDEN, JOSEPH A.
CASEY, M. B.
*CASEY, WILLIAM
BARNETT, JOSEPH
MOORE, WILLIAM H.
CARTER, ABRAM
Page 301
LOONEY, JOHN
COKER, NATHAN
WILSON, ANDREW
BURROW, HENRY
PATE, THOMAS
PATE, CHARLES
PATE, JOHN
JONES, G. W.
DUKE, JOEL
AUTRY, ENOCH
COKER, A. R.
PRATER. A.
DUNHAM, A. J.
DUNHAM, WILLIAM D.
WILSON, WILLIAM A.
HASSAN, WILLIAM
COLBURN, JOHN
BOWDON, JOHN
COKER, ROBERT
SAXTON, S. J.
LOWRY, GEORGE
LOWRY, THOMAS
WOOD, ALLEN
BAXLEY, AARON
DOWNING, ARCHIBALD
BAILEY, N.
MAHURD, WILLIAM
GRISHAM, G. B.
ARMSTRONG, S. B.
MONK, JAMES
WILLIAMS, HUGH
Page 302
JORDAN, THOMAS
WILSON, JOHN D.
FORSHEE, JOHN
ARMSTRONG, MOSES
ARMSTRONG, ROBERT, SR.
POSEY, SIMEON
ARMSTRONG, WILLIAM
HARRISON, S. D.
PICKENS, ISRAEL
RAGSDALE, MICAJAH
DICKINSON, JOEL
McINTYRE, REV.D.C.
COOPER, JAMES
SPEARS, HANNAH

HARDY, T.
HARDY, JOHN
MORRIS, WILLIAM J.
MORRIS, JOHN B.
CRENSHAW, MICAJAH
COKER, MARY
JONES, R.R.
POSEY, SQUIRE
COKER, JAMES A.
BAXLEY, SAMUEL
WILLIS, WILBORN
FINNEY, WILLIAM
FLEMMING, WILLIAM
McKEE, JAMES
McKEE, WILLIAM
Page 303
PRITCHETT, MRS.
JOHNSON, MRS.
McDANIEL, WILLIAM
FINLEY, JAMES
GLASCOCK, LOWRY
BECK, EDOM
WILLIAMS, BARROK
WILSON, ALEX. N.
WEAVER, DAWSON
JONES, ABRAM
RODGERS, JAMES
PRINTISS, DANIEL
ARMSTRONG, ROBERT JR.
EMBERSON, WILLIAM
NEWSOM, J. M.
Page 304
PINKSTON, LUCIAN
SPIGNER, JOEL
WINDHAM, SIMEON
SMITH, MALCOM
McCLURE, MOSES
CHAPMAN, ALLEN
JUMPER, JOHN G.
JAMES, SARAH
HURLEY, N.
ETHRIDGE, WILLIAM
CHAPMAN, SOLOMAN
WALL, JAMES A.
THWART, NED (man of color)
UNDERWOOD, WILLIAM
PAULDING, MRS.
HOLMAN, JOHN
HARGUS, DAVID
TERRY, WILLIAMSON
CALVIN, NATHAN
McDUFFIE, JOHN
NICHOLSON, A.B.

MOBLEY, BENJAMIN
STOKES, ALLEN
STOKES, ALLEN
STOKES, MRS.
WEDGES, NOEL
JACKSON, JOHN
OLIVER, WILLIAM K.
CHRISTIAN, JOHN
WILLIAMS, JOHN H.
STEWART, WILLIAM
BROWN, WILLIAM
Page 305
EDGING, JOHN
GRAHAM, ALEX. SR.
HATCHER, J. B.
MOORE, M. J.
TURNER, SIMEON W.
PIERCE, WILLIAM
CHURCH, MRS.
HARWELL, D.G.C.
OHARRA, W.H.
FUNDERBURK, G.W.
HARWELL, PENELOPE
CURRRY, DANIEL D.
BACHANAN, JAMES
MOORE, JACOB
JAMES, WILLIAM
MARTIN, JAMES M.
TURNER, WILLIAM
BRIGMAN, DANIEL
GRAHAM, MRS. NEALLY
WINDHAM, MATTHEW
GRAHAM, THOMAS P.
JUMPER, MRS.
WINDHAM, STEPHEN
McDONALD, DUNCAN S.
BEARD, ELIJAH
GRAY, WILLIAM
TAYLOR, ROBERT
SPIGNER, LOUIS
MORRIS, JAMES
Page 306
GRIER, MOSES
BLAKE, WILLIAM
McQUEEN, DANIEL
McARTHUR, DANIEL
SETCHER, JOHN D.
ROWE, JOHN
KENNEDY, WILLIAM
MARKET, JAMES E.
STEWART, G. A.
BOSTICK, JOHN
MYERS, JOHN P.

Coosa County

WESTMORELAND, R.
HAGERTY, JOSHUA
SULLIVAN, JOHN
LOVE, A. C.
THOMAS, D. B.
HATAWAY, MARTIN
JONES, SAMUEL P.
BIGGS, ISAAC N.
GRAY, GAINER
HUDMAN, H. J.
GURLEY, JAMES
MASINGALE, A. M.
PARKER, JAMES B.
BAKER, ABNER
BAKER, MRS. REBECCA
McARTHUR, JOHN
ROWE, DANIEL
*ROWE, JOSHUA
COOPER, ROBERT
KIMBREL, ARCHIBALD
PARKER, PETER
Page 307
WELCH, SAMUEL
FOSTER, A. W.
LOVEJOY, SAMUEL
SANFORD, C.P.
CALHOUN, DUGALD
BROWN, ELZEY
FLEMMING, JAMES
COLEMAN, JESSE
THORNTON, MAJOR
WILLIAMS, DAVID
McMANUS, JOHN
LIVINGSTON, WILLIAM
CALHOUN, MRS.
LOVEJOY, MABRY
PEAVY, MICHAEL
GINN, JOSHUA
DAVIS, MRS.
HAGERTY, B. G.
COLEMAN, A. J.
BRADY, ROBERT
ROWE, GABRIEL
TOWNSEND, JOHN
BRANAN, JAMES
SELLERS, ALFRED
DRIVER, JOHN
SANFORD, CASWELL
ULREND, MACK
PENNINGTON, FRANK
LOVEJOY, CRAWFORD
GOLDING, THOMAS
Page 308
GRAY, ISRAEL
BRADSHAW, JESSE

GRAY, ISRAEL
BRADSHAW, JESSE
BRADSHAW, DANIEL
STARKE, WILLIAM J.
HETTON, JOSEPH
BROWN, WRIGHT
TOWNSEND, SAMUEL
WALKER, THOMAS
LEA, JOHN
KIDD, SEABORN J.
SPENCER, WILLIAM
BAKER, REBECCA
SAUNDERS, WILLIAM
SAUNDERS, JOHN W.
BIECE, BRYANT
JOHNSON, JOHN A.
SHEPPARD, ANDREW
CARMICHAEL, DANIEL
GRAHAM, NEILL O.
MODESETH, JAMES
HAYNES, ROBERT H.
SPEARS, H. T.
WOOD, NATHAN
KEITH, NATHANIEL
JOINER, HENRY
STEWART, JOHN
THOMAS, WILLIAM
HUNNALY, A.M.
EPMAN, BENJAMIN
Page 309
ROSE, HOWELL
NALLY JOHN A.
DILLARD, GEORGE
TAYLOR, GEORGE
FAIN, JAMES W.
PARKER, DR. A.
CARLETON, ARCHIBALD
SKINNER, JOHN
THOMAS, DR. A.
JEOFFS, JEFFREY
GARDNER, EDWARD
OHARRA, ANDREW
ODIORUR?, WILLIAM H.
RODGERS, M. W.
CHAPMAN, BENJAMIN
SKINNER, WASHINGTON
PACE, ALEX.
ORAM, HENRY
ROWE, MICHAEL
HAYNES, WILLIAM
BOYD, JOHN
Page 310
HOLMAN, REV. ROBERT

BEALLE, DR. J.
GOULDING, JOHN
ADAMS, O.E.
BAILEY, H.B.
CHAPMAN, SOL. D.
MONTGOMERY, REV. R.
PARISH, OBED
LANIER, R.
RODGERS, WILEY
CAMPBELL, JOHN
COTTEN, JOHN
YANCEY, WILLIAM L.
FAGAN, ENOCH
BECKHAM, JULIUS
KENNEDY, LEWIS
READY, AARON
HAGERTY, ABEL
LEAK, TILMAN
WYNN, JOHN P.
LAPRADE, BENJAMIN
McMILLAN, JOHN B.
WILSON, FREDERIC
MORAN, JOHN D.
HEADEN, MICHAEL B.
FULTON, SAMUEL
HILL, REUBEN
GRIFFIN, BENNET S.
STARK, BOLLING W.
CLEGHORN, CHARLES
BILLING, DR. SAMUEL A.
Page 311
CONANT, JOHN H.
JENNINGS, C. M.
WELCH, THOMAS J.
RYLAND, R.W.
LONGSTREET, CROCHARON
LIVELY, M.C.
CARNOCHAN, SAMUEL
DEW, JOHN R.
HATTAN, F.J.
ROUSE, J.J.
ENSLEN, JOHN
CHESSON, URIAH
SKINNER, WILLIAM
JAMES, MRS.
HAWTHORN, WILLIAM
McDOUGALD, DR. WILLIAM
CRIMMINS, FREDERICK
POLLARD, JAMES A.
COOK, HENRY H.
HANNA, ROBERT
TARDY, COURTNEY

Coosa County

ANDREWS, JAMES
CARSON, WILLIAM
CRAM, JOHN
LOFTIN, JERIMIAH
DAVIS, SUSAN
HUBBARD, MATTHEW
BOYD, PLEASANT
ADAMS, MRS. ANN
WOMACK, JOHN E.
Page 312
HARRIS, SAMPSON W.
GAITHER, ELI E.
THOMAS, DR. JOHN H.
THOMAS, WILLIAM K.
FITZGERALD, REUBEN
KYLE, WILLIAM S.
DAWSON, A.B.
COOK, MRS. ANN B.
LYLE, ANDREW
GILL, HENRY
FRIOR, J. M.
HOUSE, SAMUEL W.
HOUGHTON, JOHN
FLEMMING, THOMAS W.
FOX, DR. DANIEL J.
STRINGFELLOW, WILLIAM
McNEILL, JAMES M.
SMITH, MRS. HARRIET
BYERS, JOHN M.
PENICK, DR. W.C.
LEWIS, SPENCER P.
CHAPMAN, JOHN D.
VANBIBBER, HENRY
DALE, THOMAS P.
CATER, S.
CLOCK, DARIUS
CAMP, EDWARD
HANSFORD, G. M.
BAXTER, EDWARD
GASTON, ROBERT T.
NUNNALY, WALTER
Page 313
YARBOROUGH, WILLIAM G.
BAYLIS, R. D.
McFARLAND, JAMES
LOVEJOY, SIMEON
CONIFF, P.
CAMP, SUSAN
WILKINS, DR. THOMAS T.
McCANN, JOSEPH D.
RAINEY, S.S.

FISHER, MARY
WILKINS, WILLIAM
GARDNER, BENJAMIN
HARWELL, JOSEPH
MERRITT, JAMES
GARNETT, ?
DEAN, G. C.
ROGERS, ROBERT
MASON, WILEY W.
THRASHER, MRS. E. A.
WILKINS, FRANK
STONE, S. M.
WHIFFIN, SARAH
MASTIN, W.W.
McCOY, M. B.
CATLIN, SAMUEL
GREEN, DANIEL
STEWART, JAMES
WARREN, J. W.
JENNINGS, JOSEPH B.
Page 314
SHAW, HUGH
HARRIS, JAMES H.
MASTERS, H.A.
COLE, WILLIAM R.
HAMILTON, SALLY
CLEAVELAND, JOSEPH B.
CLEAVELAND, BENJAMIN
WARD, SAMPSON
DAVIDSON, ISAAC
HORTON, JAMES
COOPER, JAMES
HILL, REV. JOSEPH
PUTTS, JOHN
WILSON, JOHN
MORRIS, JAMES B.
MORRIS, JOSEPH
FOSTER, MRS. AGNES
LOGAN, ELLIS
ELLISON, JOHN
DAVIS, G. W.
PATTERSON, ADAM
GILLIS, NEAL
WOOD, C. D.
PARKER, CARTER
TAYLOR, WILLIAM A.
ECHOLS, MRS.
WILSON, L. W.

DEKALB COUNTY

Formed 1835

Page 154
HANKINS, R. D.
CARNS, S. F.
HAWS, SAMUEL
CLAYTON, S.
WARREN, H.
ROWAN, A.
MAGERS, B.
MATHEWS, W. M.
BURT, E.
LITTLE, ISAAC
JOHNSON, J.
McPHERSON, L.
McPHERSON, GEORGE
BRIGGS, JOHN
WINSTON, J. G.
CARNES, W. Y.
BINNOW, W. M.
BERRY, B. H.
BURKET, J.
MALONE, D.
LOVELADY, H.
BYAM, W. M.
STUART, M. H.
PITTS, T.
DANNIE, D. M.
GRIFFIN, W. M.
COX, ISRAEL
GRIFFIN, N.
NEWMAN, M.C.
BERRY, B. H.

Page 155
PATEN, J.
ADAMS, SILAS
BUSSEL, A J.
MITHROE, M. H.
BROCK, A.
BROCK, H.
FINER, J.
MITCHEL, JAMES
FRASURE, J.
WITT, J.
HULER, JOHN
CHITWOOD, S.
BAXTER, F.
HILER, J.
GREEN, B. F.
HAYS, L.W.
WASSEN, B. M.
TAYLOR, H.
LEROY, A. M.

HULER, J.
HULER, M. W.
PARKER, A.
PARKER, E.
HULER, N.
GILLESPIE, J.
CUNNINGHAM, J.
BELCHER, J.
MICHAEL, Z.
PRINCE, H.

Page 156
RAINWEATHER, J.
LAWSON, J.
BLEVINS, F.
NICHOLS, J.
JOHNSON, B.
LEWIS, J.
WALKER, J. S.
RION, A.
*FRASIE, JACOB
STEEL, J.
FINKES, A.
HUMBOARD, M.P.
STONER, R.
EVANS, C.
PHILLIPS, A.
ROWAN, R.
CLABO, J.B.
COOPER, J.
CROPLIN, J.
BARKER, S.
COLLIN, J.
BEEN, J.
COOPER, J.
RITE, M. M.
WILLSON, A.
MICKS, J.
DEATON, J.
WARREN, N.
CALAWAY, J. T.
WHITEHEAD, F.

Page 157
STEPHENS, H.
CAPENGER, A.
BLEVINS, W. H.
MAXWELL, M.
GRIFFIN, J. A.
WILSON, W.
COOPER, J.
LASTON, J.

ROACH, J.
ROACH, S.
CASE, A.
BLEVINS, J.
SMITH, J.
STEPHENS, L. A.
WILLIAMS, J.
COOPER, M.
ASMON, A. D.
PUCKETT, L. A.
SISTON, J.
VANCE, W. M.
HOLDEN, R.
HUSE, J.
STEPHENS, A.
CRAGE, J.
COOK, J.
AUSTIN, E.
HAMMON, W.
NICHOLS, M. M.
DAVIS, J.
DAVIS, R.

Page 158
LAWSON, J.
FRASURE, THOMAS
HALL, E. D.
HORTON, J.
MAY, J. GEORGE
SUTTON, S.
SLAYTON, E.
SLAYTON, F.
SLAYTON, W. M.
SLAYTON, J.
DRAM, R.
DRAM, ROAN
DRAM, J.
CAR, J.
CAR, E.
BARWELL, L.
MATHIS, P.
JONES, M.
GOODNEY, H.
FUGLE, H.
SMITH, H.
BLEVINS, R.
HUSE, R.
CAGLE, C.
CAGLE, GEORGE
HUSE, W.
HUSE, G.

* military pensioner

Dekalb County

BROWN, J.
DRAIN, J.
Page 159
RITE, DISON
REACE, A.
WALKER, W.W.
DEACON, H.
MOORE, L.
VENIBLE, J.
HOGE, D.
PARSONS, L.
MONROE, G.W.
BOWIN, S.
BERRY, H.
GOODWIN, A.
HAMER, F.
BIDDLE, B.
LEE, W.
MINGO, S.C.
MALONE, R. F.
HANIS, S.
COOPER, E.
FULLER, J.
SHELTON, D.
KING, W. M.
MUSGROVE, H.
SCOTT, F.
RUSSELL, R.B.
BACON, E.
DRISCOL,. W. M.
REED, F. L.
CRAUD, B. M.
CAPEHART, F.F.
Page 160
WARD, N.W.
MCMICHAEL, A. J.
BROCK. J.
CHAPMAN, A.
BROWN, M.
WHITE, J.B.
WATTS, F. B.
COLLINS, L.
PHILLIPS, G.
WARD, N.
MAYS, S.
MAYS, J. F.
MAYS, S.
RICHUSON , J.F.
BRIDGES, M.
MINGO, J.
MORGAN, F.
BLANTON, W.

SMITH, W. C.
GIBSON, J.
COLLINS, E.
WATTS, S. B.
FURENTINE, S.
DOUGLASS, D.
SANDERS, R.
HALL, V.
BOSWELL, J.
TIDWELL, P. S.
ROGERS, F. J.
BOYSTON, F. B.
Page 161
ROSE, S. P.
HARRISON. R. P.
WARD, B.
CASE, J.
WIGGES, H.
FROST, B. H.
HARRISON, J.
GREENWOOD, J.
MALONE, N.
SCOTT, J.
LONG, B.
HASTY, S.
ELLIS, W. M.
STOWARS, C.
SHRUM, D.
TURNER, J.
NELSON. A. H.
LITTLE, R.
CASE, S.
AVERY, A.
MORGAN, J.
HAMIT, J.
WARD, J.
RAGANS, C.
PRINCE, C.
YEARGAIN, J.
SHOEMAKE, R.
DUKE, J. P.
SAUNDERS, E.
FONTAINE, F.
Page 162
MAGERS, A. W.
MOONEY, W. F.
GARRETT, F.
LYONS, J.
SMITH, J.
WALKER, WILLIAM C.
LONG, A.
BALLARD, F.

NICHOLS, J.
DAVIS, G.
HAWKINS, R.
NICHOLS, THOMAS
LEWIS, J.
STINNET, H.
HAMMONS, C.
BARNES, J.
BARNES, J.
BERRY, S.
CLARK, J.
JOHNSON, S.
BERRY, E.
CLARK, D.
HOOD, B.
WITHERSPOON, F. A.
SHANKLE, J.
REED, J.
LEMON, J.
CASEY, W. P.
WRIGHT. G.
Page 163
WRIGHT, J. C.
DUCKWORTH, J.
TAYLOR, M.
BISHOP, WILLIAM
BISHOP, J.
RUSSEL, E.
GOGGANS, E.
BISHOP, J.
DITTS, J.
BERRY, A. J.
BUSTER, M. W.
STILES, A.
REED, J.
GILLAND, B. A.
CASEY, J.
REED, S.
BERRY, J.
WARD, S.
BRIDGES, H.
PATRIC, F. A.
GUYLER, J.
OLIVER, M. B.
PLANT, S.
PITTS, J.
BROCK. J.
CURLEY, J.
MADOWS, M.
HANKINS, S.
GUYLER, A.
KEENER, D.

Dekalb County

Page 164
STEWART, H.
WILSON, E.
SIDES, A.
ELLIS, L.
ELLIS, WILLIAM
SIDES, A.
BLY, WILLIAM
SHINAULT, WILLIAM
BASS, J.
BURGESS, J.
ROSS, G.
CALLAHAN, H. F.
TINGLE, J.
REESE, J.
JOHNSON, J. B.
ROSS, A.
GLAYSNER, J.
FORTUNE. M. W.
BAR, S. P.
BROWN, B. H.
MICHAEL, WILLIAM
MICHAEL, J.
BROCK, H.
CLAYTON, S. C.
BAKER, L. G.
NICHLESON, M.
THOMPSON, J. R.
RUSSEL, F.
FINDLAY, A.
DOVE, J. F.

Page 165
RODEN, B.
RODEN. W. B.
JONES, J. W.
DOBBS, J.
GRADY, J.
FURGESON, A. F.
FURGESON, B.
FURGESON, E. B.
NAINE, J.
LACEY, W.
ROBERTS, J.
ROBERTS, R.
FUCKER, N. F.
PEARSON, E.
PINSON, E.
POTTER, J.
LACY, S.
TAYLOR, F. A.
SNIDER, D.
CLAYTON, S.
DRISCOLL, W.

ARMSTRONG, A.
MILLER, F.
DANIEL, M. M.
FRUIT, W.
WEBB, B. B.
FUNSTEN, W. B.
RUSSEL, A. J.
HENDIX, J.
SAMPLES, J.

Page 166
SIMON, A. H.
CONE, S.
LOONEY, WILLIAM M.
SIMPSON, WILLIAM
READ, B.
MITCHEL, B.
MITCHEL. J.
LAMPKIN, JAMES
COPLAND, J.
FINER, C.
WHITE, S.
SMITH, J.
ROBERTS, M.
PATEN, B.
CAMPBELL, E.
RICHEY, E.
MITCHEL, J.
GADDY, J.
MITCHELL, JAMES
MITCHELL, WILLIAM
HARGSONER, WILLIAM
LUMPKIN, L.
HOGE, J.
HARRIS, S.
SMITH, S.C.
RUSSEL, O.
HONEYBUT, A.
FINDER, J.
EDWARDS, L.
GINYARD, J.

Page 167
HUSTOLLS, H.
MILLER. H.
FRANELL, F.
THURMAN, J.
HASSETT, F.
THARPE, WILLIAM
GARRISON, M.
GILBREATH, B.
BURRUS, C.
GILBREATH, E.
RUSSEL, F.

MALONE, L.
DUNHAM, J.
HARISS, F.
JONES, A.
CUNNINGHAM, H.
HARRISON, A.
BRUCE, G. W.
BRADEN, S.
CLAY, S.
BURRIS, J.
LOVINS, W.
RODES, V.W.
NATIONS, E.
LOVINGS, L.
MALONE, D.
GILBREATH, W.
JONES, W.
HANKINS, R.

Page 168
FIELDS, A.
RODEN, J. F.
GILBREATH, G.
HORTON, A.
HORTON, A.
SCOTT, WILLIAM
WALKER, G.
*WALKER, WILLIAM
LANIER, G.
SCOTT, G.
WHITE, WILLIAM
THRASHER, G.
THRASHER, J.
THRASHER, H.
WHITE, S.
LANKFORD, R.
MARTIN, R. J.
BROOK, J.
MORRIS, D.
WELCH, EDWARD
BROWN, C.
SMITH, J.
LITTLEFIELD, J.
GRAY, WILLIAM
LEMON, J.
GILLILAND, W. B.
GILLILAND, D. M.
EDWARDS, J.
SCOTT, L.
CALAHAN, J.
BURNETT, J.

Page 169
ELLIS, WILLIAM W.

* military pensioner

Dekalb County

MASSIE, P.
BISHOP, J.
SCOTT, L.
MORGAN, L.N.
FLETCHER, W.
SCOTT, D. B.
HOLCOMBE, J.
STOCKSTILL, J.
RAY, LEWIS
SHARP, WILLIAM B.
DRAKE, J. M.
SARTON, S.
DICE, JACOB
RAY, R.
SAULS, S.
MONK, H.
SHOTE, J.
RAMSEY, F.
EVES, N.H.
MURPHY, G.
RAMSEY, R.
RAMSEY, J.
RAMSEY, A. C.
BURGESS, C.
BETHUNE, S.
SHUFFIELD, J.
McBRIER, S.M.
McBRIER, D. M.
KEMP, N.
Page 170
MORGAN, M.
McBRIER, H.
ELLIS, J.
RINK, J.
MAYES, J.
EDWARDS, J.
ALLEN, J.
TAYLOR, J.
HOWELL, F.
PARKER, O.
WALKER, J.
SIDES, J.
TOWLE, D.L.
STAFFORD, J.
TANT, WILLIAM H.
HILL, WILLIAM
COOPER, J.
FURGESON, J.
LOWRY, WILLIAM
CRUMP, B.
WARD, A. J.

SIDES, J.
CALAHAN, JAMES
THOMAS, WILLIAM
McBRIER, F. J.
INGLE, S.
INGLE, M.
SAWLS, A.
KEENEN, J. M.
CALAHAN, J.
Page 171
INGLE, R.
MALONE, C.
UPTON, G.
*UPTON, GEORGE
HUMPHRIES, D.
ANDREWS, WILLIAM
ANDREWS, THOMAS
LITTLEFIELD, L.
BURGESS, M.
STAFFORD, H.
READ, J.
STEPHENS, F.
MILLER, M.
EDWARDS, J.
FURGESON, W. J.
EDWARDS, WILLIAM
RICKS, S.
RICKS, MOSES
JET, J.
MULLINS, WILLIAM
GARRETT, J.
STEPHENS, JEREMIAH
TECEARGE?, J.
REAVES, J. A.
COATES, JOHN
SIBERT, D.
MALONE, G. B.
TEAGUE, J.
HOOD, R.
PARKER, B. H.
CLEVELAND, S.
Page 172
GILAND, DAN
BATES, P.
ACESINGE?, B.
CAGLE, H.
BRISTOE, MASSIE
RICHERSON, M.
GILIAN, E.
JOHNSON, R.
DESUMPER, H.

BROWN, WILLIAM M.
CRAM, J. M.
DILBECK, N.
HAYS, G.
BURRUS, E.
ATKINSON, J.
BOATMAN, D.
CRANE, J.
NICHLESON, L.M.
BOATMAN, W.
CHANEY, J.
PITTS, J.
CHASTEEN, R. C.
MAYFIELD, F.
CASTEEL, M.
ROACH, M.
RODEN, J.B.
FLEINKRN, R.
GILBREATH, N.
MALONE, E. C.
RODEN, JEREMIAH
Page 173
McDONALD, A.
STAFFORD, H.
BASS, THOMAS
WADE, E. H.
ROBERTS, JOHN
JONES, JOHN
KEITH, WILEY
GILBREATH, H.F.
EURY, JOSEPH
STEWART, JAMES
KING, H. W.
BALIS, JOHN
SPRINGIN, JACOB
WRIGHT, BRANTY
WHITEHEAD, THOMAS
CARROWAY, J. T.
ADAMS, J. L.
BAKER, JAMES
HUCKSON, JEREMIAH
CARPLIN, THOMAS
HOLLAND, JOHN
BOLIN, REUBEN
ROPER, H.
MORGAN, LEWIS
BOOKHOUSE, JOHN
ROPER, DAFFA
CILDER, MARGARET
NOLAND, ELIZABETH
BRUCE, MEMPLEY

*military pensioner

Dekalb County

BRUCE, SARAH
Page 174
SIMS, GILBERT
KELLY, LEWIS
LOWRY, JAMES
DAVIS, NANCY
BRANDON, A.
ELSEY, JOHN
BRANDON, GEORGE
BRANDON, LEWIS
TUCKER, ISAAC
HICKS, A.L.
HOLCOLM, NATHANIEL
SMEALY, GEORGE
ELSEY, JOHN
GARRETT, JAMES
HILL, JOHN
BRYANT, JOHN
SMEDLEY, WILLIAM
TAYLOR, JAMES
TANT, DAVID
TANT, ALEXANDER
YATES, B.W.
BROWN, ELISHA
JAMES, JAMES
SWADER, FRANCIS
CROW, ROBERT
CROW, GEORGE W.
THOMAS, N.B.
Page 175
FRENCH, JOHN C.
BELCHER, ELIZABETH
HILLS, JEREMIAH
KING, RICHARD
TILLMAN, B.
TATE, J. M.
SMITH, E.
KILLIAN, A.
WITT, P.
WILLIFORD, KING H.
WITHROW, R.
WASHINGTON J.
GUESS, ISAAC N.
WITHROW, J.
JOHNSON, P.
TATE, H.
TATE, P.
KILLIAN, CAIN
HENDERSON, W.W.
FORSYTH, SOLOMAN
SMEDLEY, JOHN
DAVIS, W.

ROGERS, E.
GRADY, A.
BEATY, J.
CHITWOOD, E.
BEATY, R. J.
CUNNINGHAM, JESSE
BASTER, JESSE
Page 176
SMITH, ELISHA
THOMAS, SAMUEL
BOUDEN, ELISHA
BOUDEN, ELISHA
STANLEY, A.
THOMAS, A.
SADLER, F.P.
COOK, B.F.
GILBREATH, THOMAS
LOWRY, A.
PANTER, JAMES
PANTER, NATHANIEL A.
JAGS, A. J.
ZOLLARD, MYRAH
BLANCOT, GEORGE
LEE, A.
CADWELL, MARY
CAUSEE, WILLIAM
NICHOLS, B.
BOWDQN, RICHARD
BOOKHOUSE, MARY
JONES, JOSEPH M.
CEEGLES, JOSEPH
RAND, MOSES
SHEARER, L.D.
BINGE, GEORGE
BLANCOT, WILLIAM
LAPUST, SAMUEL
COOK, JAMES, C.
WHITE, JOHN
Page 177
PO, AMY
GIBSON, T. W.
GASSOWAY, JOHN
NELSON, Z.
GRAHAM, GIDEON
PARMER, JOHN
DAVIS, JOHN
HALL, JOHN
HALL, B.
ROWAN, JOSEPH
LIVINGSTON, P.
GIBSON, GRAVILLE

FRANKLIN, JOHN
GIBSON, GEORGE
EUSTACE, REUBEN
BRADSHAW, THOMAS
BRADSAW, WILLIAM
HANNER, JOHN
WARD, DAVID
WEAVER, SAMUEL
McDONALD, J.K.
McDONALD, ARCHIBALD
ESTES, B.
BECK, THOMAS
CUNNINGHAM, J.
TOKE, JACKSON
CUNNINGHAM, D.
DENNIS, JONATHAN
CROWNOVER, DANIEL
WARD, JAMES
Page 178
VENABLE, EZEKIEL
WRIGHT, BENNET
SWADER, WILLIAM
WILLIAMS, JOHN
WILLIAMS, JOHN
WHITE, JOHN
BENNETT, W.
SUTHERLAND, A.
REED, Y.
REED, FRANCIS
LANKFORD, JOHN
SMALLEY, JOSHUA
MATHENY, JOSEPH
PENNY, HANIBAL
BOHANNON, W.
AMATHROUGH, S.
ARMSTRONG, SAMUEL
RUSE, DAVID
HARRINGTON, L.
RUSE, DAVID
HARRINGTON, L.
BIPIN, HILLEY
CUNNINGHAM, H.
VENABLE, JOSEPH
RONALDS, S.H.
CUNNINGHAM, S.
STRANGE, EDWARD
STEWART, S.
STEWART, R.
STEWART, W.
GASSAWAY, W.

Dekalb County

Page 179
CAMPBELL, JOHN M.
RIDDLE, F.
CLAYTON, E.
WHITE, F.
CHITWOOD, M.
THOPSON, WADE
EVERETT, LARKIN
PARKER, JOHN
CANNON, A.
COOK, R. M.
FRIFFINSIDES, J.
DUTTON, D.
WARREN, S. S.
NEWKIRK, H.
GOGGAN, R. F.
DAVIDSON, JOSEPH
HENSON, R. S.
HOUSE, A. L.
HUFF, JAMES
YOW, HENRY
BOYD, JAMES
SOUTH, N.
CHINALT, THOMAS
SYTHE, THOMAS
LANKFORD, W.
RINOLA, G.
SMITH, WILLIAM H.
HILL, J.
SHITWOOD, LARCINIUS
SHELTON, P.

Page 180
KING, SOLOMAN
BEESON, J.G.
BARNES, W.
VENABLE, ISAAC
CUNNINGHAM, JOHN
CUNNINGHAM, J.
BLACKWELL, T. P.
FEATHERSTON, J.
WARD, JOHN
THOMPSON, H.
McSPADEN, THOMAS
VANCE, LANIUS
McSPADEN, M.
MATHENY, THOMAS
WILLBORN, L.
WILLBORN, T.
ATWOOD, JOSEPH
McFARLAND, LETITIA
DUKE, R.
TODD, R. L.

LORINAS, NATHAN
HOLMAN, WILLIAM
DAVENPORT, JAMES
CROUSE, JOHN
BALEY, H.
DUKE, DANIEL
HOWELL, JOHN
PANKING, W.
CAPERTON, H. B.
CAPERTON, ADAM

Page 181
LOWRY, LERI
ALEXANDER, S.
CAMMACK, JAMES
CARDEN, DAVID
ROWAN, MARY
ROWAN, SAMUEL
ROWAN, WILLIAM
ADAMS, WILLIAM
HAMMOND, WILLIAM
HAWK, H.
DRUTON, JAMES
DOTON, DYSON
PEARSON, JOHN
THOMASON, Z.
McNEW, W.
MAHEFFY, WILLIAM
ELLEDY, REUBEN
VENABLE, MARY
HAMMOND, PHIL
GILLEY, PETER
BUNDON, C.
CROWNOVER, D.
WRIGHT, GILBERT
WELLS, ANDREW
DEATON, WILLIAM
BUNDOND, JAMES
LIZMORE, JOHN
MARSHALL, JOHN
WRIGHT, JAMES

Page 182
CROWNOVER, S.
HENSON, J.
CUNNINGHAM, J.
HENSON, J.
BATEY, JAMES
BRISTOW, E.
MEEKS, S.
BOATMAN, R.
COKER, H.
HENDERSON, J.

BOHANNAN, P.
CRAGE, CAROLINE
GUESS, JONATHAN
GRIGERY, J.
SHARPE, WILLIAM
EDWARDS, WILLIAMS
HESTER, PBD.
PANE, L.
FRANKLIN, W. H.
HAWKINS, R. D.
MURPHY, R.
NOBLES, J.
RUSSEL, LORENZO
KEMP, J. M.
WILSON, R. J.
LANKFORD, V.
NEWMAN, S.C.
GARDNER, J.
PATEN, T.

Page 183
GENTRY, S. R.
BANSTER, JAMES
McKENZIE, L.
*FRAXIL, JACOB
McCURDY, N.M.
SWAFFORD, M.
FISLAS, GILBERT
LAUFORD, PETER
BURT, ELISHA
JACKSON, DAVID
MUSGROVE, N.
CLINCH, THOMAS
ROBERTS, C.H.
WASSEN, JOSHUA
CANDEN, HIRAM
*WALKER, WILLIAM
JACOBS, JOHN
GAMBREL, W. S.
STRICKLIN.B.
*UPTON, GEORGE
LANDERS, T.
NICHLESON, W. R.
NORTON, B.
MORGAN, JOHN
ADAIR, JAMES
ROBERSON, JOHN
MICHAEL, Z.
PERKIN, A.
MORGAN, JOHN
BUSHY, JOHN
HEARD, M.

*military pensioner

Dekalb County

BLAKE, B.

Page 184

WATERS, W.
HINES, N.B.
BURNS, L.
VANDIGRIFF, THOMAS
HUFFSTUTTER, J.
RODEN, GEORGE
SMITH, JAMES
FRANCIS, GEORGE
STONE, WILLIAM
OWENS, H. W.
ISBELL, B.
HAMBLETON, JOHN
HARRIS, JAMES
SIMONS, JOHN
SMITH, B.
SHADRICK, THOMAS
SHADRICK, JOHN
TUGGLE, W.
DANIEL, STITH

Macon County

Page 2
STOUDENMIER, LEWIS
SCOTT, J. M.
STOUDENMIER, JACOB
CARGILL, JASON
PITTS, J. J.
SANDERS, DANIEL
GLASCOW, JOHN
HOLLANDSWORTH, LIDIA
RAMSEY, NEAL
THOMPSON, HARRIS
RAMSEY, DANIEL
CLEASE, NORMAN W.
TAYLOR, JOHN
McWHORTER, JOHN
BOYDE, ALFRED
LYNCH. C.G.
BETHUNE, RIDEN K.
JACKSON, A. J.
SMITH, H.H.
BOOTHE, N.
KERKSEY, DRURY
McCLEOD, A C.
BUGBY, JOHN
HATHORN, RIAL
McCLENDON, WILLIAM
WILLIAMS, FRED
FINGER, JOHN H.
WEEKS, JOHN
CURRY, JOHN
JOHNSTON, SAMUEL
JORDAN, H.D.
JORDAN, JOHN
KEENER, SETH
PURSER, HENRY
BUNKLEY, JONATHAN

Page 3
KASKEY, JOHN
NELSON, J. R.
HARRIS, L.W.
MOORE, L. G.
LAUTER, W. R.
SHEPHERD, NANCY
HAZARD, G.
THOMPSON, JOHN
FITZPATRICK, ELUM
WILDER, JOHN
DEAK, WILLIAM
HAPE, BURTON
ADDAMS, S. G.B.
JENKINS, B.
SALLEY. R.
MULDER, W. R.

STUBBLEFIELD, THOMAS
CARBERSON, T.
BARKLEY, JOHN
ABOCRUMBY, L. (estate of)
HOUSTON, JOHN
WILLIAMS, WILLIAM
WALKER, T. L.
BARDEN, WILLIAM
STUBBLEFIELD, C.
HALE, REBECCA
CRADOCK, J. H.
JOHNSTON, THOMAS
BRADLEY, C. L.
CONEL, NANCY
PIERCE, WILSON
PIGGINS, R. H.
NOLIN, STEPHEN

Page 4
CARGIL, MICKAJA
*BREWER, BARROT
COUSINS, LAVICA
McCLANE, CHARLES
McSWAIN, J. C.
BURNET, J. H.
McHALL, ARCHIBALD
CLAY, JOHN W.
YOUNGBLOOD, JAMES
HOUGH, C. J.
DEAL, JAMES
TATAM, WILLIAM
DOSIER, J. M.
KEENER, L. T.
TALBOT, BEN
COCKROSSE, W. L.
CRAWLEY, J. H.
ROTTEN, L.
McBETH, J. C.
KEADEHAMER, LEWIS
OWENS, ELI
McKAY, JOHN
CRANE, WILLIAM W.
RUMPH, JAMES
THOMAS, F. G.
GAINES, J. G.
COOK, JAMES
TAYLOR, WILLIAM
TAYLOR, J. A.
LAYTON, HENRY

Page 5
NICHOLS, ROBERT
GARVIN, THOMAS S.
JORDAN, WILLIAM

LAUTER, LENOAH
EVANS, STOKELY M.
BLACKWELL, N.
EALY, W. N.
HINSON, J. W.
BEAUCHAMP, GREEN
WILLIAMS, J. L.
BALDWIN, BENJAMIN
EALEY, MIKEL
MITCHEL, C. G.
UNDERWOOD, THOMAS
BALDWIN, J. H.
HIX, H.H.
McCLANE, KINETH
WILSON, R. C.
KELY, WILLIAM P.
MONROE, ANDREW
TALBOT, HESIKIAH
ROTTEN, W.L.
COCKROSS, THOMAS
DEVANPORT, ISAC
BRUCE, WILLIAM
BUSH, R.
ADDAMS, BAKER
DEAS, JINNET
BUSH, WILLIAM
WILLIAMS, ALLEN
BUSH, DAVID
HOOKS, CHARLES

Page 6
HOOKS, DANIEL
SLAUTER, MATHEW
MILES, HAMLIN
SIMMONS, WILLIAM
FENDELSON, JOHN
DANIEL. R.L.
DENSON, A. R.
WHITE, JAMES
COLE, DANIEL
THOMPSON, W. C.
PERRY, JOHN
GERMANY, G. W.
COLE, RANSOM
THOMPSON, BENJAMIN
PARKER, LATTIMORE
LASLEY, H.
MELONE, JOHNSON
DEVERAUX, SAMUEL
DEVERAUX, ALFRED
DEVERAUX, J. L.
CALLAWAY, LAWRENCE
TARKENTON, WILLIAM

*military pensioner

MACON COUNTY

POWEL, N.B.
GIGSEY, JESSE
LARLEY, MARGARET
THOMPSON, MOSES
GERMANY, WILLIAM (older)
GERMANY, WILLIAM
BONDS, W. B.
LARKINS, JAMES

Page 7
MERWEATHER, G. M.
FITZPATRICK, ALVY
ELMORE, H. W.
FITZPATRICK, BIRD
CHAPPEL. A. H.
LASONBY, AARON
HARRIS, MOSES
GAINEY, JOHN
WILSON, JOHN
GOLDEN, NANCY
TARPLEY, MARGARET
RUSH, C. G.
McNEAL, SAMUEL
HOWARD, JAMES
WOODARD, THOMAS
PINKARD, WILLIAM
HARRIS, PETER C.
TARVIN, RICHARD
DRAKEFORD, JAMES
WILLIS, BEDELL
PRICE, JAMES N.
BASCOMB, S.P.
STONE, GEORGE
BULLOCK, S. R.
BULLOCK, A. M.
NIX, ELISY
SIMMONS, S. D.
COLEMAN, ERBIN
MILLER, JOSIAH
CRAWFORD, WILLIAM

Page 8
VANN, LINDEN
GILDER, WILLIAM C.
TEMPLES, JOHN
SHARP, JAMES
HARRIS, AUGUSTUS
NIX, WILLIAM
HATHHORN, WILLIAM
GUDDEN, WILEY
KEMP, WILLIAM
BRADLEY, S.

DAVIS, THOMAS
COOK, CHARLES
GRUMBLES, G. W.
OSWORT, GEORGE
CONNEL, MIKE
McGRUDER, W. R.
COOK, J.
STRADFORD, RICHARD
ABOCRUMBIE, CH.
McINTOSH, ALX
ABOCRUMBIE, MILO
CLIANT, THOMAS C.
SMITH, WILLIS
THOMPSON, JESSE
MITCHELL, COLUMBUS
WETHERTON, TOLIVER
MAN, MARGARET
WILKINSON, JOHN
LUKE, J. D.
MATHIS, EMANNUEL

Page 9
ADAMS, EDWARD B.
OLIVER, WHITING
SIMMONS, WILLIAM H.
CUNIGAM, JAMES
ARWOOD, JESSE
NORRIS, T.
BUTTER, SOLOMAN
LAPAN, J. G.
BRUMBY, R. H.
DRUSICK, JAMES
McKAY, MARY
NOLAN, ALONZO
QUADDLEBUM, WILLIAM
STIGGINS, GEORGE
COOPER, DAVID
JOHNSTON, DANIEL
JONES, DARLEN A.
JONES, ELIAS W.
SAUNDIN, JAMES
HENSON, MATHEW
McGILL, ARCHIBALD
GILLIS, JOHN, JR.
GILLIS, JOHN, SR.
JAMES, EDWARD
KILEREALT, JEREMIAH
PARKER, J. M.F.
McHAUL, JOHN
HARWELL, AMBROSE
HILL, JOHN H.

Page 10
CLOUGH, GEORGE
JOHNSTON. W.
DAVIS, A. A.
PULLINS, A.
DUN, H.
MAYER, W. N.
MULLINS, J. M.
DAVIS, D. D.
DAVIS, H.
FINLEY, A.
PUGH, J. W.
ROBINSON, JAMES P.
GINDRAT, JOHN
GLEATON, NANCY
GLEATON, J. C.
PUGH, H.P.
PUGH, R.L.
COUSINS, P.
KELLEY, JOHN
CLOUGH, JOSEPH
BULLOCK, RICHARD
DRISKELL, PETER
SEIGNS, JACOB
RAY, H.
CRITESBURG, JOHN
SIMPSON, D. B.
SCROGGINS, T. R.
JOBETH, JOHN
ROBERTS, J. E.

Page 11
BENNET, WILLIAM
KING, JAMES
KING, WILLIAM
DEPREST, J. A.
WADKINS, S.
WALKER, C.
ROCKER, ALS.
TINDAL, D.
BRASIL, AARON
BRASIL, C.
FREEMAN, WILKINS
FREEMAN, B.
LAURENCE, THOMAS
HORTON, L.
PERRY, W. J.
FARISS, JOHN
FITZPATRICK, R. F.
NUNN, SAMUEL
QUARLS, DAVID
ECCLES, O.

-55-

Macon County

CROW, ISAC
SHAW, W. A.
SHAWTER, S. W.
MASON, JAMES
MOORE, AMOS
JACKSON, A.
ARNOLD, ALLEN
LORTEN, J. R.
SALLEY, JESSE
THORNTON, J. H.
Page 12
BENNS, JOSEPH
BRITTON, JOHN
DELBRIDGE, JAMES
MACON, PLEASANT
ALLEN, W. C.
RUSSEL, WILLIAM
CATENHEAD, MARTIN
CATENHEAD, JOHN
CATENHEAD, THOMAS
CATENHEAD, -ROM ?
BAILEY, WHITEHILL
APLIN, THOMAS
STEPHENS, THOMAS
STEPHENS, SOLOMAN
JOHNSON, JESSE
ALLEN, JAMES T.
BIDDLE, MICHAJAH
SMITH, G.
SMITH, ELIZABETH
HEWLIN, ANDREW
BIDDLE, T. J.
GRISSOM, MRS. MARY
BIDDLE, JOSEPH R.
STEEL, T. M.
PHILLIPS, R.
JONES, JAMES
BRADSHAW, C. H.
CARY, D.
JONES, W. B.
JAMES, MESHACK
RUTLIDGE, D. A.
Page 13
THORNTON, HENRY
DONALD, MARY
SLAUTER, SEPTEMUS
ISLEN, M. R.
SPORE, D.
MOREHAM, JAMES
COONER, JOHN
FORSYTH, NANCY
MOTLEY, T.

SEIGNER, JACOB
SEIGNER, URIAH
SEIGNER, LEMUEL
RAY, DANIEL
VANN, WILLIAM
OWENS, D.
ATKINS, C. J.
JENNINGS, T. L.
LARTON, J. R.
BRITTON, THOMAS
VICKERY, J. H.
BEMON, W.L.
CHAPMAN, WILL
CHAPMAN, LEVY
CHANDLER, JOHN
MOBLEY, THOMAS
WILLIAMS, E.
HUDDON, N.
HENDERSON, THOMAS
O'DANIEL, JOHN
Page 14
NEAL, A. H.
DEASON, WILLIAM
JONES, LEVY
BEARD, BERRY
WILKINSON, H.
SMITH, R.
SCROGGINS, H.
MINGS, JESSE
MOORE, J. Y.
McCALLISTER, JOHN
CASERTY, W.
COX, WILLIS
CARNS, SAMUEL
ROGERS, WILLIAM
JACKSON, R. H.
HOBBS, W. A.
CLARK, JOHN
CHESUR, JACOB
LANEY, JOHN
HATTERWAY, C.
HOUSE, W. H.
MOORE, SPENCER
MOORE, E. R.
COX, R. N.D.
ALDERSON, JOHN
ESTERS, E.
POTTS, JAMES
OWENS, L. B.
GLADDEN, H.
LAUTER, THOMAS
Page 15
SMITH, J. H.

RUNNELS, J. N.
HERINGTON, E.
FLANIGAN, W.
CANEDY, H.
LAWSON, J.
HARISON, J. H.
MEHANE, E. F.
TURNER, SAMUEL
KEY, W.L.
WYNN, LITTLETON
STAR, S. W.
TURNER, MATHEW
WILLIAMS, JOHN
CONNER, M.L.F.
CHRISTIAN, L.
LAURENCE S. J.
OUSLEY, JOHN
OUSLEY, J. C.
EDDY, T.
HARPER, J. J.
LANFORD, H. N.
MIHAN, WILLIAM
NUNN, W. J.
HOLDEN, WILLIAM
SANDERS, JULIUS
OUSLEY, W.B.
SCOTT, N. J.
CLARK, THOMAS
Page 16
ROOF, JOHN
GRAHM, J. A.
HARRIS, F. L.
PETTEWAY, M. C.
WAGGONER, GEORGE
BUSHBY, JACOB
NORRIS, JOHN
BUTTS, NATHAN
HENDERSON, W. M.
BALDWIN, W.O.
BLACKMAN, JAMES
NICHOLSON, JAMES
DENT, JAMES
COX, PREASTLY
SEIGREST, G.B.
HARDY, ALFRED
CHAPPEL, JOHN D.
CAMERON, J. M.
BEAS, WILLIAM
BRANDON, JAMES
ALLEN, JAMES
PULLEN, JAMES
SEGREST, R.

-56-

MACON COUNTY

SEIGREST, D.
MAY, NATHANIEL
PETERSON, BATTLE
MORELAND, W.F.
HENDERSON, J.C.
LEGRAND, W. C.
Page 17
ECCLES, JAMES
WILLIAMS, S.
GRISSEL, C.
FAG, BETSEY
DISMUKE, J.
OVERSER, REAVES
POWRIDGE, R.
FAULKENBERG, ISAAC
FRANCE, JOSEPH
TAYLOR, JESE
TURNER, O.B.
SKINNER, BENAJAH
DOBSON, W.
RUSSELBINE?, S. B.
PARSON, D. J.
MORRISON, A.
CAPS, JOHN
BENNET, MARTIN
DOBSON, C.
TANTON, NUSOM
PATTERSON, JAMES
SKINNER, EPHEM
WATSON, A.A.
ATWELL, A.
HARDY, A.
HALEY, JOHN
BREWER, JOEL
BREWER, ENG.
BREWER, W.
TARVER, W.
Page 18
WILSON, WILLIAM
FILES, JOHN
*FILES, ADAM J.
PAUL, ROBERT
GREEN, AMOS
CUNIGAM, JOSEPH
SKIRLOCK, PRIESTLY
SKIRLOCK, LUCENA
VEASEY, JAMES
TREADGIL, H.
TEDDER, MARTHA
BRITTON, ISOM
DURANT, A. J.

McNEAL, D. W.
CHAPMAN, W. H.
BOYDE, C.L.R.
BRITT, PHILIP
DARBY, AUGUSTUS
ROBERTS, JAMES
SANDERS, J.W.
PIGGERS, J.L.
JOHNSTON, ALEX.
HOWARD, J. H.
COLE, J.L.
DURANT, LACKLEY
GREEN, R.
BELL. W. H.
BELL, ALEX N.
ROOF, P.
PEN, W. S.
Page 19
WHITE, GEORGE
JETER, JAMES
CALLOWAY, BENJAMIN
FUNDERBIRK, J.F.
SEALS, ARNOLD
ROBERTS, LUCY
QUARLS, DAVID
FLOURS, STEPHEN
GATES, ANN
WARE, J.L.
PICKET, J.R.
MARSHAL, A. G.
MILHAM, JAMES
SHEPHERD, FLOYDE
SHEPHERD, W.
WHITE, G.
PITTS, W.C.
WHITE, W.
TARVER, JAMES
PICKET, GEORGE
GIL, WILLIAM
ENGLISH, THOMAS
BEVERLY, JOSEPH
HARVILL, SAMUEL
CLACKLEY, J.L.
GLEN, T.
SHELTON, WILLIS
COLE, N.B.
McCLEMORE, S.W.
Page 20
MURPHY, R.R.
CAR, SAMUEL
CAR, JOHN
GRIGORY, R.

GARDNER, W.
NOLIN, THOMAS
NOLIN, JAMES
GRAHAM, D.
McKASKEL, MURDOCK
GRAHAM, ALEX.
McCRORY, J.J.
JOHNSTON, J.J.
TERRY, W.
VAUGHN, HENRY
BOLIN, J.A.
BEST, REDDEN
TALBOT, EDMOND
ADDAMS, J.T.
HARROD, WILEY
NICHOLSON, GILLOM
COLEMAN, THOMAS
TULLUS. P.
SAYRE, GEORGE
TOD, W.
STINSON, SIMON
BLACKMAN, W.
BLACKMAN, WILLIAM
CALLAWAY, HENRY
PUGH, J. N.
DEVENPORT, MIKJA
Page 21
DAY, STEPHEN
BRUMBY, J.G.
WESTMORLAND, ELIZABETH
McCALPIN, D.
GOODE, S. W.
GRIFFIN, SAMUEL
MITCHELL. W. H.
CLOUGH, T.
BUTLER, RICE
THOMPSON, W.
WEAVER, ARTHUR
STRANGE, L.B.
RUGELY, H.
DENT, WILLIAM
LUCAS, W.
HADEN, R. G., SR.
RUNNELS, ROBERT
HADEN, ALEX.
ROBERTS, CHARLES
McKINIS, GRACY
SIMMONS, THOMAS
BLAKEY, BOLIN
CRIM, CHARLES
McGILL, DANIEL
GRAHAM, WILLIAM

*military pensioner

Macon County

HADEN, R. G., JR.
HADEN, J. F.
HADEN, J.
BOYDE, JAMES
BOYDE, CHARLES
Page 22
DEASON, A.
KIDWELL, JESSEE
YOUNGBLOOD, OSBEEN
HARRISON, C.B.
LOE, JOHN
RAY, DANIEL
RACER, ARTHER
DEAN, REUBIN
JOHNSTON, STEPHEN
SCOTT, U.
OWENS, W.
WILLIAMS, JOHN
YOUNG, MIKAJA
WILSON, G. W.
LAURENCE, IVY
LUNEAU, SAMPSON
TAYLOR, JOSEPH
NOBLE, JOHN
EVERIT, WILLIS
BREDLOVE, LEWIS P.
JACKSON, A. B.
SMITH, LARKIN
HOWARD, R. H.
STAFFORD, W. H.
HUFMAN, LEWIS
THOMPSON, G. W.
COOK, BENJAMIN
HARRIS, T. M.
Page 23
GLEN, M. R.
MACON, W. H.
JONES, L. M.
MILLS, R. M.
SMITH, J. H.
GINNINGS, E.
PRICE, J. N.
HADNOT, W. F.
PINKSTON, C. A.
WINGATE, E.
MOORE, W. J.
STACY, MARTHA M.
SCOTT, ELIJAH
ANSLEY, W.
HOWARD, JOHN
MITCHELL, ROBERT
BAGERLY, A. D.

LAURENCE, D. H.
LEWIS, W.L.
RAGLAND, W.
DAYMON, G. H.
VAUGHN, M. E.
TRANOM, W. T.
BREDLOVE, M. B.
WALKER, E. W.
GUIN, T.
GINNINGS, ELIZABETH
WINIKEL, D.
CAMPBELL, MOSES
HUDNAL, JOHN
Page 24
GARTMAN, DANIEL
PUGH.J. M.
MARTIN. E.M.BRYANT
SIMMONS, SIMEON
HUNTER, H.G.
GOODWIN, R. T.
NOLEN, ROBERT
WAFER, J. T.
BEAUIN, J. T.
RIGHT, CHARLETON
MANSFIELD, GEORGE
CARMIAL, GILBERT
GIE, MARY
RAINS, ALLEN
RAINS, JACKSON
MEDLEY, ELIZABETH
CLANTON, N.H.
GREEN, LUCY
CHAPPEL. T. M.
PIGGERS, MALIKIAH
NOBLE, PHILEMON
JINKS, REAS
SMITH, JAMES
GINKS, URIAH
MATHIS, WESLY
MIMS, LITTLETON
HEWLIT, JOHN
BROWN, M.
LAND, J. D.
PEDDY, JEREMIAH
Page 25
RANDALL, HENDRICK
TATUM, A.L.
WILLIAMS, WILLIAM
HARRIS,OROSS
LISENBE, AARON
RUTLAND, MARTHA
DENSKER, THOMAS

ADAMS, ROBERT
BARRETT, WILLIAM
WILSON. G. W.
MINFIELD, WILLIAM
KEY, PHOEBA
HARRISON, HEARTWELL
COLEAU, WHITFIELD
JACKSON, H.R.
DAVIS, B. E.
GORDIN, W.
WILSON, JOHN
DEA, J..P.
McKINNON, JOHN
PHILLIPS. A.
DENSLEY, H.L.
TATUM, HAMLIN
DRIVER, J.
MIMS, GEORGE
OWEN, JAMES S.
GRINNIT, JAMES
LEE, ASA
HODGES, WILLIAM
ARRINGTON, PETER
Page 26
WINGATE, E.
DUKES, N.
GADDIS, J.
PADGET, H.
TURNER, T.
DRAKE, P. H.
DUKES,__(none given)
BLANKS, L.B.
HARPER, JUDGE
NUCKELS, G.B.
JONES, W.
WICKER, JOHN
COSTASNEY, J. H.
COSTASNEY, J. J.
GRIZZEL, L.
GRIZZEL. J.C.
RIGBY, A.
HYMAN_ ELIZABETH
HEWIT, W.
MITCHELL, JOHN
RIGBY, ELI
MITCHELL, JAMES
PAIN, J.
LOFTIS, J.T.
WATLEY, SIMEON
MOTES, R.
STORES, L.B.
STORES, B.A.

MACON COUNTY

ECCLES, ROBERT
Page 27
SHARO, STEPHEN
FLANIGAN, SIBERN
FERRIL, W.B.
McKAY, ADDAM
MILES, ELIJAH
DAVIS, PHILOP
HARPER, JAMES
SMITH, SAMUEL
MELTON, J.
MATHIS, JOHNSTON
MOORE, W.W.
PATILLO, NATION
FLEMMING, OLIVER
HILL, ISAAC
PAROM, W.B.
SCOTT, ALX.
POMENTS, FARIS
SLEDGE, HIRAM
BAKER, BENAJA
JONES, WILLIAM
JONES, CHESLEY
MIHAN, J.A.
CHALKER, W.H.
LANGFORD, H.H.
McFARLIN, R.T.
COGBURN, H.
COGBURN, SCIRUS
GINKS, WILLIAM
SPINKS, BAKER
Page 28
SMITH, JOEL
SMITH, HENRY
GINKS, WILSON
KILCREAST, E.
GREEWAY, JOHN
HORTON, L.
BAILEY, URBIN C.
SHELTON, W.
PRICE. W.
GASET, J.V.
DIXON, JOHN
JOHNSTON, STEPHEN
LANFORD, B.
NEUGENT, L.
SANFORD, W.
STEPHENS, J.P.
STEPHENS, B.
PEAL, J.
BELL. J.

JINNINGS, JAMES
HARDY, W.
BALLADi, L.
BALLAD, D.
COONER, JOHN
MILES, JOHN
HARDY, JAMES
MILES, JOHN, SR.
DAY, JOHN
IVERSON, W.
JONES, W.
Page 29
BORING, JESSEE
BALDWIN, T.
BALDWIN, DAN
BALDWIN, WILLIAM
DOLES, JAMES
DOLES, WILLIAM
WOODRUFF, P.D.
McKINLEA, WILLIAM
TURPIN, A.S.
BORUM. B.F.
CROCKER, E.E.
ROYAL, E.
GREENWOOD, WILLIAM
McGUIRE, JOHN
TALBOT, ELIHEW
McGAN, JOHN
EVERIT, MILLS
BELYEU, BERRY
MEHONE, T.M.
READ, NATHAN
GRIGGS, R.L.
HARDEN, ADAM
THOMPSON, SAMUEL
GERMANY, J.J.
DAY, JOSEPH
COLLINS, N.
STEWART, BEN
CAPS, D.B.
COLQUIT, JOHN
ESTES, THOMAS
Page 30
HIX, WILLIAM
HARE, JAMES
McCLENDON, F.
WIMBERLY, H.F.
WHITLEY, W.L.
GRAS, P.W.
MENEFIELD, R.
ELLIS, W.
CLEGHORN, A.

ADKINS, T.B.
McCRARY, P.R.
MULLIN, THOMAS
HOLT, R.A.
BROWN, J.W.
ECCLES, A.
FOSTER, B.
STEWART, B.
LEVERTON, S.
CALLOWAY, P.M.
JORDAN, T.G.
KELLEY, R.
McGRATH, R.
PERRY, S.
APPLEBY, P.
SESTRUNK, JOEL
TORBERT, JAMES
MILLER, C.
MILLER, H.
SMITH, H.
Page 31
GILDER, G.P.
WILLIS, M.P.
PADGET, J.R.
PADGET, H.R.
HARPER, T. H.
MIAMS, S.W.
FREEMAN, W.M.
YANCEY, S.W.
McGEEHEE, W.D.
STANTON, S.
MIMS, H.
SIKES, JOSIAH
DUKES, H.
FAULKNER, WILLIS
TARGINTON, W.A.
HAUGHTON, F.R.
NEAL, W.B.
ELI, JOHN W.
HERON, W.
TRANAM, SUSANNAH
BLACKMAN, H.

MARSHALL COUNTY

Page 72
SMALLWOOD, ROBERT C.
DOWNS, JOHN L.
DELVIN, THOMAS
JONES, SALATHIAL
HIGGINS, JASON
HENSON, REUBENE
TIPTON, JOSEPH
ASHLY, JOHN
STURGIS, WILLIAM F.
BAGGET, UZZLE
PETERS, EMANUEL
EVANS, JAMES M.
UPTON, JESSEE
AVERY, HENRY
GOSS, RICHARD
AVERY, DAVID
SMITH, BRYANT
DERICK, TOBIAS
ROSE, WILLIAM
HIGGINS, WILLIAM
HOWEL, MICHAEL
SMITH, DRURY
WILSON, JOSEPH
SMITH, JAMES
CARLAND, GEORGE
PITTS, THOMAS
SMITH, WILLIAM R.
SWEARINGIN, SAMUEL
WILSON, JEREMIAH

Page 73
SMITH, JOHN
WILSON, JOHN R.
HIGDEN, CHARLES
McCAULESS, JAMES
LAW, PEYTON, JR.
CAMPBELL, JOHN W.
TATE, THOMAS M
CASS, ANDREW
SAMMONS, LEWIS
BAESHART, RUDOLPH
GIPSON, JAMES
HERRON, DANIEL
COLE, JOHN W.
LAW, JEFFERSON
SHAW, ELISHA
BOND, WRIGHT H.
PETTON, DAVID
BAESHART, L.D.
THOMAS, WILLIAM C.
BLACK, WILLIAM

PILE, SEBRON
FLETCHER, JOHN
BARTON, JANE R.
CARTER, JAMES
PENDERGRASS, JOSEPH
RAINES, WILLIAM
PENDERGRASS, JASON
SMITH, JOHN A.
MANNING, LEWIS

Page 74
BOHANNON, ERVIN
WILEMAN, ISAIAH
TIDWELL, JAMES
DAVIS, ABRAM
McLEMON, JAMES
McPEARSON, SPENCER
WILDMAN, THOMAS
THOMAS, RICHARD
CUNNINGHAM, SAMUEL
MAYFIELD, JOHN
RAINEY, THOMAS
BOHANNON, DANIEL
BARTON, JAMES
EMBRY, DANIEL
GARLAND, ABRAS, JR.
DUNN, ANN
CHAMBERS, RANSOM
ORE, WILLIAM
ELLIS, BRADDOCK
McKINCY, JACOB
CLARK, DAVID
BARCLAY, WILLIAM
BENSON, WILLIAM
MURPHY, THOMAS
GARLAND, AMBROS, SR.
WARD, WILLIAM
WARD, THOMAS
WILDMAN, BENJAMIN
WILDMAN, BAILEY

Page 75
BURKS, GRANVILLE
O'BAR, ALEXANDER
BURKS, JANE
O'BAR, CASWELL
WARD, CHINA
BAESHART, DAVID
LOWE, THOMAS
DAVIS, JAMES
READ, SAMUEL D.
MOORE, THOMAS

STARNES, ISHAM R.
DUNCAN, PETER
TUCKER, JOHN, JR.
DENNIS, HEZEKIAH
TIDWELL, WILLIAM
JONES, JOHN
FAITH, JOHN S.
HERRON, ELIJAH
STEPHENS, NOAH
WOODALL, PRESLEY
MICKEY, MATHEW
KENNAMORE, STEPHEN
DODBS, JAMES
KENNAMORE, JACOB
KENNAMORE, SAMUEL
KENNAMORE, ROBERT
PAGE, LEWIS

Page 76
BARCLEY, JOEL
KENNAMORE, DAVID
HILL, SUSAN
KENNAMORE, LEVI
HILL, SAMUEL
WRIGHT, JOHN W.
CLINE, JACOB
CLINE, ANDREW
HITT, MARTIN
STEPHENS, ELI
KENNAMORE, SA.
PAGE, JOHN P.
LAW, JOHN
WRIGHT, JAMES
WRIGHT, ISHAM
WILDER, SAMPSON
PERKINS, JABAZ
WHITE, JOHN
GARLAND, JOHN
CANNON, HENRY
KENNAMORE, ZACHERIAH
BAXTER, JOHNATHAN
PARISH, LEVI
WRIGHT, ISAAC
BROWN, DAVID
BEVELL, HAWKEYE P.
GRAYSON, MARY
MORRIS, WILLIAM
WHITECOTTON, JAMES

Page 77
LEE, JOHN
LEE, GEORGE

MARSHALL COUNTY

RIGGINS, NACY
HEDGES, WILLIS
DERICK, GEORGE
EDINGTON, DAVID
BOMAN, JESSEE
MORRISON, WILLIAM
WRIGHT, JAMES
McNABB, DAVID W.
GREEN, CASWELL
EVANS, MARGARET
WHITAKER, SUSAN
WHITAKER, NATHAN
CRAIG, ELIZABETH
JONES, WASHINGTON
FLETCHER, PEGGY
CRAIG, WILLIAM
MORROW, GEORGE
WHITAKER, WILLIAM
STAPLES, AMOS
CRAIG, LEONARD
MORROW, WALKER
RICHE, WILLIAM
KEY, SAMUEL
WINKLE, NANCY
WHITAKER, CRISTIANA
NORMAN, WILLIAM
DAVIS, THOMAS
Page 78
HILL, WILLIAM
PRICHETT, PHILLIPE
REVIS, EDWARD
SIMPSON, SAWYER
McGAHA, BURGESS
WILEY, SAMUEL
CLARK, GEORGE R.
SIMPSON, ELIZABETH
MOORE, ISAAC
SIMPSON, RICHARD
MERRELL, BENJAMIN
PALSON, WILLIAM
POE, ANDREW
LOONEY, ELIJAH
KEMPER, SIMON
BLASENGAM, JESSEE
BROWN, JAMES R.
SIVLEY, WILLIAM A.
SIVLEY, JOHN A.
WEST, WILLIAM
BURNTSIDE, ANDREW
BURNTSIDE, JOHN
BENSON, JOHN
BRUNSON, DANIEL M.

BRUNSON, DAVID W.
SPENCER, JAMES
BURGETT, EPHRAIM
JONES, WILLIAM
JONES, FEDERICK
Page 79
STEPHENS, NICHOLAS
STEPHENS, HENRY
JOHNSON, HANNAH
WATERS, GAINER
RANDALS, THOMAS
MITCHELL, AMOS
FENNELL, FRANCIS M.
FURGESON, HORATIO
WALKER, JOHN
WALKER, WILLIAM L.
MORROW, ISAAC
TIDWELL, FRANKLIN
MORRIS, THOMAS G.
HARRISON, LAURENCE
SHAW, FRANKLIN
GARRISON, SAMUEL
DAVIS, MARY
JONES, MICHAEL
COFFEE, JOHN
NICHOLS, LAWSON
WALKER, WASHINGTON
ROBBINS, EDWARD
BARNES, JAMES
RAGSDALE, WILLIAM, SR.
BARNES, EDWARD
COPELAND, JAMES
DAVIS, CLARA
BASTER, JOHN
COOPER, THOMAS
Page 80
DUNCAN, BENJAMIN
BURKET, JOHN
BANE, MOSES
HILL, THOMAS H.
DAVIS, JOHN
LASETER, JACOB
KIRKLAND, RICHARD
IVY, CHARLES
PARKER, BERNY
BRANSFIELD, JOHN A.
ROMAN, JEREMIAH
ADAMS, GEORGE F.
LAW, WILLIAM
PIERCE, ROBERT
LILLEY, EDMOND
GREEN, THOMAS
GROSS, GEORGE

DERETT, THOMAS
DERETT, SARAH
ANDERSON, WILEY
WEDGEWORTH, JOSEPH
WEDGEWORTH, ROBERT
MILLS, JOHN
HAMILTON, GREEN
BIRKWELL, MOSES
SULLIVAN, CRAVIN
MARTIN, LEWIS, SR.
MILLER, GEORGE
Page 81
RICHE, WILLIAM
CORDELL, WILLIAM
SIMS, ASA
SIMS, THOMAS
FREELAND, JOHN
SIMS, WILLIAM
SUTTON, JOHN C.
PACE, CORNELIUS
HARPER, ROBERT
CORDELL, MILLIGAN
BAYLES, HEZEKIAH
TURNER, WHALE
ENGLAND, ROBERT
GARRETT, JOHN
RECTOR, ELIJAH
JONES, JESSEE
JONES, RICHARD
TAYLOR, WILLIAM
DAVIS, JAMES
SHELTON, JOHN
FOSTER, GEORGE
JOHNSON, BENJAMIN
DAVIS, HILLIARD
WOODS, JOSEPH
CONNALLY, JOHN W.
JOHNSON, ALLEN
HANES, GEORGE
BYRD, SAMUEL
JOHNSON, JAMES, SR.
Page 82
HANEY, ISAAC
MARTIN, BYRON B.
SUMMERS, JOHN D.
PARISH, NOEL
PARISH, JAMES
SMITH, ISHAM
BROWN, JOHN G.
GADDIS, WILLIAM
MILLER, LEWIS
CHILDRESS, ISAAC

Marshall County

CHILDRESS, JOHN
MILLICAN, JOHN
BEARDIN, JAMES
BEARDIN, AMEL
PARKER, LEWIS
MAYO, DANIEL
WEBB, JOHN
HORNBUCKLE, WILLIAM
HORNBUCKLE, FRANKLIN
WALKER, ROBERT
LOVE, JOHN
BANE, SIMPSON
WEDGES, CALLOWAY
BANE, ALEXANDER
MARTIN, JOHN J.
BANE, ROBERT
TAYLOR, THOMAS
CLAGHORN, WILLIAM
BIDDY, JAMES
Page 83
WILDMAN, ELIAS
KING, BARNEY
SMITH, BARTHOLOMEW
PATE, JOHN
FRY, WILLIAM L.
CHILDRESS, JAMES
FURLOW, JOHN
PENDERGRASS, RALEIGH
PENDERGRASS, MOSES
BARNES, JOHN
NEWMAN, SHADRACK
PENDERGRASS, ATHA
McDUFFIE, DAVID
LEE, SARAH
PHILLIPS, WILLIAM
McDUFFIE, ANGUS
ROMAN, PETER
RANES, BRAXTON
SCHOOLER, NATHANIEL
TOLAFAIRO, NANCY
WILLIAM, ABSALAM
PENDERGRASS, BENJAMIN
LEE, HENRY
SOUTHERLAND, EVAN
CHAMBLESS, JOEL
PATE, THOMAS
FURLOW, NANCY
SOUTHERLAND, ALFRED
SOUTHERLAND, WILLIAM, SR.
Page 84
BEARDIN, JAMES
ROSWELL, PETER

LUCAS, SANIEL
ROSWELL, JAMES H.
SWADER, SAMUEL
SWADER, JOHNSON
RANEY, HENRY K.
RANEY, WILLIAM
GALLOWAY, THOMAS
LOCKETT, RICHARD
OLIVER, BENJAMIN
SOUTHERLAND, JOHN
PENDERGRASS, PHILLIP
PENDERGRASS, JOHN
STORY, JOHN
SOUTHERLAND, ALEXANDER
SOUTHERLAND, ADAM
SOUTHERLAND, HENRY
REYNOLDS, JOHN
WILLIAMS, JAMES
WILLIAMS, JACKSON
WILLIAMS, HENRY
KELLY, NATHAN
BAITEY, WILLIAM
SANDERS, ISAAC
JONES, WILLIAM
COFFEE, LOGAN
SINCLAIR, PASCAL
BEEDLE, POLLY
Page 85
SWAFFORD, WILLIAM
GRISSOM, ASA
CARTER, JOSEPH
CLARK, DELIA
HASTEN, STEPHEN
MORGAN, WILLIAM
OSBORN, PATIENCE
COFFEE, ELIZABETH
GAUTNEY, DARIUS
PARTON, WILSON
RODEN, SPENCER W.
DOUGLASS, EZEKIEL
DIXON, FREEMAN
HOLLAND, RANSOM
MINICKS, ABNER
BARBOR, ELISHA
COGGINS, DANIEL
BRADLEY, JOHNATHON
WOOSLEY, THOMAS
MARTIN, LEWIS, JR.
JOHNSTON, JOHN
RAGLAND, BURRELL A.
EVANS, JEFFERSON
BURKET, WILKINSON

CHILDRESS, ROBERT
MARTIN, JOHN
KENNAMON, ZACHARIAH
McDUFFIE, MACOM
DICKEY, EDMOND
Page 86
GOFORTH, SARAH
RANSOM, GEORGE
FINLEY, BUSHROD
CULVER, GEORGE W.
ARMSTRONG, GEORGE C.
EVANS, WILLIAM
NORMAN, JOHN M.
COOK, ELIJAH
WHITWORTH, WILLIAM
ROYALL, ELISHA
FONSE, PETER
FONSE, PHILLIP E.
MARTIN, ALLEN
WALKER, ROBERT
BUSH, WILLIAM
BANE, JOHN J.
DODD, JOHN C.
YOUNG, WILLIAM
HUGHS, WILLIAM
CULVER, JESSEE W.
FREMAND, ROBERT S.
BOATNER, PHELAND
SMITH, ISAAC
PATE, JOHN C.
HOGUE, ROBERT
VAN CLEAVE, GEORGE W.
CHINNAULT, GEORGE
MAJORS, JAMES
TIDWELL, RICHARD
Page 87
CRYER, WILLIAM J.
SMITH, THOMAS
ROBERTS, JOSHUA
MARTIN, HENRY
WILLIAMS, WILLIAM
BRIDGES, EPHRAIM
ROBINSON, JOHN
ROBINSON, CATHERINE
INGRAM, WILLIAM M.
JOHNSON, BENJAMIN
STILL, JOHN
ROGERS, CALEB W.
WEBBER, SAMUEL
SMITH, BURRELL
PARKER, JOSEPH
HOLLY, MARSHALL

MARSHALL COUNTY

HEASTERLY, JOHN
COLLINS, WILLIAM
HEARNE, EZEKIEL
SMITH, JOHN G.
SMITH, BRYANT, SR.
CRUTCHER, JAMES
NOBLE, MARK
CALLOWAY, WILLIAM H.
SLOAN, JOHN
NEWMAN, STEPHEN
BISHOP, ISAAC
MOORE, JAMES
COFFEE, WILLIAM S.
Page 88
KEIGS, THOMAS
HINES, BYRAN
GULLION, WILLIAM
COLLINS, FEDRICK
BRISON, JOHN W.
DERICK, ALEXANDER
DERRICK, ANDREW
BERRY, ZADOCK
HINES, CALVIN
RAGIN, EPHRAIM
WOOLEY, BAZZLE
FEEMSTER, SAMUEL W.
HATCHETT, CALDWELL
CHEEK, JESSEE
CASEY, LEVI
PATTESON, THOMAS
WEBB, JULIUS
GRAVES, JAMES
MORTON, JOHNATHAN
RIGHT, HORATIO
BOMAN, CHARLES
NOBLE, YANCY
HENRY, WILLIAM
WALKER, LANDEN C.
EMBRY, JAMES
DRINKARD, PRESLEY
DRINKARD, ELIZABETH
LEE, ELIZABETH
WILLIAMS, POLLY
Page 89
COOPER, JOHN
McBROOM, DAVID
BAXTER, RUEBIN
KING, BENJAMIN
JOHNSON, JAMES
EVANS, LORENZO D.

MORGAN, JOSHUA
SMITH, JOHN
PITTS, SUSANA
PRENTIS, WILLIAM
RIDGEWAY, ELIJAH
RAGSDALE, WILLIAM W.
RAGSDALE, PETER M.
PARMER, CALEB
JONES, ZACHERIAH
YOUNG, EDMOND
MARTIN, MILES
QUEEN, ELIZABETH
HINES, JOSEPH
FREEMAN, MICHAEL
RECTOR, JESSEE
PUTMAN, MARTIN
DONALDSON, JOHN
CULBREATH, JOHN
HESTERN, JOHN
PARKER, WILLIAM
McALLISTER, JANE
NOBLE, SARAH
MOONEY, JACOB
Page 90
MOONEY, PETER
ELGIN, MARY
GAILBREATH, ALEXANDER
GILBREATH, WILLIAM
LONG, NATHANIEL
STEPHENS, WILLIAM P.
BIGGS, ELIAS
PARISS, CHAMPION
HINES, MARY
TUCKER, PETERSON
SUMMERS, JAMES A.
CARP, CULLEN
BECKWORTH, SIMON
KING, WILLIAM
SMITH, WILLIAM
BRADLEY, JOHN
COLLINS, THOMAS
BLESSING, JACOB &
  JONES, SAM
NOBLE, JAMES
MORRIS, WILLIAM
COLLINS, THOMAS
WATSON, PATRICK A.
SCRIVNER, ESTILL
WALKER, JOHN V.
CULVER, JOHN W.

CULVER, ICHABOD
CULVER, GEORGE
ARMSTRONG, WILLIAM
BOMAN, WILLIAM
Page 91
BOMAN, JESSEE
REAVIS, JOHN
YOUNG, WILLIAM J.
VAUGHAN, HIRAM
BILLINGSLEY, JANE
HARLEY, JOHN
GREEN, WILLIAM
NIXON, JAMES
WOOTON, RICHARD
RANES, JAMES H.
KIRKSEY, GEORGE
NEAL, SAMUEL W.
WESTERN, ELIZABETH
CAMPBELL, CHARLES
TOLBERT, WESLEY
WOOTON, JOHNATHAN
BROWN, JAMES
POLLOCK, BENJAMIN H.
FARISS, JAMES
LITTLE, CLARA
SMITH, JOSEPH
SMITH, MARY
ROPER, PHILLIP
WALLIS, ELIZABETH
ODEN, ISRAEL
GOLDEN, WILLIAM
FIELDS, GOLDER
HICKMAN, JOHN
SWINDLER, JOEL
Page 92
KELSO, WILLIAM
WEST, JUDAH
PETT, JOHN
PETT, NAOMA
HAM, MANNE
HAM, ALLEN
CARLTON, HENRY
EASTERS, JOHN W.
JORDAN, WILLIAM G.
MURPHY, LEVI
EVETT, JAMES
MORTON, DRURY A.
BANKS, JAMES
MORTON, JOSHUA
GRIGORY, JANE

MARSHALL COUNTY

MORTON, JAMES
GAITER, JOHN
GAITER, DILY
MORTON, WILLIAM, JR.
CHAMBLESS, WILLIAM
MORTON, JOEL, JR.
MORTON, JOEL, SR.
THOMAS, GREENBERRY
MORTON, MARSHALL
MORTON, MARSHALL, JR.
DAVIS, PHILLIP
WINDSOR, WILLIAM
COX, EDWARD
Page 93
RICE, JOHN B.
SMITH, GREEN
BANKS, ARISTO C.
NEELEY, JOHN J.
COLYER, MOSES
GIPSON, EDWARD
CARPENTER, MOSES
DOUGAN, AARON M.
ST. CLAIR, HUGH
NUNNALLY, NANCY
STANLEY, WILLIAM
SMITH, JOSEPH J.
BURNS, MARY
BURNS, RANSOM
HUGHS, RICHARD B.
WEST, BUTCHER
*WEST, SAMUEL (103 yrs, old)
SWEETON, JOHN
BUCK, JAMES
TURNER, HENRY M.
RAMSEY, JOEL
WORDSWORTH, WILLIAM
DERICK, TOBIAS C.
CONNALLY, CHARLES
READ, GEORGE
RICHE, DAVID
BAXTER, STEPHEN
MARTON, FRANCIS
CARTER, KINCY C.
CALDHARN, SLAXTON
Page 94
SOUTHERLAND, WILLIAM JR.
ISBEL, WILLIAM
ISBEL, LEVI
NIGHT, JAMES
DUNCAN, JOHN
JOHNSON, JAMES

MILLER, GEORGE
WILDMAN, THOMAS
McKAIN, SARAH
NICHOL, JESSEE
THOMPSON, JOSEPH
KENNADY, JOHN H.
DONALDSON, ALEXANDER
TILLAY, WASHINGTON
ROSE, JAMES
KING, ANDREW
STINNETT, LINA
CONNALLY, GEORGE
TAYLOR, JANE
HARPER, LEVI
CHAMBERS, JOHN
BUSBY, DANIEL
MAJORS, JACOB
WATSON, GEORGE W.
Page 95
BEARD, A. C.
FINLEY, SARAH
CHARMIR, SUSANNAH
BROWN, ELIJAH
HATCH, RALPH
WELLMOTH, GABRIEL
WILLMOTH, GEORGE
GLASCOCK, K.B.
MATHEWS, MARY
HART, JOSIAH
ANDERSON, JAMES
FINLEY, JOHN
SMITH, ANDREW
CASS, LARKIN T.
RICHBURG, ABIJAH
CASS, WILLIAM
WOODS, PETER
GRIFFETH, SARAH
DERICK, ALFRED
CHEEK, ----
DERICK, JACOB
GRIFFIN, RICHARD
HANBY, ELIZABETH
ALLEN, WILLIAM G.
PILCHER, JOHN
CAST, SAMUEL
DERICK, WILLIAM W.
NEELEY, JOHN
SMITH, KEZIAH
NEELEY, JAMES B.
Page 96
GRIFFIN, SARAH

GRIFFIN, WILLIAM M.
SUTTON, BENJAMIN
NEELEY, RICHARD
LAW, PEYTON, SR.
HEALE, THOMAS
BRALTON, COLBERT
PHILIPS, NELSON
LEFEW, JOHN H.
GREEN, THOMAS B.
GOBBLE, JOHN
ANDERSON, ROBERT B.S.
HAMILTON, MARTHA
STEELE, SARAH M.
BOLIN, ALEXANDER
DANIEL, JAMES M.
WHALES, WILLIAM H. E.
GARRETT, JOSEPH G.
NICHOLS, SIMON
BURNS, SARAH
WILSON, JOHN
DUNKIN, THOMAS
SMITH, WILLIAM
RECTOR, THOMAS B.
RECTOR, FIELDING L.
SMITH, TURNER
ABLE, JOHN
ABLE, JOSEPH
CAMPBELL, ELI
WOOD, THOMAS
Page 97
McDANIEL, MATHEW
CROPLAND, GEORGE
PACE, ---
ROBINSON, REBECCA
PRICE, ABNER H.
PRICE, REESE
ROBINSON, GEORGE W.
TUCKER, RUSSELL
LEWIS, LEONARD
JOHNSON, KENNEDY
LEWIS, HENRY
JOHNSON, JOSHUA
MARTIN, GEORGE W.
PATTERSON, SPENCER
THOMPSON, EPHRIAM
BAKER, WILLIAM
FINLEY, JAMES
TUCKER, ARCHIBALD
SMITH, JACOB
RUSSELL, JOHN
MILLS, BENJAMIN

*military pensioner

MARSHALL COUNTY

ANNY, PHILIP
CHAPMAN, MARTHA
PARKER, WILLIAM
WOODS, NANCY
PIPKINS, ZILSHA
JOB, AARON
LASOR, MARGARET
WHITEHEAD, WILLIAM
BOUMIT, MARTHA
   Page 98
CLAPP, BARTON
TIDWELL, JOSIAH
BERAL, WILLIAM
*BRADLEY, JOHN, SR.
BIRD, RILEY
HERRIN, EPHRIAM
BRADLEY, JOHN JR.
BOADLER, ALEXANDER
PARKS, THOMAS
JONES, JOSEPH D.
STARNES, PETER
EMERY, GEORGE W.
SUTTON, DALIER
STEWARD, WILLIAM
STARNES, PETER A.
TROUP, JAMES
COBB, TRAVIS M.
TACO, JAMES
MATSEN, JESSE
TACO, JOSEPH
EVANS, CHARLES G.
CHAPLE, HENRY
BOWEN, MORDICIA
MANNING, CHIRNAS
MANNING, NANCY
SINT, JOHN B.
PARKHILL, DAVID, JR.
PARKHILL, DAVID
JONES, JOHNATHAN
   Page 99
PHILIPS, LABION
GRAMMAR, WILLIAM
WILLIAMS, JOSHUA
MARONEY, JOHN A.
MANLEY, WILLIAM
ROBINSON, JAMES
WATTS, WILLIAM
MAY, DANIEL
NEWMAN, RANDOLPH
RICKETTS, DAVID
FENNELL, ISHAM

PARKER, ALCANER
BAKER, DAVID
ROBINS, PLEASANT
MCKEE, WILLIAM
RECTOR, CASWELL
GUYIER, CHARLES
TAYLOR, GEORGE
WOODS, WILLIAM
BAKER, JOHN
EVAN, WILLIAM
NEWMAN, RICHARD
ALLEN, ROBERT R.
TUCKER, WILLIAMSON
SULLIVAN, SARAH
NICHOLS, CHARLES
STARNS, JOHN
CAMPBELL, MARGARET
STARNES, PETER C.
RICKETTS, THOMAS
   Page 100
McMICHAEL, WILLIAM L.
RODEN, BENJAMIN
RODEN, SHELTON
RODEN, MARGARET
RHEA, JOHN
HENRY, HUGH
LEWIS, ROBERT
ANDERSON, ROBERT H.
MANLEY, JOHN B.
MARTIN, JOHN W.
BARCLAY, JAMES
KITE, MARTIN S.
TRIPLETT, ABNER
JOHNSON, SAMUEL
KITE, CISSE
*CARGILE, THOMAS
IVY, GEORGE
DEARMAN, B.
LEWIS, LOREN R.
CHISLOM, WILLIAM
BRIDGES, EDMOND
PARKHILL, MYLES B.
HOLT, ABRAHAM G.
MORRIS, HIRAM
TIDWELL, URIAH
TANT, THOMAS
TANT, ELISHA
SUTTON, JAMES M.
*DOTY, THOMAS
KIRKLAND, WILLIS
   Page 101
HOLT, ROBERT G.

JOHNSON, WILLIAM
TACO, JOHN W.
SIMS, THADEUS
SIMS, JOHN
HIGDON, THOMAS
ALDRIDGE, DRURY
JOHNSON, ARRON
BIRDWELL, ABRAHAM
LOGAN, WILLIAM S.
FLETCHER, JORDON
FLETCHER, JAMES
KIRKLAND, JOHN
CLACK, JOHN
ELLISON, ELIJAH
RENNS, JAMES
WRIGHT, JOSEPH C.
WOODS, WILLIAM
HAMPTON, JOHN
COX, JOHN
WILLIAMS, ROBERT
WILLIAMS, JANE
DAVIDSON, JAMES
McDONOUGH, WILLIAM
BOGGESS, TARNES
DONGAN, SHARP
LAMSTER, JOHN
GEORGE, PRESLEY C.
BOGGESS, HENRY H.
HUSE, MOSES
   Page 102
WOOD, DANIEL
*RAINS, ROBERT
FLEULLEN, WILLIAM
MARSH, JOHN S.
MARSH, DANIEL
MARSH, THOMAS M.
AUSTIN, JESSE
GARRETT, NEWTON
MILLSAPS, WILLIAM
MacREYNOLDS, HUGH
EDWARDS, JANE
GOODWIN, JAMES
HENRY, ALBERT G.
HOYLE, DAVID L.
BAYLESS, ROENNA
QUEEN, AGNES
RANDLES, RICHARD S.
TYLER, SAMUEL
HALE, THOMAS
HELTON, WILLIAM
JONES, ALEXANDER

*military pensioner

MARSHALL COUNTY

MacFARLANE, WALTER P.
WIGGS, WILLIAM H.
CALDWELL, WILLIAM
LITTLE, AMELIA
BUSH, WILLIAM
CARMICHAEL, WILLIAM L.
BELL, GEORGE W.
BAYLEY, CARR
CHAMBLESS, HENRY

Page 103
DOUGAN, MARY
CRIPS, JOHN
CRIPS, JACOB
ADAMS, JAMES M.
THOMAS, GEORGE
SHORES, HILLAS R.
TODD, WILLIAM T.
FIELDS, DANIEL
JOHNSON, JOHN
SARLES, CHARNEY
DAVIDSON, EDWARD
KING, GEORGE
KING, ISAAC
McCONNELL, JOHN
GOLDEN, RICHARD
CHILDRESS, DAVID
STEPHENS, HARDY
RAYBORN, SAMUEL R.
USERY, GILBERT
ALLEN, GEORGE W.
HOWELL, ANDREW
LOVELESS, ALLEN
METCALFE, JAMES
THOMAS, JOHN
HAYS, MARIA
FAINSTER, ANN
PARIS, ABNER
PARIS, JOHNSON
HAINS, HENRY
PARIS, ELIZABETH

Page 104
McCREDY, ANDREW
RUSSELL, ALFRED
DURAN, JOSEPH E.
TERRELL, CHARLES R.
TERRELL, JESSE
EASON, JOHN W.
TIGON, JAMES
KILFOYLE, PETER
DOSS, JOHN
KENNEDY, ROBERT

WYATT, WILLIAM H.
STEELE, ELIZABETH
MYRICK, Z.
WILLIS, DAVID
GRIFFIN, ANDREW T.
SCHRIMSHAW, JAMES
WILLIAMS, ROBERT M.
MATHEWS, EDWARD
KIRKSEY, HENRY
WINDSOR, WILLIAM
WILLOUGHBY, JOHN H.
BELTON, HENSON
CONNALLY, THOMAS K.
MOORE, JAMES M.
GARMESON, WRIGHT
STEPHENS, HURBERT
TIDWELL, JACKSON
COAL, JOHN
COLBERN, ROBERT
ARMSTRONG, ROBERT

Page 105
HUDSON, ALEXANDER
MABSON, JOHN
GEE, JAMES M.
ANDERSON, MARK
GLOVER, JAMES
GARRETT, SIMEON
HARPER, SAMUEL
HARRIS, CHARLES P.
WILCHER, JOHN
HIGGINS, JOEL
KILCHINS, MAHALA
WOOLARD, SWAIN W.
HICKEY, JOSEPH
THOMAS, JOHN T.
CONAWAY, ABLE
WILLOUGHBY, JOHN W.
BISHOP, JOHN
ARNETT, WILLIAM
SWORDS, JOHNATHAN
SMITH, ELISHA
WHITLOCK, JAMES
HERRIN, CURTIS
WRIGHT, JOSEPH E.
DYE, LACEY
MARSH, JAMES
MARSH, THOMAS
RAMSEY, BENJAMIN B.
CAROT, RUFUS
FINLEY, HUGH
PATRICK, JAMES

THORNBURG, THOMAS
Page 106
JONES, JOHN
GARRETT, EDWARD
WELLS, THOMAS C.
WILLIAMS, GARY
KELLEY, EDWARD
BOLIN, JAMES
KELLEY, ELIZABETH
POLLARD, MILLER
ROBINS, ISAAC
COWAN, GARRETT
COWAN, FRANCIS
DICKSON, JOEL
ALAWYNE, JACOB
BAYLEY, ZECHARIAH
COOK, CLAYTON
PATRICK, ELISHA
NICHLES, WILLIAM C.
WHITWORTH, JOSEPH
WHITWORTH, CLAIBORNE
WHITWORTH, JOHN
BODIN, CATAVIN
HAMNER, DANIEL
HAMNER, JOHN
HAMNER, RICHARD H.
PATRICK, JOHN
PATRICK, RICHARD
MACKEY, WILLIAM O.
POWER, EDWARD
HERRON, ASA
BAYLES, TOM
BOATNER, LEWIS

Page 107
PRATT, JESSE
SWINGIN, SAMUEL
SEXTON, ROBERT
BOYLES, BARNEY
STREET, OLIVER D.
AKINS, JOHN
AKINS, GEORGE
AIKINS, WILLIAM H.
HOWARD, ELIJAH
ADKINS, THOMAS
EASLEY, JOHN
SHARP, BENJAMIN
BERRY, JOHN H.
DERRICK, JOHN H.
FRY, MARY
BRIGHT, BOWLEN
BRIGHT, RACHAEL

-66-

MARSHALL COUNTY

BRECK, WILLIAM
PARKS, CATAVINA
ALEXANDER, ANTHONY
FRY, WELLBORN
CHILDRESS, JAMES
CHILDRESS, AGNES
KENNEDY, CHARLES
HILL, JOHN
HILL, ELIZABETH
SMITH, JOHN
FINLEY, JOHN B.
WOODALL, B. D.
BARNETT, JOHN W.
MORELAND, ELISHA
   Page 108
BUCKHANNON, MARGARET
LOWRY, THOMAS
RAGLAND, JOHN
HOPE, SAMUEL
COXE, ADAM
HAMILTON, RUSSELL
LOWRY, SAMUEL
FRY, HENRY
FRY, SOLOMAN
DITTO, MICHAEL
McKAN, ABRAHAM
LUMMUS, JAMES
BEARD, SAMUEL
MILFORD, JAMESON
MILFORD, JAMES
MILFORD, THOMAS
TOWNS, JOSHUA
MACKEY, WILLIAM
COXE, JOHN SR.
MILLS, ALEXANDER
CASS, JOHN
ANDERSON, JOHN
ANDERSON, SUSAN
BAXTER, ARCHIBALD

RANDOLPH COUNTY

Page 192
MAGEE, JOHN
HUMBER, A. P.
WALKER, E. C.
PELMAN, JAMES M.
CARDMILL, WILLIAM
MICKLE, JAMES M.
HATHORN, HUGH
PERRY, JAMES W.
WEATHERS, WILLIAM W.
EDWARDS, ELISHA
McMURRAY, T. J.
McKNIGHT, WILLIAM
OSBORNE, W. H.
FAILES, REBECA
AGERBON, DEMPSEY
CUMMINGS, JAMES
COAL, JOHN
PHILLIPS, HARRINGTON
HOUSE, THORNTON
WINDSOR, ANN C.
LUNSFORD, HENRY
GAY, HENRY M.
PEERSON, JAMES S.
SHOEMAKE, J. F.
GLENN, WILLIAM
WILLIS, R.S.
WARD, WILLIAM
SHURANS, Q.G.
WALKER, HENRY
CONNOR, JOHN
Page 193
BURKHALTER, A. M.
BOX, JACOB
HEADON, JOHN
SECKORY, JOHN
SHANDFIELD, RICHARD
VAUGHN, JARED
WALKER, WILLIAM S.
PINKARD, PEYTON
HEFFLEN, WYATT
EAST, JESSE
DABNEY, A.B.
COGBURN, JARED H.
MICKLE, JEREMIAH
RALBON, JOHN W.
DUKE, THOMAS
MICKLES, THOMAS F.
CLEMENTS, WILLIAM
NUNN, ELIGAH
JONES, JAMES B.
WOOD, WILLIS
KENNEDY, SAMUEL
CARLEE, JAMES

NORTHAM, JOHN M.
CHILDS, RALPH R.
FINCHER, JOSHUA
WOOD, WILLIAM
PEERSON, URNEY
CRAWLEY, GEORGE H.
GREEN, TABITHA
Page 194
HARTEFIELD, A.T.
LEVERETT, ROBERT F.
GREEN, PETER
GRIFFIN, THOMAS
POOL, THOMAS A.
BREWER, MARTHA
POOL, P.V.T.
INGRAM, JOHN C.
NOEL, RICHMON
PERRY, WILLIAM
DELLAH, NATHAN
HARMELTON, JAMES
MONIEES, BENJAMIN
DINGLER, WILLIAM
HARRIS, J. M.
PERRY, HUGH
PINCKARD, THOMAS C.
HANSON, JOHN C.
BARRETT, ROBERT
EAST, BENJAMIN
EAST, ZEALOUS
WOOD, A.E.
ROTTEN, W. J.
POOL, W.P.
HANES, PARMENAS
PHILIPS, ELIJAH
PATE, JAMES
TAYLOR, FREEMAN
MUNKUS, WILLIAM
Page 195
LATIMORE, EDWARD
CLARKE, WYATT
HARKINS, JOSEPH T.
DANIEL, THOMAS T.
BLAGG, C.J.
GILILAND, THOMAS
McKNIGHT, WILLIAM
ALLMAN, WILLIAM
HENDON, ROBERT
HEELEY, JAMES S.
LEE, SOLOMAN
PRICKETT, WILEY J.
BAZEMORE, B. H.
HESTER, TAPLEY
ALSOBROOK, A.G.

GELASPY, JOHN G.
SHELNUT, WILLIAM
JOHNS, ZACHERIAH
SPIVEY. E.P.
BENEFIELD, WILLIAM
STITT, ROBERT
GOODMAN, MICAJAH
STONE, MICAJAH
GLADNEY, WILLIAM
GLADNEY, THOMAS
SPEARS, MICER
CUSE, JOHN
FOWLER, JOHN
POOL, ROBERT C.
Page 196
CURRY, THOMAS
HARPER, GREEN K.
BRUMBELOE, E.G.
YATES, DARLING
SMITH, JOHN E.
ROGERS, JOSEPH
McDONALD, ANGUSH
MORTON, GREEN
YOUNG, SAMUEL
BAILEY, TOMAS J.
DANIELL, CHARLES W.
WILLIAMS, ROBERT
CROSBY, CHARLES
PRESNELL, M. F.
MILLER, MARTHA A.
COALMAN, JOHN
LONG, ROBERT
MISBON?, ELIJAH
CHILDRESS, ABRAHAM
TWILEY, JAMES M.
SNOW, JEREMIAH
SURRY, THOMAS
NARON, THOMAS
BELLAH, REUBEN
BOATNER, JOHN
WILLIAMS, WILLIAM
BEAN, WILEY J.
HARCROW, HUGH
BEAN, JOHN
Page 197
KENARD, BARNETT
*KENARD, JOHN
PEVOUGHN?, ISHAM
WILLINGHAM, JESSE
CORLEY, RICHARD W.
CORLEY, EDWARD
CORLEY, WILSON
JORDON, WILLIAM

*military pensioner

RANDOLPH COUNTY

Page 197

CLAGBURN, BENJAMIN
CLAGBURN, DANIEL C.
BILLINGSLEY, WASHINGTON
ORR, JOHN
LINSAY, JOHN
WOODRUFF, IRVIN
ASHCROFT, THOMAS
YOUNG, ISAAC
BOX, EDWARD W.
YOUNG, RICHMOND
ASHCROFT, JOHN
COCKRELL, SIMEON
TAYLOR, JOHN
BEAN, WALTER
HARCROW, DAVID
JOHNSON, PETER
FERRELL, JETHREW
FERRELL, HENRY
HANNERS, NOAH
OWENS, WALTER
OWENS, THOMAS

Page 198

PARKER, FRANCIS
LUNDEL, THOMAS F.
LYLE, WILLIS
POWELL, ELISHA
JORDON, MARY
PENOUGH, FREEMAN
ROBERTS, HARDY
WOODS, WILLIAM W.
EAST, AMOS
JONES, SEBAIN
WILSON, VALENTINE
HAWTHORN, JOHN B.
HAWTHORN, JAMES
McGLEN, EDWARD
McCOY, EDWARD
REEVES, THOMPSON
WRIGHT, WILLIAM
McCLENDON, WILEY M.
LUCAS, B. E.
HUFFMAN, WILLIAM
SMITH, TOMAS K.
GATES, ELI
TREDWELL, STEPHEN
LEE, JEPTHA
McDONALD, JOHN
CASCE, CHARLOTTE
COSNIMS, BENJAMIN C.
BLACK, MARY
LAMB, WILLIAM

Page 199

WALLIS, JEREMIAH
WALLIS, HENRY
WILSON, LEANDER
COAL, JAMES G.
MALLETT, JESSE
McDANIEL, SAMUEL
COAL, HASEY
WHITE, CARTER
SMITH, JOSEPH
FRAZIER, SAMUEL G.
ROBERTS, ALLEN
LOVEN, JAMES
LEDBETTER, HARRY
LEDBETTER, ISAAC
WARD, JESSE
WEBLEY, ROBERT
GARRISON, THOMAS
PERRY, JAMES
WILKERSON, ELKANAH
DUBERRY, SILES
PENNINGTON, A.S.
SMITH, JOHN
NIGHT, FLOYD
SMITH, JEPTHA V.
JACKSON, C. R.
HUDDLESTON, WILLIAM
HEDMAN, SAMUEL
GRESHAM, WILLIAM
MOORE, ISAAC

Page 200

STONE, JEREMIAH
SKINNER, JOHN H.
KILPATRICK, JOHN P.
TAYLOR, WILLIAM W.
HEARD, JOHN
YATES, PETER
CARTER, URIAH
CARTER, WILLIAM
SCROGGINS, HENRY
PARIS, WILLIAM C.
POWELL, GEORGE C.
COOK, CASWELL
BASS, CALVIN
WEATHERS, JESSE
SHELNUT, THOMAS
WAKEFIELD, JAMES
COPELAND, GILBERT
WELDON, ISAAC
LEE, JOHN
COPELAND, GAINS
SPERRY, BEVERLY

SPERRY, BEVERLY
HESTER, TAPLEY
POSEY, SEABORN
WEATHERS, ISHAM
EDWARDS, DANIEL
FREEMAN, HUGH
CUNNINGHAM, WILLIAM H.
BLACK, ROBERT
GOLDMAN, WILLIAM

Page 201

LAMB, JOHN
LAMB, NICHOLUS
LAMB, GREEN
DARDEN, ZACHERIAH
LAMB, JOSHUA
BRIGHTON, T. J.
SPEARS, DANIEL
BROWN, ALLEN
WATWOOD, JAMES
ABBOTT, JAMES W.
CLEMENTS, JAMES M.
CROOK, JEREMIAH
MONTGOMERY, HUGH
HODGE, ANDREW
BERRYHILL, JOHN
KNIGHT, HENRY
WILLINGHAM, WILLIAM
HARRIS, HUGH W.
HAY, CHESLEY
BLAKE, THOMAS
BLAKE, WILLIAM
JOHNS, WILLIAMS
NIXON, JOHN
HIGHTOWER, WILLIAM
HIGHTOWER, JOSHUA
THOMPSON, ASA
BURNES, ELIZABETH
PARKER, CATHERING
WADE, JAMES P.

Page 202

JOWERS, BENJAMIN
SMITH, JAMES
GOODWIN, IZIAH
GOODMAN, WILLIAM
INGRAM, EDWARD
McKINNES, ALEXANDER
MILLER, JOHN A.
JOHNSON, JESSE
PENSON, HARRISON
STEWART, ANDREW J.
MOORE, SAMUEL

RANDOLPH COUNTY
Page 204

DOWDY, JAMES
BRADS, JACOB
ANDREWS, WILLIAM
CRESLER, ABRAHAM
WEPON, W.W.
WELLS, CARBER
MORRISON, T. J.
SWEET, ROBERT
PENSON, JAMES
THRASHER, THOMAS
GOODEN, JOHN
BOULEN, JOHN
OWEN, DAVID
HUNNECUT, JAMES
MORRISON, JOHN S.
SMITH, JOHN
PRUETT, ANDREW H.
SEARS, DAVID

Page 203
TOWERS, JEFFERSON
RAGAN, WILLIAM P.
REYNOLDS, JESSE
NEWSOM, SILAS
McKEE, WILLIAM
TOLBERT, ALLEN
McDOW, JOHN
FEATHERSTON, WILLIAM
MULLOLLY, WILLIAM
DAVENPORT, GEORGE
HOLOWAY, JOHN
SMITH, MOSES
DOWDEY, JAMES, JR.
RATTEN, HENRY
ROJERS, WILLIAM
MILLER, JOHN A. D.
McCOY, NEELY
MILLER, ANDREW
HURST, WILLIAM
SIMPSON, WILLIAM
*SIMPSON, JAMES
KENNEDY, JOSEPH M.
PRUETT, ANIEL
BANKS, JOHN
ALLAN, NATHAN
BOLING, SAMUEL
DEBMORE, JOHN
GILBERT, SIMON
HURST, ROBERT
ELLIOTT, JACOB

SPEARS, WILLIAM
McWHORTER, SAMUEL
RUSTON, BENNET J.
URSURY, PETER
LEOPARD, JOHN
LEOPARD, WILLIAM
SKINNER, SAMUEL
LEOPARD, ROBERT
FALKNER, WILLIAM G.
PARKER, MARGARET
SKINNER, JOHN
BARNES, ELEANOR
REEVES, JOHN
HUDSON, C.D.
ROWELL, JOHN
BAKER, JOHN T.
STONECHER, MALINDA
DUNCAN, MATTHEW
MANGRUM, JAMES
ALLEN, FRANCIS
CROWSLEY, MARTHA
SAWYER, JOHN
FALKNER, JOB
URSERY, ELVIN J.
WILKS, OSBURN
LEWIS, VINEY
BREED, JOSEPH
LANIER, WILLIAM W.
CONALLY, JAMES

Page 205
BONNER, JAMES
CROMBY, REUBEN
CARDLE, ELIZABETH
McPHERSON, ELIZABETH
GREEN, JAMES
VANCE, CHARLES W.
KERKLEY, JAMES
KERKLEY, JOHN
PEELER, JAMES
VANCE, ADAM
SMITH, JOHN E.
BAYLES, BURRELL
OLIVER, THOMAS
PROTHRO, JAMES
McPHERSON, JOHN
HARPER, MILES
YOUNG, ANDREW
ALLAN, JAMES W.
SHERROD, WILLIAM P.

VANCE, ROBERT R.
BOLT, ISHAM
REEVES, JAMES W.
HARRIS, JOHN
STEWART, TEMPLE T.
VOWEL, NANCY
VOWEL, NATHANIEL
MOORE, MOSES
KENNEDY, ROBERT D.
BAYLIS, LARKIN

Page 206
DOBSON, JOHN
GLADNEY, SAMUEL
SPEARS, JOSHUA T.
SPEARS, JOSHUA
HOGAN, WILLIAM
ALLISON, WADE H.
CLARK, CRAFT
WILLIS, JOHN T.
BAKER, ELIZABETH
FINCHER, MOSES C.
FINCHER, BENJAMIN
STEWART, JOHN
BENNETT, EVELINE
JONES, MARY
ALLAN, WILLIAM
TARVER, HEZEKIAH
JENNINGS, COLEMAN
BARDEN, JAMES
MULDREW, ISAAC
BARNES, LAMB
YANCY, WILLIAM
CARDMWLL, WILLIAM
WALKER, SYLVANNUS
TRAUNT, JOHN
HOUSE, WILLIAM
STRICKLIN, CALVIN
STRICKLIN, D. G.
WINDSOR, JOHN D.
MULDREW, DAVID

Page 207
SAWYERS, ARCHIBALD
REALS, PHEBY
REYNOLDS, ZACHARIAH
HUDSON, WILLIAM
HUDSON, JOHN W.
RYAN, LACY
STRIPLEN, BENJAMIN O.
SEWART, SAMUEL

*military pensioner

RANDOLPH COUNTY

SEWART, HIRAM
STEWART, WILLIAM
HEATH, JOSEPH
HAVERSON, JAMES
CAMP, PINCKNEY
BRYAN, MARGARET O.
CLAYTON, WILLIS M.
CAMP, SUSAN
McPHAIL, JOHN
ADRAN, JAMES
SMITH, WILLIAM
HIGGINBOTTOM, WILSON
ELLIS, IRVY
WARDWORTH, MARBEN H.
CAMPBELL, DANIEL
FULCHER, RAYMON
CHAMBERS, PRESLEY
CAMP, JONATHAN
WHITE, JANE
WALKER, LARKIN
   Page 208
MORRISON, JOEL T.
BUCHANAN, DEWARD
STRONG, SAMUEL
SWEET, ROBERT
SWEET, LUKE
MORRISON, M. R.
HATTON, JOHN
BURSON, J. C.
FOUSTER, FREDERICK
CRAIGHEAD, R.B.
BURSON, KIDDIE
SHIP, JESSE
McCULLERS, ANDREW
McCRELESS, JAMES
VICE, ABNER A.
McKENSAY, A.
MORRIS, WILA
FLIN, B. A.
REHAUG, FRANCIS
PUTMAN, SIMON
PUTMAN, MADISON
ARMSTRONG, JOHN
PUTMAN, MONROE
ABLES, JOSEPH
ABLES, JOHN B.
McKINEY, JAMES
SHIP, JOHN
ADRAIN, F.F.
   Page 209
CASPER, GEORGE H.
CASPER, JOSEPH B.M.

CASPER, JOEL H.
FRAZIER, ELI
HARRIS, BRITTON C.
HARRIS, BENJAMIN
DANIEL, JACKSON
RIGSBY, JOHN
SEXTON, JAMES
FOSTER, WILLIAM T.
STRIBLING, JAMES M.
STEWART, CALVIN
McDONALD, SAMUEL
DYSON, THOMAS
RIGSBY, WILLIAM T.
FRAZIER, S. G.
RUSHAM, JOSEPH
JONES, THOMAS
TINDLE, JAMES
HOWARD, SAMUEL
HOWARD, THOMAS
HOWARD, DAVID
KERR, JOHN Y.
BROWN, JAMES
BROWN, JESSE
BLALOCK, GILES
CASPER, WILLIAM
GORRES, B.F.
RIGGSBY, THOMAS C.
   Page 210
TYREE, WILLIAM M.
WILLIAMS, AVINGTON
McBURNETT, THOMAS
MUSIC, DAVID
HARRIS, ELBERT
CASEL, ARVINGTON
DANIEL, ISAAC B.
TRAYLOR, WASHINGTON
STROUD, WILEY
BURDEN, EDWARD
MOORE, RICHARD
CHANDLER, JOEL
SMITH, RANSOM S.
MOORE, SIGNA
WATSON, HARMON
COLEMAN, JESSE H.
BURDEN, JAMES
BADDATT, JOHN
WORLEY, ADAM
HODGE, RICHARD
HENSON, WILLIAM
HENSON, JESSE
HERREN, ELISHA
BOLT, BERRYMAN

WILSON, HENRY
COLE, RICHARD
CADDLEMAN, RHEUBEN
THOMPSON, ISAAC
CAWFIELD, WILLIAM H.
   Page 211
BOWEN, JOHN D.
DANIEL, JAMES B.
KID, JOHN
BREED, WILLIAM S.
STIFLE, R.M.
KNOWLES, GEORGE W.
HOPSON, ABSALOM
RIGSBY, SAMUEL
ROSS, JAMES
WHITE, J. F.
BERRETT, THOMAS
BERRETT, ANDREW
BARROW, RICHARD
MISE, WILEY
THOMAS, GARRETT
HOLMS, JAMES
HOLMES, LAWSON
WHITE, JANE
WILLIS, NOAH T.
BURTON, JACOB
LAKE, JAMES
HULL, RICHARD
GLADNEY, THOMAS
APEENEY, ROBERT
FALKNER, JOEL
CROWSON, THOMAS
RIGSBY, ALLAN
BURRETT, THOMAS
BREED, RICHARD N.
   Page 212
BARETT, FRANCES
COTTON, ELIJAH
TAYLOR, JOHN S.
NUNN WILLIAM
SMITH, JAMES M.
WAFER, THOMAS B.
PARKER, WILLIAM
LANCASTER, WILLIAM
BAILEY, IRVIN
DOUGLASS, J. M.
GARRETT, JOHN
DEAL, JOHN
BAILEY, JOHN
THOMASON, A.M.
HENSON, JAMES
McSWAIN, DENNIS

-71-

RANDOLPH COUNTY

BARNS, WILLIAM
STALLINGS, JEREMIAH
BAKER, ISAAC
FALKNER, JEFFERSON
INGRAM, GABRIEL
GRESHAM, PARIS E.
DOUGLE, SAMUEL M.
FALKNER, WILLIAM
BURDEN, JAMES
FORD, WILLIAM
FALKNER, ELIJAH
SEALY, A.
PARKER, JOHN
Page 213
HOWELL, PETER
MORRIS, H.
WEBB, GIDEON
GLOVER, ISAAC
ELLIS BENJAMIN
HANNAH, JOHN S.
TUBMAN, HIRAM
DONALDSON, HUGH
DAVIDSON, T. A.
DONALDSON, ELIZABETH
METCALF. ANN
SHIP, RANSOM
BROOKS, JAMES
REYNOLDS, MITCHELL
REYNOLDS, JOSEPH
ABLES, JAMES
MILLER, C.
McCASKILL, GEORGE
ARNOLD, ANDREW
MURPHY, JEREMIAH
BROWN, M.
CASKEY, THOMAS
ADAMS, JAMES
BROWN, JOHN
BENNETT, JOHN S.
ABLE, THOMAS
WHEELER, JOHN M.
DONALDSON, ROBERT
ROBERTS, JESSE
Page 214
SMITH, R. H.
BURNHAM, ANDREW
LAMBERT, JAMES
ROBERTSON, JAMES B.
ARMSTRONG, WILLIAM
PARKER, HENRY H.
ARMSTRONG, JAMES
HULL, WILLIAM

DOWNS, JESSE M.
HULL, JAMES
MILLER, SAMUEL
HOLIFIELD, JOHN
BENNETT, WILLIS P.
THOMAS, JAMES
BARNES, R. G.
GARRISON, JAMES H.
KNIGHT, F.
SALE, J.
COLLINS, WILLIAM
FINCHER, LEANDER
HARRIS, REYNOLDS
KENT, EDMUND
LATIMORE, A.
SMITH, JESSE
BURGESS, JOHN H.
HENDRICK, JOHN
WILDON, A.
MICHEL, WILLIAM P.
COCKRELL, T.
Page 215
LEE, WILLIAM G.
LENDVILLE, WORLEY
HOWARD, F. J.
LEE, IVEY
CLARKE, JOHN E.
EVANS, DAVID T.
MOULTON, JOHN
O'HARROW, H. H.
O'HARROW, A. H.
*CAID, HUGH
DONALDSON, JAMES
RUSSELL, WILLIAM
PETTY, MOPHEN
PELL, MITCHELL H.
PEIRCE, JACOB
SMITH, R. H.
STEWART, WILLIAM
PARIS, LARKIN H.
CROW, GREEN
HOWELL, SANDERS
FUGRESON, NEAL
HARRIS, GEORGE
PUTMAN, SILUS M.
GOODMIN, SANFORD
WARE, SAMUEL B.
OTWILL, WILLIAM H.
TONAHAM, JOHN
HOUSE, SION
CAMARON, JOHN
JONES, JAMES M.

OTWELL, SAMUEL
Page 216
HOWELL, ALBERT
McCLENDON, T.W.M.
JOINER, WILLIAM
JARRETT, JOHN
JONES, RICHMOND
RUCKER, FIELDING
HENSON, JOHN
HOWELL, SUSAN
HOWELL, JEFFERSON
McBURNETT, ALBERT
THOMAS, ISAAC
McCLENDON, LEWIS
CASKEY, ROBERT
PEELER, JACOB
McDOUGALL, J.
PORE, JACOB
MANNING, MICHAEL
MANNING, DANIEL
HAGERTY, JAMES M.
BRADSHAW, J. W.
HEARN, ASA
MORROW, JOHN
BURTON, MARTIN
BENTON, JOSEPH
SHARBUTT, JANE
WILLINGHAM, JOHN
PRIDDY, LEMUEL
CHILES, DANIEL
Page 217
PARKER, DAVID S.
JOHNS, WILLIAM
DUKES, JAMES
MARTIN, DANIEL
HARRINGTON, JAMES
THOMAS, DAVID
SMITH, UEL
CULLENS, DAVID
SHEPP, ROBERT
THOMAS, LEWALEN

*military pensioner

RUSSELL COUNTY

Page 2
TATE, THOMAS L.
MARTIN, WILLIAM B.
MYRICK, HOWEL
McGEHEE, ISAAC
COX, MOSES
ROUT, HENRY
McKISSACK, JEREMIAH
CAPMAN, MOSES
WILLIAMSON, WILLIAM
BAKER, BENJAMIN
WOOD, JOHN
BARNETT, LUNDY
GEDRY, PETER
OWEN, WILLIAM C.
MOORE, E.E.
DUDLEY, WILLIAM
PHILIPS, STEPHEN D.
BACON, JOHN E.
SIMS, JOHN
BRYAN, D. C.
MARTIN, JAMES N.
BRYAN, HENRY
STRATFORD, E.
POK, JOHN
THOMPSON, M.H.
FERGISON, JAMES
DORSEY, ISHAM
ASKEW, JOHN
HARVY, WILEY
GREEN, THOMAS

Page 3
TANIER, JOHN
ROBERTS, WILLIAM
MANGHAM, THOMAS B.
WYNN, GREEN B.
TATE, JOHN B.
SHARP, JOHN M. E.
WILLIAMS, STEPHENS
CIRKLIN, JOHN
HOPKINS, BEDFORD
PARK, E. E.
PERKINS, JORDEN
RUSSEL, JOSEPH C.
HENDERSON, WILLIAM
SHADAWICH, JOHN
GROM, COUNCIL
KINDRIC, P.E.
BENNET, E.
HOOTEN, WILLIAM
SHADAWICK, L.
SHADAWICK, ROBERT
SHADAWICK, JAMES

TURNER, THOMAS E.
SCARBOROUGH, A.
JOHNSON, ISAAC
BROWN, THOMAS
LONG, N.W.
WATSON, GEORGE
ALLEN, JANUS
CHILES, WILLIS
JELKS, WILLIAM
SCARBROUGH, B. J.
MILLS, R.K.

Page 4
THREDGILL, WILLIAM
SCROGGINS, GEORGE
KINDREN, ALX.
WILLIAMS. A. J.
DORMAN, WILLIAM
ALLEN, ROBERT
SMITH, JOHN
LEWIS, P. A.
MORELAND, JEFFERSON
LEWIS, NEWTEN R.
PORTER, URIAH
McDUFFIE, DUNCAN
HADDOCK, NOAH
VANCE, D.
VANCE, JOHN
THORNTON, YANCY
SWIFT, SHELDON
REDWINES, J. L.
TAWBS, M.
CATTENHEAD, JOY
GODWIN, WELLS
GREEN, GEORGE W.
GREEN, WILLIAM
RICH, E. R.
SMITH, HUGH A.
HARISON, EATON
JOHNSON, RILEY
TAFF, GEORGE
HEDGE, JOSHUA
JONES, WILLIAM
JACKSON, JAMES B.
HINSON, W. J.

Page 5
BABB, MERCES
HURST, WILLIAM
PARKER, LEMUEL
WARD, EZEKIEL
CILLERS, WILLIAM
WHITE, WM. JACKSON
WHITE, CYRUS

AKIN, JAMES
TILLERY, REBECCA
TEEL, BRADBERRY
SMITH, ABEL
AARON, PETER
GIBSON, WILEY J.
PERRY, JOHN
HAYS, JAMES
MAUGHAM, ARTHUR
TROTTER, WILLIAM
MYRICK, WILLIAM
HARISON, LEVI
BOLLING, WILLIAM
CILLS, HENRY
SMITSON, BURNEY
BENNETT, JAMES
EDWARDS, LOXLE
ASKEW, JAMES H.
YANCY, ABSALOM
GARREL, RANDOLPH
LEWIS, JAMES
PALMER, M. G.
FARMER, GEORGE P.
PALMER, A.P.

Page 6
RUSE, JOSEPH B.
MEIGS, JAMES
BAR, SAMUEL
HAMIL, H.W.
LEWIS, RU
SHARP, WILLIAM L.
STEPHENS, MARY
WALKER, WILLIAM B.
HOLLAND, DAVID
LEGGET, JOSHUA
NATIONS, CHARLES
ELTAN, ABRAHAM
JONES, ERATIS, W.
HUNT, HENRY
PERRY, BURWELL
LOCKHART, JOEL L.
DAVIS, WILLIAM
McCANE, HUGH
STEWART, CHARLES
PERRY, JOHN M.
DEARING, SIMEON
GARNETT, WILLIAM H.
ROBINSON, WILLIAM C., JR.
ALDRIDGE, JAMES
PITMAN, ALFORD
MATHEWS, LODWICK
COLQUIT, THOMAS

RUSSELL COUNTY

DAWKINS, REUBEN
BAKER, WILLIAM H.
BROOKS, TERRILL
GIPSON, WILLIAM
Page 7
MILLS, JAMES A.
STUART, W.L.
MANGHAM, WILLIAM, G.
COTTON, CYRUS
STUART, ADAM
BURT, WILLIAM W.
WADE, THOMAS
WHITE, THOMAS
SHARP, JOHN H.
HOLKINS, WILLIAM
POAG, HORATIO
WILLSON, JAMES
SMITH, JOHN B.
THOMAS, MICHAEL
ADAIR, JOHN
GIPSON, ROBERT
NEWTON, WILLIAM
FARMER, E.
WALLACE, J.G.
HEATH, BRITTEN
JORDEN, JACOB
SHEARMAN, JOHN
HARTLY, HENRY
GAUK, ISAACK
DELOSEY, N.R.
ROBERTS, DEMPSEY
MILES, W. GREENE
HUTSON, STEVEN
BAMSY, JAMES
RENFROE, ALFRED
Page 8
PEN, JOHN T.
MILTON, LEWIS
HUNT, DANIEL
SHEARMAN, JAMES
ELIOT, STEPHEN W.
WHITE, MOSES D.
ARRBRIT, REDDICK
FIELDER, B.B.
KNOWLES, PARKER C.
WHITE, CYRUS H.
WILLS, JOHN
PITTS, NATHAN
WHITE, PLEASENT
GOLDEN, MITCHEL
SMITH, SAMPSON
KING, HEARIS

WILLIAMS, BENJAMIN
SUDDETH, JAMES
BLACKMAR, BURWELL
BLACKMARR, JOSEPH
LAWRENCE, LABON, B.
ALFORD, JOHN C.
WASHINGTON, GEORGE
BARNES, HYRAM
BARBOR E. L.
PREST, JOHN
WITHERINGTON, WILLIAM
SUETS, JAMES P.
CAPS, JOHN
Page 9
TILMAN, WILLIAM
SMITH, JOHN T.
KING, COLLINS
THREDGILL, RANDOLPH
ALLEN, JOSIAH
REPOE, NATHANIEL
JOHNS, JESSE B.
SPILLARS, SILUS
SCROGGINS, JAMES
MARCUM, JAMES
BAGGET, WILLIAM A.
BRIT, GEY
JOHNSON, ROBERT
RUNELS, WILLIAM
DAVIDSON, FOUNTAIN
HILL, HARDY
MOODY, JOHN
MOODY, HENRY
RICHARDS, JAMES
WITSTER, WILLIAM
SHIPTER, JOHN
SHIPHER, MARTIN
WILCOX, IASAH
THIGPEN, N.S.
BYRD, WILLIAM
ODEN, DIMPSY
RALLS, MOSES
PRESLEY, WILLIAM
Page 10
RIGHT, CATHARINE
McKAY, THOMAS
MCKAY, HUGH
GARNER, JOHN
HARIS, JOSEPH
BUCKNER, LEONARD
BALDWIN, JOHN C.
COOB, JACOB
HOOD, ALX.

PEED, HENRY
BROOG, EPHRAIM
MANYHAM, B.L.
CRAWFORD, R.B.
NAPIR, CALIP
MOONEY, MICHAEL
ADAIR, GEORGE
FARROW, TOMAS
JARRELL, JOSHUA
BOYD, ELIAS
CRAWFORD, CHARLES
PARKS, WILLSON
McCUCKING, MARK
YORK, SINGLETON
GARNER, CHARLES
BUFORD, WILLIAM L.
BUFORD, SARAH D.
CHAMBERS, JAMES
CHAMBERS, EW.
DRENNON, JAMES
BRANNON, B.
HARIS, FRANCIS B.
Page 11
WALKER, GEORGE A.
DAY, DAVID
HOLLAND, JAMES
HOLLAND, SAMUEL
JOHNSON, JOSEPH
LASOR, RICHARD
TURNER, THOMAS
RED, WILLIAM
TURNER, ABRAHAM
LOWE, WILLIAM
CONWAY, WILLIAM, JR.
CONWAY, CAMPBELL
CONWAY, WILLIAM, SR.
GOLDEN, LATEN
GARNER, CHARLES
THOMPSON, A.
SMITH, SPIRA
PARKER, GAIL
RIGHT, ALX.
HURST, BILLINGTON
ARON, PETER
AARAN, WILLIAM
GANT, WILLIAM
GAMILION, HENRY
GRAY, ANN
SAINT, JOHN
JACKSON, W.
FOSTER, LUDWELL
DAVIS, JAMES

RUSSELL COUNTY

NICKSON, JAMES
McCLINDEN, WILLIAM W.
ARON, NEWEL M.
SMITH, RACHEL
MARTIN, FRANCIS
MARTIN, GEORGE W.
OSBURN, DANIEL
SMITH, JOHN
DOTSON, LABON
SPIER, WILLIAM
TODD, ANDREW
MADDEN, HASTING
ARINGTON, DRURY
JONES, SAMUEL
ROBINSON, WILLIAM P.
PRICE, THOMAS
BOLTON, JOHN
ARRINGTON, YONG
ENFINGER, HENRY, JR.
ENFINGER, HENRY, SR.
CRAIG, ANDREW
HINES, JOHN
BURGESS, HYRAM
STOKES, MATHEW
PEIRCE, WALTON
WOOD, WILLIAM
MADDEN, ABRAHAM
MILROY, WILLIAM
HALL, JESSE
LUMPKIN, EDMOND
JOHNSON,, DAVID
Page 13
JOHNSON, JAMES
RATCLIFF, JOSEPH
WADE, JOHN
HICKEY, WILLIAM
HARRELL, ISAAC
COLIER, BENJAMIN F.
ALDRIDGE, MATHIAS
WADE, PETER B.
PERMENTER, JOHN
SHARRED, ELI
STUBBS, WILLIAM
BRADLEY, ELIZABETH
BISHOP, JOHN
REED, STEPHEN
PRIDE, JOHN
DANIEL, JAMES
ALLEN, WILLIAM H.
DRAKE, MARTHA E.
BELEMA, WILLIAM

WILLIAMS, WILLIAM
GELHORN, MILES
MEIGAURT, JAMES
TURNER, THOMAS E.
TOMPKINS, B.
BEASLEY, JACOB
BENNET, THOMAS
CROWEL, JOHN
BENNET, JEREMIAH
LOYD, LEROY
KELLY, JOHN
Page 14
HANCOCK, ISHAM
LEVERETT, W.
GORDY, ABEL
LEWIS, NANCY
ANDREWS, SAMUEL R
CATTENHEAD, WILLIAM
FARES,, ABEL
JONES, SAMUEL
WEST, JOHN
BARD, JOHN
PERRY, THOMAS W.
WELLS, ABNER F.
CUTHBRITT, CONRAD
DURHAIM, ALSEY
WETHERSBY, A.
SLAUGHTER, HENRY P.
JOHNSON, DAVID
DURHAM, FIELDEN
LOVITT, ALX.
ADAMS, WILLIAM R.
DAVIS, THOMAS C.
LEDBETTER, E.
BRYANT, ALEN
EDWARD, NATHANIEL
RAMSEY, ISHAM
RUNNELS, ANDERSON
KENADAY, SAMUEL
KENADAY, JOHN, JR.
KENADAY, JOHN, SR.
CALHOUN, EZEKIEL
Page 15
JOYCE, WILLIAM
BROUGHTON, JOHN
JOHNSON, ENOCH
CAMPBELL, A.M.
LACY, BENJAMIN
STALLINGS, POLLEY
BARKER, WILLIAM
HICKS, THOMAS
FISHBURN, E.B.

HOWARD, RALPH
HEERIN, WARREN
EVANS, M.R.
CHAMBERS, J.
OWENS, E.
OWENS, J. N.
OWENS, WILLIAM H.
CALHOUN, E.
JOHNSON, DAVID
LESTER, L. D.
HURN, WILLIAM
DANCE, MATHEW
PERRY, WILLIAM
ELLIS, THOMAS
SCARBOROUGH, DAVID M.
HENDERSON, RICHARD
BROWN, BENJAMIN G.
WATKINS, REUBEN
YOUNGBLOOD, WILLIAM
YOUNGBLOOD, ALEN
SPENCE, WILLIAM D.
LIPSEY, H.
Page 16
JORDEN, JOHN
GOOLSBY, JOSEPH
CILGORE, BENJAMIN
CULBETH, JOEL
HALSEY, GIDEON
PERSONS, SEXTIUS
HOLIDAY, THOMAS D.
WHATLEY, WILLIAM C.
MCCRACKEN, ROBERT
MITCHELL, JORDEN
HARIS, AMOS
DEBARDELEBBIN, M.D.
BURK, SOLOMON G.
GILBERT, WILEY
HAWKINS, SAMUEL
STURNS, JOHN
WOOD, JOHN
HALL, TOLIVER
REED, ELIAS
JELKS, ROBERT
KINDRED, HENRY
SCROGGINS, GRIFFIN
McTYRE, JOHN
SHADWICK, DANIEL
INGRAM, LEMUEL
MOLTON, TURNER
CALHOUN, JOHN L.
Page 17
BATTLE, ISAAC

-75-

RUSSELL COUNTY

WARD, JOHN J.
WILLIAMS, DANIEL
TAMLIN, JESSE
BASS, STERLING
CARLILE, E.
LIVINGSTON, LEWIS
COHAN, JAMES
MORELAND, TURNER
BASS, HARTWELL
WILLSON, JOEL
JOHNSON, ZACHA
TRAYWICKE, HENRY
ABERCROMBIE, A.
ABERCROMBIE, CHARLES
ROCKMORE, Z.
ABERCROMBIE, JAMES
BLACKMAN, JOEL
WHATLEY, MAVEN
MARTIN, MARTHA
FOWLER, A.M.
COGWILL, MARY
BARNETT, LANDY
SIMPSON, CATHARINE
CLAY, P.G.
LYNCH, THOMAS
COLIER, P.
HALL, SAMPSON W.
RILEY, WILLIAM H.
LEOPARD, JOHN
 Page 18
COLWELL, NATHAN
COLWELL, WILLIAM
SIMMONS, JAMES
WRIGHT, WILLIAM J.
BROWN, SACKVILLE
READ, A.P.
MILES, ELIJAH
McCLANE, HUGH
CRAWFORD, ARON
BRYANT, ALMON
HALL, HENRY
ENNIS, DAVID
NICKS, JOSEPH
SNIDER, HENRY
CHAMBERLIN, JAMES
RITTER, F.
SHIVERS, THOMAS
NILES, JONATHAN
BRIGMAN, THOMAS
SMITH, DAVID
HILL, M.
RUSSEL, H.

RUTHERFORD, H.
LEWIS, ULYSSES
BIRCH, GERARD
HARIS, W.B.
KENT, ELIJAH
DAVIS, M.
STUART, JAMES
COOPER, GILFORD
 Page 19
GARNER, JAMES
SMITH, HOPSON C.
WORSHAM, JOHN G.
GRIFFIN, WILLIAM
PEABODY, JOHN B.
PEABODY, CHARLES A.
MORE, S.
KING, AMOS
REEVES, COLMAN
THOMAS, WILLIAM
NAULS, JONATHAN
HARWELL, DRURY
WHITTLE, PEDY
COLLINS, CHARLES
LOVE, NATHANIEL
LUMMARY, PENERY
PENNOYER, EDWARD
MOORE, JAMES
TIDWELL, C.
SIMPSON, JOHN
WILLIFORD, W.
BECKWITH, L.G.
RIGHIGHT, JAMES
THOMPSON, DANIEL
DILLARD, G. W.
MUNK, SILAS
STROUD, JOHN
SHEPHARD, JOHN L.
JORDEN, IRBY
 Page 20
SILAS, DRED
McKENNON, WILLIAM
KENMORE, WARNER P.
KENMORE, H.J.M.
FRANKLIN, GOODMAN
LUMPKIN, DICKSON
BULLARD, HENRY
BURNSIDE, DAVID
BURNSIDE, MATTHEW
WILLS, JAMES
STORY, JAMES
HICKEY, EZEKIEL
WHITE, WILLIAM

BRAZIEL, WILLIAM
REESE, HUGH
HATHCOP, ISAAC
GLANDS, ELEN
TANNER, WILLIAM
JONES, WILLIAM
ALDRIDGE, CLARK
ELLIS, WILLIAM C.
COLLINS, GEORGE
HOWARD, WILLIAM
HOWARD, SIMEON
BAKER, WILLIAM
BRAZIEL, CORNELIUS
MALONE, DUCAN
PRICE, G.L.
FOSTER, JOHN W.
COMIERE, HENRY
 Page 21
WHITE, WILLIAM
SHORES, JOHN
WILLIAMS, SHEPHERD
LAUSON, J.P.
THORNTON, J.J.
EDWARDS, BENJAMIN
WHITE, JONATHAN
LESICER, SAMUEL
WARLOCK, HYRAM
DALLIS, GEORGE W.
GARRETT, D. N.
CHILDS, WILLIAM
LANEY, WILLIAM
MANGHAM, ARTHUR
WHITE, JOHN
HUNTER, JAMES W.
PEARCE, GEORGE
SHANK, JOHN T.
KNIGHT, BIRD
MEIGS, STEPHEN
TROTTER, JOSEPH
HARRIS, JOHN H.
BROWN, SAMUEL
HORN, ABNER
SHOCKLEY, DELINDA
JOYNER, BENAJAH
MIZELL, WILLIAM
WILLIAMS, WILLIAM
LOCK, WILLIS
ATWELL, BENJAMIN
 Page 22
MARTIN, B. A.
WILEY, CYRUS
JOHNSON, JAMES

RUSSELL COUNTY

BATSON, CAROLINE
PORTOWINE, JAMES
INGERSALL, L.M.
POMROY, CHANCY
HALL, H.
WALKER, G.A.
TOMLIN, JACOB
McCONNELY, WILLIAM B.
BROWN, J.F.
CAY, JESSE
BROWN, R.H.
CURINCE, JOHN W.
CARY, A.
STEPHINS, WILLIAM
GODWIN, JOHN
MARCHEL, ELI
DICKSON, JOHN
WADE, Y.H.
DICKSON, JOSEPH
PRINCE, HENRY
GRAVES, WILLIAM
VINSON, JOHN
McMICHAEL, LEMUEL
DOWD, WILLIAM
LANEY, DANIEL D.
WINDURN, WILLIAM
MOTE, DRURY
LEARS, ANDERSON
Page 23
WILLIAMS, WILLIAM
WELCH, WILLIAM
WILLIAMS, WESLEY
JACKSON, CARIL
WILLIAMS, WHITFIELD
PETTIT, W.B.
PETIS, STEPHEN
DUPREE, JOHN
ANDREWS, GEORGE Q.
MITCHELL, JOHN
BUGG, J.C.
HAMMOCK, W.
PERRY, MICHAEL W.
ELKINS, SAMUEL
SHADAWICK, L.
STRICKLAND, S.
ADAMS, SAMUEL C.
LANIER, ALEN
WALKER, CLEMENT
PARKER, JOHN W.
BYRD, ASA
TAYLOR, HENRY R.

CARLISLE, ROBERT
THOMPSON, AMTHEW
POSTER, H.B.
BRANFORD, JAMES A.
THOMPSON, JOHN
MURRAY, P.I.
POOL, MATTHEW
BRANNON, J.W.
DAVIS, MARTHA
*POOL, SAMUEL
Page 24
LEGAR, JOHN
HOLLOWAY, JAMES W.
CARTER, JOHN B.
FLORENCE, O.
ALLEN, ANDERSON D.
GARDNER, THOMAS H.
BURNS, OS
MURPHY, MICHAEL W.
PRIDDY, JOHN
MITCHEL, WILLIAM
EDWARDS, BENJAMIN
ALEXANDER, WILLIAM
FULLER, WILLIAM
CANADAY, JESSE
BRADLY, FORBS
WHATLEY, TYRE
RITE, ELIZABETH
BENTON, D. C.
BENTON, ABRAHAM
BURDICK, LYSANDER
THORNTON, JONATHAN M.
NUCKLES, NATHANIEL
FORTUNE, JOHN
ASHLY, SIMON
PATTILLO, SIMON
EVANS, THOMAS C.
TURKE, WILLIAM
ARMSTRONG, JAMES F.
HOLLAND, WILLIAM
RICHARDSON, RICHARD
HAWKS, LEWIS
Page 25
FREEMAN, N.
MOORE, JOSHUA
COLQUEHAUR, ALX.
PHILIPS, ICHABOD
MIMS, D.
MIMS, ALEN J.
PAULK, URIAH
MOORE, GEORGE A.

McGEE, THOMAS J.
SAWEARINGANN, JOHN B.
GERBO, JOSEPH
BURR, JAMES
STWART, JOHN D.
WIMBERLY, JOHN
ANGLE, THOMAS
MAN..., DR. W.
CANADAY, ALX.
LUCAS, WILLIAM D.
BOUDRE, MARY H.
GODFREY, JAMES G.
CHAPMAN, ALEN
McKEM, WILLIAM P.
SCHLEY, GEORGE H.
TOWNSEND, LEWIS
ELLIOTT, G.W.
ADORN, JOHN
BENNET, LARRY
BASINGAME, B.F.
DAVIS, GARDNER H.
WOMBLE, EDMOND
LOVE, ANDREW
Page 26
McDUFFIE, JOHN
CHAPMAN, JESSE
SHADAWICK, EDMUND
FORTNER, STEPHEN
PERSONS, JOHN
BRYANT, MARGARET
THOMPSON, WILLIAM T.
CRADDOCK, ROBERT
WICKER, JULIUS A.
HANEY, THOMAS
POOL, M.H.
BLAIR, G. W.
MANGHAM, HENRY
SILLS, WILLIAM
CURETON, JOHN
BISHOP, DAVID
RANFROW, EDWARD
BISHOP, JOHN
PHILIPS, PLEASANT
WATT, A.P.
KING, G. C.
WATT, JAMES M.
SNEAD, WILLIAM H.
MAXWEILL, NATHAN
HASKINS, JOHN M.
ARDIS, JOHN
ARDIS, ISAAC

*military pensioner

RUSSELL COUNTY

Page 27
BARNETT, WILLIAM
BRADLEY, E.
FOLLIER, E. M.
TERRILL, PHILIP
BALLARD, E. M.
PATERSON, C.R.
TAYLOR, T.W.
HIGHTOWER, L.
STWART, GEORGE W. H.
CASK, THOMAS P.
HODGES, MATTHEW
BANKS, J.B.
PACE, THOMAS
BOON, BENJAMIN
IVY, B.
GATING, EDWARD
STWART, SAMUEL
O'REAR, JOSIAH
MILES, E.
SMITH, WILKINS
HURT, JOEL, JR.
HURT, HENRY, SR.
PHILIP, JAMES
HAWS, BENNET
CLOUD, J.T.
HARGROVE, WILLIAM D.
HURT, WILLIAM
LEWIS, PEARCE, L.
PRUET, JAMES
JOHNSON, THOMAS
JOHNSON, OBEDIAH
PRUET, WILLIAM
LEGARE, JEREMIAH
SEWEL, GREEN B.

Page 28
STOKES, WILLIAM
HURT, JOEL, SR.
INGRAM, BURWELL
OWENS, LUCINDA
COVINGTON, DAVID
WILKERSON, SMITH
GREEN, HARTWELL
COWEN, JAMES
MACKEY, L.
RUSSEL, RICHARD R.
KINDRED, JOHN C.
WALKER, DAVID
MORRIS, KINCHEN
COX, B.
McGEE, WILLIAM
BALDWIN, JESSE
WEST, D.

GOINGS, BERRY
INGRAM, B.
HAMMOCK, H.
WRIGHT, E. W.
GRIGG, WILLIAM
RICHARDSON, JOHN A.
WHITE, BENJAMIN
BURK, DAVID
McCLENDON, DENNIS
MASSEY, JOHN
MIMS, ROBERT
FRAZIER, F.
HARDWICK, CHARLES A.

Page 29
RUTHERFORD, A L.
HUDSON, GRANBERRY
TRAYWICK, MOSES
COOK, HENRY
CANIFOX, BENJAMIN
ROBERTS, JOHN A.
WILLIAMS, BENJAMIN
TAYLOR, N.B.
HUTCHISON, T.B.
TARVER, SHILTON
ADEM, DAVID
COUR, JAMES
JACKSON, BURWELL
McDANIEL, J. F.
HENSON, MARTIN T.
HEARN, ELIJAH
HOWARD, JOHN
HOLOMAN, WILLIAM
STURGIS, ELI
HARRY, HYRAM
JOHNSON, STEPHEN
JOHNSON, CHARLES
GULLEDGE, JEREMIAH
HANEY, CALVIN
HANEY, JOHN
WILLIAMS, NANCY
BRIDGES, JAMES
BELL, ISAAC
WHITE, JOHN
SATTERWHITE, STEPHEN

Page 30
IVY, BENJAMIN
KING, MICHAEL
TUCKER, JOSEPH
BURR, LEVI
ODUM, JACOB
WILLIAMS, GEORGE
BROWN, AUGUSTUS

DAVIS, E.L.
MARSHEL, A.
BURK, B.B.
GRIFFIN, RICHARD
HAYS, JOHN G.
ELKIN, DAVID
ELKIN, J.W.
MURPHY, JAMES M.
MACE, EZEKIEL
RADFORD, R.W.
KEMP, HENRY
SLAPPY, F.
MUZLE, JOEL
LEVAN, HARISON
HARDEN, JOHN
TYSON, MOSES
McCRARY, JONATHAN
EDGE, JESSE L.
BLALOCK, HARDEN
PRUET, JOHN W.
THOMAS, A.B.
JETT, MORDICA
ROBINSON, WILLIAM

Page 31
LOWERY, BIRD T.
ROBINSON, WILLIAM
ROBINSON, W.L.C.
MOFFET, HENRY
BOYKIN, STERLING
RUSE, JOEL
GRIMES, HENRY H.
RED, ELIZABETH
MATTOX, WILLIAM
CROWEL, SARAH C.
CROWEL, JOHN, SR.
LANEY, NOAH
SHIVERS, JAMES
WHATLEY, C.
McDOOGALD, DUNCAN
HARDAWAY, ROBERT L.
HUDSON, SARAH
RUTHERFORD, JOHN
VENAWAY, WILLIAM
BENTON, FRANCIS
HENDERSON, DAVID
HUMPHRIES, S. OR L.
PORTER, P.
McCOY, E.
BRYAN, J.L.
LASSITTER, JOHN C.
HARIS, B.D.
KIBBER, WILLIS

RUSSELL COUNTY

LOGAN, WILLIAM
FLOID, D. W.
Page 32
BABBELL, E.C.C.
MONTANE, MARTHA
SEATON, JAMES
WHITE, ZAHA
BUCKHANON, H.B.
ALDRIDGE, REUBIN
ALDRIDGE, NATHAN
NELMS, HYRAM
LERVENT, THOMAS
PITTS, STERLING
HITCHCOCK, ISAH
LONG, WILLIAM
LOWE, JAMES P.
MILFORD, ROBERT
LARSESENT, JAMES, SR.
LARSESENT, JAMES, JR.
LARSESENT, RICHARD
MCKAY, McKINNEY
CORLEE, WILLIAM
CORLEE, FLOID
CHILES, LEAH
NICKERSON, GEORGE W.
MORGAN, REUBEN R.
NANCE, WILLIAMSON
NANCE, WILLIAM L.
WILLIAMS, ELI
ALLEN, WILLIAM
CHAPMAN, ELBERT
HATHCOX, ISAAC
CHALCER, WILLIAM
Page 33
MANGHAM, WILLIAM
MORRELL, WILLIAM
COLE, WILLIAM
TALLEY, JOHN
WALLIS, JOHN
GILES, JOHN
MUZLE, AMIAS
BALLARD, DANIEL
LOCKHART, DAVID
BENNETT, A.B.
WADKINS, EVERETT
MIZLE, LUKE
BULLARD, JAMES M.
ASHLEY, ROBERT
McCINON, JOHN L.
COTTON, LARKIN W.
HAYWARD, MARTIN H.
GRAYHORN, JOHN
DICKSON, JAMES J.

KELLUM, BXTER
LOWE, ROBERT
GRANBERRY, THOMAS
DUNCAN, BRYANT
GRIFFIN, JAMES
PRINGLE, JAMES
BRITT, SOLOMAN
BOYD, DAVID C.
SHARP, PETER
HORTON, JOHN F.
HACKLY, JOHN A.
Page 34
COX, A.B.
MORGAN, EDWARD
CORMACK, FURNEY
CORMACK, FEDRICK
CORLEE, M.
WITHAM, JOSEPH
THORNTON, RUBIN
SPENCER, EDWARD
THOMAS, WILLIAM T.
CRAFT, PLASENT
LOCKWELL, WILLIAM
WHITE, THOMAS A.
LAWRENCE, S.
HAYS, JAMES
EDWARDS, AMBROS
WATSON, THOMAS
GREEN, HENRY
GUY, TOMAS
HICKEY, GORDEN
BROWN, JOHN
NIGHT, EPHRAIM
CARTER, R.
MANGHAM, JAMES G.
THOMAS, JACOB
SCALES, WILLIAM
DOSS, GREEN
CLARK, JAMES
MACKEY, WILEY
WHATLEY, JOHN
WHATLEY, WILLIAM
Page 35
FLAKE, WILLIAM G.
DUKE, WILLIAM
FAULK, RICHARD
EDWARD, WILLIAM
CHISLOM, PHILIP
EVANS, LAVINA
PITMAN, ALFORD
BROOKS, POSEY B.
TOLES, SWIFT
ROPER, ELDRED

RADEL, CHARLES
MATHEWS, MATHEW
BAGBY, A.S.
HUFF, DANIEL
FOSTER, JOHN
WOLENS, STEPHEN
SLAPPY, GEORGE W.
GILBERT, JORDEN
INGRAM, ELIJAH
DICKSON, JOHN K.
COR, DAVID
SIMMONS, JOHN M.
INGRAM, MOODY
CARMICHAEL, JOHN
ALLEN, CORLEE
THOMPSON, HENRY B.
BERRY, WILLIAM
OLIVER, BERRIAN
THOMAS, JOSEPH
HALL, WILLIAM
HARRIS, HENRY L.
Page 36
BOOTH. F.
BLAKE, LUTHER
DAWSON, HENRY
CALHOUN, HERN
KENNEYMORE, MICHAEL

TALLADEGA COUNTY

Page 250

THOMPSON, ELIZA A.
HAYS, JAMES
HUEY, JAMES G.L.
CHANDLER, MORDICAI
DERITY, MILTON
LAWLER, LEON R.
ROWE, C.H.
EDWARDS, JOHN S.
JOHNSTON, PATRICK
McGUIRE, M.S.
ABERCROMBIE, JAMES
LEWIS, LEWIS C.
GILLILAND, MARY
CAVER, THOMAS
KENNERLY, SHELTON
WALKER, DAVID
WARE, BENNETT
BRYANT, JOHN
REYNOLDS, JOHN
FRIERE, MARTHA
ALBRIGHT, JOHN
SCISSON, THOMAS
ALBRIGHT, MICHAEL
DULANEY, DANIEL
KENDRICK, JOHN
DOUGLASS, ROBERT
HANKINS, THOMAS J.
TURNER, WILLIAM
DUNCAN, MARCUS M.

Page 251

POE, WINSHIP S.
TOMPKINS, J.F.
WAUGH, DAVID T.
SMITH, A.L.
HINKLE, JOHN
DICKEY, GEORGE
BERRY, JOHN D.
MOORE, THOMAS
WHITE, JOHN
LYLES, MICAJAH
WILSON, ROBERT C.
SIMS, A.G.
HANDCOCK, JAMES
BRADFORD, J.L.
YARBOROUGH, JOHN
DURHAJOU, LEWIS
MURRAY, TITUS
CALDWELL, W.H.
ROZELL, JAMES
SIMS, HENRY
GAREY, JAMES

FROST, J.R.
CARTER, B.R.
CORE, ALEXANDER
BEST, WILLIAM B.
RICHARD, CHRISTIAN
HARRELL, BEATTIE
KILLOUGH, JAMES

Page 252

STARRIS, ELIJAH
KENNEDY, W.M.
RHINEHART, MARTIN
McLELAND, W.B.
BLACKWELL, DAVID
GOGGINS, THOMAS
TRUP, THOMAS
MILLER, WILLIAM
CARTER, JOHN W.
CARTER, MATHEW
BUREN, WARREN
COTTEN. A. J.
LAWRENCE, NOAH
LOGAN, AVILLA
McREYNOLDS, JOSEPH
SATCHER, ELLIS
DOBBS, JOEL W.
COPELAND, GEORGE W
HAMMOND, SAMUEL E.
GRAY, WILLIAM
MAYFIELD, AUSTIN
McWILLIAMS, WATSON
SISSON, DAWSON
SISSON, WILLIAM
MITCHELL, EZERIAH

Page 253

HAMMOND, SARAH ANN
SMITH, CHARLES
MASER, JAMES
HARPER, JOHN
TAYLOR, DICY
SARTIN, JOHN
BARNES, CARREWAY
AUTERY, JAMES
JEATER, DANIEL R.
CROW, AUSTIN
SEESON, JOHN
BREWER, THOMAS J.
RILEY, ALLEN W.
RICHIE, DANIEL
McLELLAND, THOMAS J.
MARTIN, WILLIAM
TURNER, JOHN

PLOUGHMAN, GEORGE P.
SHELLEY, WILLIAM P.
ALLEN, SHEROD
MILLER, CHARLES
COMPTEN, JOHN V.
LEFTWICH, JOHN S.
JOHNSTON, GARRETT
GRIFFEN, DAVID A.
JAMISON, ROBERT
PEARSON, P. EDWARD
SMITH, DANIEL
MORGAN, ANTHONY
BOAZ, ZEDKIJAH

Page 254

DODSON, ELIJAH
YOUNG, SAMUEL K.
MARTIN, SOLOMON
BYNUM, ELIJAH
HARMON, JOHN
PINSTON, MARY
JONES, SEABORN
HILL, GEORGE
JACOBS, ISAAC
MOORE, WILLIAM H., JR
FANT, ABRAM E.
MEDLOCK, JOHN
DOUGLASS, SIMEON
RICE, H.W.W.
HALCOM, THOMAS M.
TRUP, JAMES
McCAIN, WILLIAM
HENDERSON, SAMUEL
BISHOP, LEWIS
BROWN, HENRY L.
TERRY, JOSIAH
WILLIAMS, JORDON
McELHENY, WILLIAM H.
HEACOCK, JOSEPH B.
FUNDERBURGH, JOHN M.
EDWARDS, Z.A.
FORMAN, JESSE
CHILTON, THOMAS
CHILTON, WILLIAM P.
RICE, SAMUEL F.

Page 255

McLURE, WILLIAM P.
ROBESON, MARK
HALL, JOHN W.
MADDON, ABRAHAM
RANDALL, DUDLEY
RANDALL, SAMUEL

TALLADEGA COUNTY

HOWELL, REESE
MACKLIN, WILLIAM J.
BAILY, WYATT
ROWE, ASA
KAREKINS, EDWARD
MADDEN, ZERINE
THOMPSON, SABRE
HALL, JOSEPH
JACK, JANE
BAGLEY, DARIUS
DONEY, JAMES
KIRKLEY, ISAAC
ROBERTS, WILLIAM T.
MONTGOMERY, JAMES
HARDIN, JESSE
FORMAN, JOHN W.
DODSON, RILEY
HENRY, WILEY
DAVIS, PEARSON
DILL, ANDERSON
DAVIS, WILLIAM
LOWE, CEREY
BURNS, JAMES S.
Page 256
KIETH, THOMAS
KIETH, JOSEPH
DRINKARD, FRANCIS M.
NORTHCUT, ROBERT
BOYD, JAMES
AUTERY, ADAM
SCRIMMONS, VINCENT
TOMPKINS, THOMAS
LAWSON, JAMES
KIMBRELL, DAVID
ENGLISH, JOHN
NORTHCUT, WILLIAM
BRANDON, JOHN
BRYANT, JESSEE
HARRIS, BENJAMIN
BORUM, JOHN
LAWSON, JOHN
SMITH, DAVID
HARE, PETER
BLACK, MARCELLUS
MAULDING, SAMUEL
HOUSTON, LREOY
STRACENER, HENRY
HOUSTON, JOHN G.
BLACK, ROBERT
FERGUSON, ISAAC
BRYANT, FRANCIS
SHEASTLER, JOSEPH

WILLS, JOHN W.
TAYLOR, ALLEN J.
Page 257
HUNTER, DAVID
PERKINS, WILEY
LEE, FRANCIS
BANE, ANDREW C.
CHERRALL, STEPHEN
RUNYAN, ISAAC
MASSEY, DAVID
LOWRY, WILLIAM
JETT, JAMES
WESSON, WILLIAM N.
GOULDING, WILLIAM
MILENDER, JESSEE
WELCH, OLIVER
WELCH, NATHANIEL
CHAPEL, THOMAS
WARD, HENRY
McELROY, MARTIN
BUTT, F.A.
ANDERSON, MARTHA
NORRIS, WILLIAM B.
PRICE, THOMAS
CLACK, N.B.
RAY, PLEASANT
LOWRIE, JOHN R.
RHINEHART, ABRAHAM
KELLEY, GEORGE
RUNYAN, ATELEY
SMITH, BENNETT
CAMPBELL, THOMAS
GILL, JAMES N.
Page 258
HARRISON, RICHARD J.
TOWNSEND, JOHN H.
LANSDALE, JOSEPH
DIXON, ELIZABETH
LAROE, JOHN
BENTLY, CORIAH
KEATERS, WILLIAM
GIVINS, JAMES A.
GRIFFITH, WILLIAM
THOMPSON, WILLIAM
McDOW, ARTHUR
HAYS, MADISON P.
FOWLER, JAMES A.
WADDELL, WILIAM A.
HENSSEY, ALLEN
HAYS, JOHN
QILSON, WILLIS
BOMAN, MARY

SEESON, LEMUEL
PATTERSON, REUBIN
PATTERSON, JOHN
LITTLEJOHN, WILLIAM
MORRIS, WILLIAM
HUBBART, JOHN
GALTEN, GARRETT
CONNOR, HESTOR
LEARLEY, WILLIAM
LEE, JOHN L.
LEE, MATHUS
HALE, WILLIAM
Page 259
RHODES, POLLARD
HENDRICKS, WILLIAM
SAWYERS, WILLIAM E.
MUNROE, JACOB F.
CUMMINS, JAMES M.
GADDY, MARTIN P.
LITTLEJOHN, JOHN
HARPER, WILLIAM D.
KILLOUGH, DAVID
WATKINS, FRANCIS
ESTILL, ISAAC
SMOOT, BENJAMIN A.
SCOTT, WILLIAM
RAGLAND, GEORGE L.
GRAY, ROBERT
BURCHFIELD, THOMAS J.
HOBBS, LEWIS
EDWARDS, WILLIAM
SEAY, WOODSON
CARTT, THOMAS A.
DUNN, SOLOMON W.
ALBERSON, ZECHARIAH
KUPS, GEORGE
DOYL, ANDREW J.
BARCLAY, HUGH G.
BARCLAY, A.R.
STENNETT, RUFUS
PERESTON, JOSIAH B.
CHANEY, HEZEKIAH
GRAHAM, MARGARET
Page 260
HENDERSON, JOHN F.
LAWSON, ROBERT
SHORTRIDGE, ELI
SHELLEY, JACOB D.
ALLEN, JOHN J.
FAGAN, THOMAS
REPPETOE, A.H.
McMEANS, EDWARD

TALLADEGA COUNTY

McLERKIN, SAMUEL
CURRY, WILLIAM
GOULDING, JOHN N.
FINN, DANIEL W.
WADSWORTH, JOHN
WADSWORTH, THOMAS
MOORE, WILLIAM
GOULDING, WILLIAM
DWYER, JOHN
ENGLISH, ALEXANDER
CONNOR, JOHN
SMITH, LUCY
BOWIE, ALEXANDER
BENNETT, MICAJAH
McLEOD, GEORGE
SAWYERS, DRURY
SMITH, THOMAS
SMITH, STEPHEN
BRITT, JOSEPH J.
BAIRD, ANDREW
DERION, AGNES
ENGLISH, ALEXANDER

Page 261

McKEY, JOHN
McGOWYER, WILLIAM
RODGERS, JOHN H.
RODGERS, LEVI
WEST, WALTER
WARDLAW, ABSOLUM
SEWELL, BALDWIN H.
McALESTER, A.W.
COBEY, JAMES M.
SNAPE, NATHANIEL
SPARKS, STEPHEN
MILLER, GEORGE
RUBEL, PETER
WEATHERS, ALLEN J.
WATSON, JAMES S.
WILLIAMSON, GEORGE
HOGAN, WILLIAM
BARRETT, M.H.
MITCHELL, FRANCIS
McCONNELL, F.T.
GIVINS, EDWARD A.
WALDRON, WILLIAM R.
SIMMONS, P.D.
THOMPSON, GEORGE W.
FAGAN, A T.
SHOUTTS, JOHN W.
GAINS, JOHN

DEFRUE, HIRAM A.
LAWSON, JAMES
EAST, RICHARD W.

Page 262

HUGHS, WILLIAM
HUGHS, MOSES
BRIGHT, CHARLES P.
MOORE, JOHN
PILES, LEWIS
MIRES, GEORGE
VICE, MERRADY
COCHRAN, ANDREW
BOGG, HENRY
COCHRAN, ROBERT H.
COCHRAN, JAMES
COCHRAN, EDWARD
THOMAS, JOHN F.
BOGS, SAMUEL O.
HANEY, ROBERT
SMITH, EDMUND
BROCK, HANNAH
JACK, SAMUEL A.
ARCHER, PHILLIP
RAVAN, WILLIAM
CUNNINGHAM, MAHALA
WILSON, HUGH M.
MADDISON, WILEY W.
ANDERSON, TOMAS M.
GERIT, DANIEL
WATSON, WILLIAM B.
WATSON, DEMPSEE
BAGLEY, NATHAN
FUNDERBURGH, PETER
COOPER, ADAM

Page 263

CARPENTER, WILLIAM S.
HILL, JOSIAH H.
CATHEY, JOHN C.
SEAY, JOHN L.
MATSON, SARAH
MAY, NANCY
BROWN, JOHN A.
JONES, McMIN
DYE, JAMES
SHOCKLEY, LEVI
McELDRY, THOMAS
DODSON, JOEL
WEATHERLY, JOHN P.
BASS, JOHN
BASS, WILLIS

NORWOOD, RICHARD S.
BASS, JORDON
WALKER, JAMES A.
BUSEY, JARAMIAH
MAY, CLAIBORN, B.
LORENZ, WALTER
WOODWARD, JOHN S.
TARRANTT, RICHARD
BALL, SPENCER
ARTHUR, CHARLES D.
BALL, A.B.
FAIRES, TEMPERANCE
JENKINS, S.G.
KENDRICKE, KANCE
BANISTER, EDWARD W.

Page 264

McNIELL, ARCHIBALD
CARMICHAEL, DANIEL
COLEMAN LEVI D.
ROBESON, MORDICA
SMITH, DANIEL
WILSON, ANDREW
HARWEL, SAMUEL S.
MARTIN, SAMUEL
MARTIN, EPHRAIM
BROWN, JOHN B.
CAMPBELL, JOHN A.
MORRIS, JACK
MUNROE, DUNCAN
CAMPBELL, WILLIAM A.
LEGALE, LEWIS
HESTER, ABRAHAM
HARTWELL, NATHANIEL
BULL, MARTIN
BULL, WILLIAM P.
HARRIS, JAMES S.
WILDER, EZEKIEL
EVANS, JOSHUA
EVANS, SEABORN
SOCK, WILLIAM B.
FARIT, JOSEPH C.
MATSON, JESSEE
FANT, ELIJA
BARRETT, JOSEPH
JOHNSTON, SAMUEL

Page 265

McRIGHT, ROBERT
PRITCHETT, ELI
CAMPBELL, JOHN M.
PRITCHETT, LEWIS

-82-

TALLADEGA COUNTY

ALLEN, JOHN
WILSON, ABASIYAN
MOORE, SOVERIGN
SIMMONS, MOSES W.
LAMBERT, THOMAS
BRADDY, GIDDEON
BETHUNE, CATHARINE
PATTERSON, GEORGE M.
MORRISON, DANIEL
GRAHAM, MARGARET
SIMMONS, JAMES B.
KEAHEY, ISABELLA
BROWN, WILLIAM C.
PATTERSON, JANE
BROWN, DUNCAN
TOMLIN, SHEROD
EVANS, DANIEL
BULLARD, ALLEN
KIRKLAND, JAMES
COOPER, DANIEL
HARWELL, ABSOLEM
ROBESON, THOMAS J.
HARWELL, HENRY
LANE, DANIEL M.
EVANS, JOSHUA
GRAY, THOMAS
Page 266
LESLEY, THEODORE J.
WRIGHT, JACOB
BREWER, JOSEPH
BITTLE, JACOB
JORDON, JOSIAH
SPREWELL, NIMROD
EDGE, NATHAN
VINES, SEABORN
BITTLE, GEORGE
BRADFORD, THOMAS M.
KILGORE, SOLOMAN
RYAN, WILLIAM G.
CAMPBELL, WILLIAM H.
ISBEL, JAMES
KNORS, JAMES C.
COWSAR, ELI E.
STONE, GEORGE W.
RESPESS, RANSOM
McAFEE, GREEN S.
MILLICAN, JESSEE
WYNATT, RUFUS M.
ELSTORE, ALLEN
BLYTHE, WILLIAM
BEST, JOSHUA
ROBISON, JAMES

SAWARIT, LEONARD
HARDIE, JOHN
McLEOD, DANIEL
McCULLOUGH, DAVID
MILLER, BENJAMIN
Page 267
COKER, JAMES
JONES, SEABORN
LACKEY, EDY
JONES, WESLEY
HARRIS, NATHANIEL
FANE, JESSE
COKER, JOSEPH
CARPENTER, JAMES
HENDRICK, JOHN
McRIGHT, JAMES
CAMP, WILLIAM M.
MANNING, LEWIS
ADAMS, GABRIEL
ADAMS, JOSHUA
ADAMS, JAMES
CARTER, STEPHEN
ADAMS, ELIAS
MUSSELWHITE, WILLIAM
BALL, REUBEN
STRICKLAND, T.C.
HARIES?, WILLIAM
BALL, BENJAMIN
BROOKS, THOMAS
PERREN, WILLIAM
LAMBERT, JOHN
SANFORD, ROBESON
HAGGARD, DRURY
MASHBURN, MARSHALL
CULLINS, JOHN
OWENS, JUDGE
Page 268
HOUSTON, SAMUEL
HASTY, WILLIAM
FLOYD, ALSA W.
HOUSTON, MARGARET
WHITTENBURGH, ANDREW
CARPENTER, REUBEN
MORROW, MALINDA
CARPENTER, CHARLES K.
FRANCIS, JOHN
CLICK, HENRY
McMEANS, JOHN
LEDBETTER, JOHN
CAMERON, THOMAS
MILLER, JOSEPH
CALDWELL, CHARLES
*CALDWELL, DAVID

TAYLOR, JOHN K.
WEAVER, WILLIAM A.
LEE, BURRELL
WATKINS, GEORGE J.
PORTER, JAMES B.
DUKERSON, SHADERICK
BAIRD, THOMAS
POWELL, LEWIS
HARWELL, FRIEF
ELEOTH, THOMAS
LEE, MARTHA
MASHBURN, DANIEL
TRAMMELL, ASA
INZER, JAMES
COCHRAN, WILLIAM
Page 269
WYATT, WILLIAM H.
ELLIOTT, WILLIS
CARTER, CHARLES
HALL, WILLIAM
FRANKLIN, WILLIS
RUTLEDGE, HENRY A.
ALISON, DANIEL
HALL, JAMES
HARN, JAMES
SIMS, WADE H.
LOVETT, WILLIAM D.
MOORE, S. J.
SCALES, NICHOLAS
ELROD, GEORGE
GUTHRIE, JAMES S.
CUNNINGHAM, SAMUEL
LUNDIE, WILLIAM Y.
HENDERSON, JOHN J.
GOVER, SAMUEL
RANDELL, TABITHA
MOORE, WILLIAM H.
BEST, THOMAS L.
GRAHAM, JAMES
WATSON, JAMES B.
GARRAWAY, HOWELL
DAWS, ISAAC H.
RENTFROW, JOHN
RIDEOUT, GORDON
SEALES, THOMAS H.P.
RIDEOUT, WILLIAM
Page 270
WILLIAMSON, THOMAS
PARK, MARGARET
LINSEY, DAVID
FARIT, DAVID H.
PORTER, MITCHELL

*military pensioner

TALLADEGA COUNTY

BORUM, EDMUND
RYAN, MARTIN K.
EARLY, WILLIAM
RANDELL, JOHN J.
JAMES, BENJAMIN
GASKELL, EXOM
TALIFERIO, HARDIN
DOUGLASS, ALEXANDER
ARMBUSTER, MICHEAL
McGUIRE, WILLIAM H.
McELHENNEY, STEPHEN H.
CATER, SILAS
McELHENNY, ROBERT W.
ADAMS, ISAAC
ADAMS, JAMES
GOODWIN, THOMAS
BASS, LAWRENCE
CAMP, JOSEPH
TERRY, JOHN C.
LEWIS, WILLIAM L.
SHAFFER, WILLIAM
SHAFFER, SIMEON
PAYNE, WILLIAM
LEWIS, ALEXANDER
FRENCH, AARON
   Page 271
CARTER, HENRY
DYE, LEWIS G.
ABERCROMBIE, J. H.
SUMNER, WILLIAM
McGEEHEE, CHILES
ATKINSON, STEPHEN
PERIN, GREENVILLE W.
THOMPSON, JAMES S.
PORTER, ALEXANDER
CHANDLER, JAMES
TATE, SOLOMON
COTTON, C.W.
COX, J. S.
GOVER, SAMUEL
HESTERLEY, J. O.
ELLIOTT, D. B.
WILSON, G. W.
LEDBETTER, F.
HOUSTON, J.T.
MOSS, ANDERSON
GRANTHAM, RICHARD
BARBER, TARPLEY
LIKENS, THOMAS M.
BOTTON, CHARLES
LONG, JOHN
LONG, JAMES

BUSH, HARRISON
THOMPSON, WILLIAM
DRIVER, GILES
McKENZIE, HENRY
   Page 272
LAWLER, LOVE W.
JENKINS, WILLIAM
DEAN, JANET
REYNOLDS, WALKER
WILSON, MARTHA
WILSON, CUNNINGHAM
BELL, MARION B.
WILSON, DANIEL
GOODGAME, JOHN
FLEMING, EASTER
DERICK, THOMAS
CARLETON, THOMAS
BAKER, WILLIAM
WALLIS, JOHN
GIBSON, ALLEN
JAMIESON, JOHN
KINGAID, JESSE
McCARTEY, JAMES
MALONE, JOHN
BULGER, JOHN
LAMB, JAMES
HERD, GEORGE
DULANEY, ELIZA
BURTON, LEWIS
THRIFT, WILLIAM
BLEDSOE, BENJAMIN
MALONE, THOMPSON
HOLLIS, AUSTIN
LINDSAY, JAMES S.
COBB, HENRY
   Page 273
FOSTER, THOMAS
ODEN, JOSHUA
SMITH, EVAULL
MYER, JAMES
SAWYER, JAMES
COLFER, JAMES
TAYLOR, JOHN
MAHON, JOHN
SINES, MARY
WALLIS, CHANEY
HENDERSON, JOHN
WATTS, PRESLEY
McMILLEN, DANIEL
JOHNSTON, WILLIAM
McMANN, JOHN
JONES, MOSES B.

HOLLEY, THOMAS
GOODGAME, FLOYD C.
COTTINGHAM, CHARLES
RAMSEY, ALISON
PARKER, JESSE
REESE, JAMES G.
GRAHAM, WILLIAM
GASKELL, EVAN
HAMMONS, JOHN J.
HENDERSON, DANIEL
HALLMARK, JAMES
RAGLAND, EVAN
OVERMAN, WILLIAM
DEEL, GEORGE W.
HERRELL, SARAH
   Page 274
WATKINS, JOHN
WATKINS, SAMUEL
CRUISE, CHARLES
McADAMS, THOMAS
RANDELL, SETH
BROWN, EDWARD
COLEMAN, HENRY W.
WARD, THOMAS
SCOTT, JOHN
ASHLEY, JOHN
CRAWFORD, B.H.
RHINEHART, ADAM
MORRIS, LUCIAN
RHEA, NANCY
FULLER, RYAN
MACHERN, WILLIAM
MITCHELL, NEROWAY
MALONE, ULDY
HENDSON, WILLIAM H.
McGEHEE, WILLIAM
CHAPMAN, BRITAIN W.
KELLEY, SARAH
McGUIRE, SARAH
FRANKLIN, PRESTON
KING, PLEASANT
CAVENDER, ELEANOR
LANE, WILLIAM M.
DAVIS, SEBE
LAJURIE, MARY ANN
DAVIS, ELIAS
   Page 275
RISER, GEORGE
LAGRONE, JOHN
MALORY, MALINDA
MALORY, NATHANIEL
KELLY, WILLIAM

TALLADEGA COUNTY

COLEMAN, ISHAM J.
OWENS, BERD S.
OWENS, THOMAS
ECHOLS, GEORGE C.
MARING, JAMES W.
HILL, PHARO
ASKEW, WILLIAM
HUDSON, ISAAC
GWINN, JESSE
COOPER, CADER
COOPER, JOHN C.
HAFAIR, JOHN
RUSSEL, WILLIAM
GRUBBS, TOLIVER H.
WALLIS, CHARNER
RUSSELL, JAMES C.
JONES, SOPHIA
JONES, JOEL
SNELL, DAVID
BALFOUR, JOHN O.
RHODEN, JOHN
DISCON, WILLIAM
TURNER, HENRY B.
BALLERD, JAMES
HARRISON, IRA

Page 176

DEES, SANIEL
BARRETT, MILES
DEES, BYANT
DEES, JOHN
DEES, CHARLES
HYATT, GEORGE
HILL, JOHN
NEAL, REUBEN
HENDERSON, PARDY
LINDSEY, JOHN
MAXWELL, POLLY
LEE, MOSES A.
RHODEN, ISAAC
PATE, STEPHEN
PATE, DAVID R.
PENDERGRASS, SILAS.
*PENDERGRASS, SPENCER
HILL, ALEXANDER
SPARKMAN, WILLIAM
HENDERSON, JAMES W.
BANCORSE, ASA
STOVER, LORENZO D.
McDONALD, JOHN
GOODGAME, JOHN
DRENNON, SIDNEY
DRENNON, JAMES
BUTTS, GEORGE W.

SMITH, JOHN G.
WOODWARD, HENRY G.
McCLUNG, WILLIAM

Page 277

PERRY, EDWIN, SR.
COUNCIL, JDM.
FERGUSON, JAMES
MILLER, EZEKIEL
KEENER, BENJAMIN
McCLUNG, HUGH
HARRISON, RICHARD
FERGUSON, LARKIN
MALLORY, JAMES
LINDSEY, DAVID
HALLMARK, ALFRED
HALL, LEANDER M.
DERHAYCE, LARKIN
ADAIR, JAMES
MOORE, AARON W.
HARRISON, EDWARD
FONNAN, JAMES J.
HAGLER, WILLIAM
STURRIT, JOHN W.
FUNDERBURGH, HENRY M.
FUNDERBURGH, WILLIAM B.
MOSLEY JOHN
CASTLETON, THOMAS S.
LESTER, THOMAS J.
HENDERSON, WILLIAM
JAMES, BENJAMIN
RAYFIELD, THOMAS
RAYFIELD, MOULTON
RAYFIELD, DANIEL
RAYFIELD, JOHN

Page 278

TAYLOR, JESSE
TAYLOR, ROBERT
COLEMAN, HENRY
LETCHER, FRANCES
ODEN, LEWIS
VINYART, BARRY
ODEN, ALEXANDER
EDWARDS, MILLER
FORSHEL, WESLEY
FORSHEL, DAVID
LAWLER, ABNER
HILL, HENRY
GOODWIN, YOUNG
GOODMAN, THOMAS
McGUFFEN, THOMAS
HILL, JOHN W.
HILL, JAMES H.
PERRY, JOHN

PERRY, CHARLES W.
PERRY, EDWARD
GORIN, MARION
MARTIN, DAVID
WATSON, ALEXANDER
LONG, JOSEPH W.
CASEY, JAMES
CASEY, EARTHEX
HENRY, EDWARD
SHROPSHIRE, GREEN
McCULLOUGH, BRYANT
GENTRY, MARTIN P.

Page 279

ASCUTT, BENJAMIN
JONES, JOHN A. C.
SHELLEY, CHARLES P.
BASKINS, JAMES C.
RADFORD, OBADIAH
MITCHELL, JAMES B.
SMITH, JOHN S.
ROBISON, HELEMS
CANTELE, JOHN
WELCH, DAVID
WASHINGTON, JOHN S.
BROWN, JOSHUA
McGRADY, ROBERT
CASEY, WILLIAM A.
DODD, ROBERT
McCOY, WILLIAM
BARKINS, HENRY W.
BARKINS, THOMAS
CRAWFORD, WILLIAM H.
THOMPSON, ALLEN B.
ROBISON, THOMAS
ROBISON, WASHINGTON
VARDIMAN, BENNETT
McDUFFIE, JOHN
REAVIS, WILLIAM A.
THOMPSON, MARGARET
THOMPSON, JAMES
VARDIMAN, PORTER R.
ATKINS, JASPER
WOOD, MATHIES

Page 280

WATTERS, HARDIN
VARNELL, BENTON
BOWLS, TURNER
MILLER, URIAH
MILLER, WILLIAM
McCLELAND, WILLIAM
WALKER, PETER J.
RINEHART, GEORGE
WARD, ELIZABETH

*military pensioner

TALLADEGA COUNTY
Page 282

DARLEY, HUGH L.
HILL, JOHN
HILL, JAMES
CROWSON, JOSHUA W.
EVANS, JABEZ
BRASHER, JOHN A.
McKEE, WILLIAM
CLOWERS, JOHNATHAN
BROCK, WILLIAM
McPHERSON, WILLIAM
COOPER, JAMES
VARNELL, JESSE
WATTERS, COLLINS
GADDY, HIRAM
WATTERS, GEORGE
GRIFFIN, SOLOMON
JOHNSTON, SOLOMON
INNMAN, HENRY
HILL, JOHN, COL.
DRENNON, SHADRICK D.
WOOD, JOHN
Page 281
POWEL, CADER
FAVOR, WILLIS A.
JIMERSON, JAMES M.
LEWIS, WILEY
McCALES, DAVID
STEADMAN, ELISHA B.
SPRINGER, JOB
KILLOUGH, RICHMOND
KILLOUGH, ALLEN
KILLOUGH, ANN
HARRISON, EZUEL S.
ADAIR, JAMES M.
HEASLIP, ROBERT H.
CASEY, DAVID
WOOD, WILLIS
WATTERS, JOHN
WATTERS, WILLIAM
VARNELL, JESSE
VARNELL, JOSEPH
SOUTH, MADISON
LAMBERT, ELISHA
HEASLIP, BENJAMIN H.
ARNOLD, SETH M.N.
HOSEY JESSE
HOSEY, JAMES
HEASLIP, WILLIAM M.
RODGERS, ROBERT R.
MASON, JOHN
THOMPSON, ALFRED

EDWARDS, BENNETT
SMITH, JOEL
WATSON, SAMUEL
PEARSON, JONATHAN
RODGERS, ROBERT
HAMMETT, JAMES
TAYLOR, HENRY
NOTT, SIMON
HILL, JOHN, CAPT.
BRITTEN, BURREL
LIGHTSEY, JOHN
SEAY, JACOB B.
MOODY THEOPHILUS
JOHNSTON, JOHN
CAMERON, BENJAMIN D.
FARIS, THOMAS J.
LEDFORD, JASON
JAMES, JOHN P.
KILLOUGH, ELIZABETH
JAMES, ROWLAND J.
RUMEL, JOHN S.
DEAROSSON, GEORGE
RITCHIE, MARY
HOBBS, CHARLES
PRICE, GEORGE W.
ARNOLD, TANDY M
HOLLEY, BENJAMIN F.
BARR, MOSES D.
JORDAN, CHARLES
HAYNES, ABRAHAM
Page 283
MOORE, MOSES
MOORE, ELIZABETH
COTTEN, PETER, JR
COTTEN, JOHN
HUTTEN, OVERTUN
SOLNE, JOHN
COTTEN, WILLIAM P.
BRADEN, JOHN
GRAVIS, GEORGE
LEE, SAMUEL M.
STEPHENS, ENOCH
WATTS, GEORGE W.
COTTEN, PETER, SR.
MITCHELL, SETH
BRADY, JOSEPH A.
RIDDLE, PRESLEY
HEARN, MOSES
YARBROUGH, FRANKLIN
HEARN, DAVID M.
WATTS, JACOB

CALDWELL, J.W.
MURPHY, JOHN
McLURAIL, JOHN
YARBOROUGH, RUBEN
SHORT, JOHN
SANDLIN, JAMES
ARMSTRONG, JAMES
HAMMONTREE, HUGH
CASADEY, JAMES
BRYANT, THOMAS
Page 284
TRIPLET, HEDGEMAN
TRESLE, JAMES
BARNES, JAMES M.
JORDAN, JAMES D.
WATLEY, TAYLOR
WARE, JIMERSON
RIDDLE, HENRY
RIDDLE, WILLIAM
ROBERTSON, DANIEL
McGOWAN, MARGARET
ATKINSON, JAMES
FOREMAN, JESSE W.
ROZELL, ENOCH R.
MERRELL, JESSE
LAWLER, ROBERT M.
LONG, JEREMIAH
HANEY, MARY
HOUSTON, JAMES
DEEL, JOHN
LONG, WILLIAM B.
LONG, MARY
SIMMONS, JOHN
STOCKS, WILLIAM
BOARING, ROBERT
BOARING, L.P.
STOCKS, ISAAC F.
SIMMONS, HOLMAN F.
FORMAN, JAMES
COOK, WILLIAM D.
MARTEN, GREEN L.
Page 285
McCONTHEY, JOSEPH
LEVI, THEODORE
SMITH, WILLIAM
COX, JOHN
GILLAS, DANIEL
McCREA, MALCOM
CHANNEL, JOHN
RUSSELL, DEMPSEY
SAXTON, BENJAMIN

TALLADEGA COUNTY

GAMBLE, WILLIAM
BURK, JESSE
HARLAND, HENRY
HARLAND, ELIAS
COCHRAN, WILLIAM
CUNNINGHAM, MATHEW
BURK, JAMES
DILLARD, JABEZ
CREG, JAMES L.
CLONCH, JOHN
WEATHERFORD, BARZILLA
STREET, HEZEKIAH
NELSON, ISHAM
FORMAN, JESSE
BEARD, ALEXANDER
FORMAN, WILLIAM
NELSON, ROBERT
GEORGE, WILEY
RASCO, JOHN
GUINN, IVERSON R.
BISHOP, JOHN W.
Page 286
METCALF, SARAH
JOHNSTON, JAMES
CLARK, SAMUEL
STONE, (not legible)
KELLEY, TOBIAS
YATES, JAMES
BURGESS, WILLIAM
McCAIN, GLOVER
BURGESS, JOHN R.
LEVERITT, ABRAHAM R.
HEARD, GEORGE W.
PACE, D.E.
HANNAH, JAMES J.
JOHNSTON, WASHINGTON
KILPATRICK, JOSEPH F.
HARRIS, BRAHAM
McCAIN, JAMES
McCAIN, SEABORN
McCAIN, EDWARD
McCAIN, JAMES G.
McCAIN, HENRY
GARRETT, JONATHON
McCAIN, JOHN
GARRETT, MANCILL
GARRETT, NEWTON
DOOLEY, WILLIAM
HOLLY, JOHN
DOOLEY, NATHAN
EIDSON, DAVID E.

HOLLEY, JETHRO
Page 287
ELLARD, THOMAS
BARNES, EDWARD
RIDDLE, THOMAS
McCAIN, CHRISTOPHER P.
PHILLIPS, WILLIAM
FEASLE, ISAAC
RIDDLE, GIDDEON
FORD, JESSE
GRIFFIN, J.I.
PETTIS, WILLIAM
CARDWELL, JOHN
FORD, BARTHOLOMEW
WATTS, MOSES
WATTS, JACOB
CALDWELL, GEORGE W.
HANEY, ELIZABETH
VICKERS, JEFFERSON
SMITH, MILTON
THOMAS, ROLA
KILPATRICK, JAMES
CLAUNCH, TRUHART
BRIDWELL, WILLIAM
CHILDERS, FIELDING
STIDAM, BENJAMIN
HAMP, JOHN
WHELASS, A.I.
RACKLEY, SHEDERICK
CASTLEBERRY, JAMES H.
LEE, GREEN B.
LEATH, WILLIAM
Page 288
CALDWELL, A.C.
PHILLIPS, RUBIN
SMITH, JOHN
CHAPMAN, ROBERT HET
BRITTEN, THOMAS
BUSH, JOHN
OSBURN, LEVIN
TATUM, THOMAS
McCLUNG, ANDERSON
RICHEY, AMEY
STRINGFELLOW, HENRY
HUBBARD, BENJAMIN
KERR, ALEXANDER
HUBBARD, ROBERT C.
GREEN, JAMES
COUNCIL, JESSE
TAYLOR, JAMES
ROBINSON, ESKRIDGE G.

DENNIS, SOPHIA A.
MUNDAY, WILLIAM
LUCAS, GUTHRIDGE
LEDBETTER, JAMES
STONE, RICHARD
STONE, ISAAC
JONES, WILLIS W.
WEAR, MARY
BYERS, MARTHA
McCARTER, WILLIAM
MORRIS, WILLIAM A.
SPENCE, SOLOMON
Page 289
DAIL, ISAAC S.
THOMPSON, ROBERT H.
LANE, JOHN
FRANKS, ELIJAH
DULANEY, BAKER
SPENCE, BENJAMIN
ROWAN, WILLIAM
FRENCH, JOHN
COOK, THOMAS
TUCK, ROBERT W.
McCLELLAN, SAMUEL
EMBREY, WILLIAM G.
EMBREY, JOSEPH
TRUSS, ARTHER
BURCHFIELD, JEREMIAH
SIDES, BENJAMIN
CRAIN, BARTLAY
BEARUS, MAGOR
LUCK, JOHN B.
DRISKILL, JACOB
CASTLEBERRY, JOSEPH H.
CONN, SANDERS
KENNEDY, JESSE C.
ANDREWS, DAVID
EMBREY, ELIJAH
BLACKWELL, ALFRED
BLACKWELL, JAMES A.
KENNEDY, WILLIAM
LEE, CARROL
DULANEY, BAKER
RILEY, DAVID L.
Page 290
HOBBS, LEWIS H.
EARLEY, BAKER
PERRY, JOHN
DULANEY, DAVID
McCLELLAN, ROBERT
KNOTT, WILLIAM

TALLADEGA COUNTY

WORTHINGTON, SAMUEL
KING, MARTHA
KNOX, JOHN W.
GOODWIN, ELIZABETH
LAMBERT, ERWIN
MILAM, JAMES W.
SIDES, JOSEPH
SCISSON, STERLING
MARSHELL, JOHN
HOGAN, SHEROD
HOGAN, EDWARD
MARTEN, ELIJAH
MARTIN, JOSEPH C.
DANIEL, JACOB J.
KING, WILLIAM
WEAVER, HENRY
HANEY, ELIZABETH
NANCE, JAMES
OWINS, DAVID
OWINS, THOMAS
GOODWIN, NEWTON
ALISON, JOHN
FORD, ISAAC
DOLLAR, SAMUEL
Page 291
CURWELL, ANDREW B.
HARMON, JACOB
COCHRAN, OBADIAH
FORD, WILLIAM
THOMAS, PETER
FUNDERBURGH, ANTHONY W.
HUTCHINSON, WILLIAM
LEUPEN, ALFRED
McLELLAND, MARY
McLELLAND, THOMAS E.
HARRISON, MILES H.
CRESWELL, HENRY
TANT, JOHN J.
REAVES, LAWSON
MARABLE, THOMAS C.
HARRIS, ALEXANDER
WILSON, HARRISON
DRISKELL, ISAAC K. L.
CRITO, ARCHELAS
BURNS, BENJAMIN
HARRISON, ELIJAH
CRISWELL, CALVIN
WILLS, GEORGE W.
PATTON, EDWARD
CUNNINGHAM, ANDREW
MONTGOMERY, WILLIAM
OGLETREE, LARUM

PRATER, JOHN
ALVIS, ELIAS H.
Page 292
CLARK, ABNER
BLYTHE, SARAH
MALORY, HENRY
WILSON, JOEL
FLYNN, WILLIAM A.
LARD, ASHLY A.
CHANY, JAMES
CHANY, BENJAMIN B.
EMBRY, JACKSON
MITCHELL, JOHN
LITTLE, HENRY
MELTON, WILLIAM C.
BREWER, JAMES L.
MARTIN, ELIJAH
GREEN, THOMAS
NANCE, SALLY
TOWNSEND, ANDREW
LEAR, P.W.
REASON, REUBEN
McCARTER, ISAAC
HOWARD, ABNER
CUNNINGHAM, JACOB
SIDES, CALVIN
FANSHER, DAVID
BLANKENSHIP, RAMON
FRASHER, DAVID C.
MARTIN, DANIEL
FORMAN, SAMUEL
WILLIAMS, WILLIAM H.
MORROW, A. J.
Page 293
MURPHY, JAMES
KNIGHT, ENOCH
JONES, MARIAH M.
BRIGHT, THOMAS
WALTON, THOMAS
POWELL, B.F.
DONALDSON, CATHARINE

TALLAPOOSA COUNTY

Page 162
HOWELL, JOSHUA
REDDEN, JOHN
INGRAM, G. W.
COX, WILLIAM
JORDAN, DEMPSEY
WHITE, G.W.
ADGUR, A.
HUMPHRIES, EDWARD
CATES, P.A.
JOHNSON, JOHN
COLLUM, J. S.
ADCOCK, J. S.
SMITH, SAMUEL R.
STOW, A. R.
STOW, JOEL
YOUNG, BENNETT
KIMBALL, BRADLEY
BRYANT, NEADHAM
JENNINGS, JEREMIAH
CARTER, DAVID
YOUNG, JAMES M.
YOUNG, JAMES
BOOTH, HENRY
CRADDOCK, DAVID
KIMBROUGH, B. T.
EDWARDS, T. J.
STERNS, WILLIAM
PATTERSON, JOHN G.
WOODEN, JOHN
Page 163
GAITHER, GREENBERRY
HARBIN, WILEY
LOVELESS, JOHN, SR.
LOVELESS, JOHN, JR.
WOOD, F. F.
BELLAH, ELIJAH
BURING, JAMES L.
FAVOR, M. A.
CAMPBELL, A. H.
WHATLEY, HANNAH
WINGO, SARAH
LANEY, HUGH
WARD, J. W.
BROWN, WILIE
BROWN, WILLIAM
MITCHAM, N. J.
MORGAN, JOHN
WARE, PHILIP
ALLISON, ELEANOR
BUTLER, JOHN W.
GAHAGAN, LAWRENCE

BURNETT, JEREMIAH
BUCKALEW, M. S.
SLAUGHTER, JOHN
GILLAM, HARRY
NARON, SAMUEL
WILDER, SIMEON
HENDERSON, JESSE
McIVER, DANIEL
Page 164
JACKSON, HENRY
HENDERSON, RICHARD
ARGO, EDMUND
DAVIS, ELISHA
WARD, RANSAM
SIMMONS, JOSEPH, SR.
EPPERSON, G.W.
KIRKLAND, N.C.
JARMAN, TRESSEY
CANE, JAMES
HAMBY, DAVID
HAMBY, RACHEL
DABBS, JOHN H.
DABBS, JESSE
HENDERSON, JAMES
BURGER, MARY
HANSE, CONRAD
TEAL, WILLIAM
SAXON, BENAJAH
HENDERSON, NATHAN
HARALSON, ALEX
PATTON, ROBERT
BURNETT, ALEX.
HENDERSON, RICHARD, SR.
SMITH, JOSEPH
BURNETT, JEREMIAH, SR.
RASBERRY, MARY
LANGLEY, MANNON
FURGASON, L. H.
Page 165
SANDERS, WILLIAM G.
SANDERS, MARY
BRESSE, M.
HARDEN, E.
WRIGHT, A. S.
FAULK, JOHN
BASSETT, KILBY
WHITE, J. B.
LEDBETTER, WILLIAM
WRAY, JEREMIAH
DUDLEY, A. D.
BLACK, JOHN

BARR, JAMES A.
DUDLEY, PETER
MILES, M. H.
MAINARD, JOHN
HUNTER, N. Y.
STEPHENS, ELI
TATUM, W. V.
HUGHS, JOSEPH
MURRAY, JAMES
CARMICHAEL, JOHN
TARVER, BENJAMIN S.
TOWLS, W. N.
DAILEY, S. C.
JOHNSON, JOSEPH A.
SIMMONS, JOSEPH, JR.
DANIEL, WILLIAM
BERRY, GEORGE M.
Page 166
SLAUGHTER, J. M.
HOLLEY. C. L.
SANDERS, R. M.
NEVES, DANIEL
BREWER, D.
HOLLEY, J. A.
GILLAM, ROBERT
GILCOAT, A.
HAMMERS, JOHN
LANGFORD, M. L.
GENTRY, RANSOM
WARE, WALTON
FORSHEE, JOSEPH
HEARD, ELIAS
BERRY, JAMES
BERRY, THOMAS D.
MOORE, M. A.
LAWSON, IRVINE
TEAL, JESSE
HOLLY, HOWELL
YOUNG, B. H.
WEST, JESSE
WILLIAMS, WILLIAM A.
MORGAN, JESSE
TAYLOR, JOB
CRAVENS, M.M.
BUCE, JOHN
McCLENDON, JACOB
BRYANT, SIMON
Page 167
FLASS ?, ALEXANDER
VINES, JABEZ
ANDERSON, WILLIAM

-89-

TALLAPOOSA COUNTY

McGUIRE, FRANCIS
CROW, WILLIAM
SMITH, A. C.
BRICE, JOHN, SR.
STANFIELD, JAMES
GIBSON, BENJAMIN
McDANIEL, DAVID
PARTRIDGE, H.
GAY, A. H.
STRENGTH, L.P.
HEMMING, T. J.
CANNADY, L.
EVANS, JEREMIAH
FRYER, GEORGE
PORCH, HOWARD ?
SMITH, ELIZABETH
SANDERS, ZACH.
McERVIN, K.
JOHNSON, JOSEPH
GODWIN, R.
KEMP, M. H.
MANNING, THOMAS
INGRAM, B.L.
JORDAN, ELIJAH
SMITH, ELIJAH
ADCOCK, A.W.
Page 168
DILLARD, NATHAN
ELEY, ELI
SHROPSHIRE,
RUSSELL. T. W.
CHANNEL, WILLIAM
BRADFORD, JOHN
HACKNEY, JOSEPH
LASSETER, ISIAH
MURRAY, G. W.
CANTERBURY, W. S.
LAUDERDALE, J. M.
THOMAS, S. T.
LOCKWOOD, J. A.
SMITH, R. W.
ANDREWS, A. G.
CANNON, JOHN
THOMASTON, M.
BAIN, ABRAHAM
HOPKINS, JOHN M.
McLEMORE, JAMES
TILLORY, B. G.
HARTT, F.
HARRIS, L. C.
MARLOW, G. C.
SENTELL, A.

HERRING, E.
BROOKS, JOHN
WILLIAMS, WILIE
*Page 168-A
CARDY, ALLEN
FOWLER, WESLEY
EASTRIDGE, H.
SCROGGINS, PHILIP
KING, T.T.
ROBINSON, G. W.
SEAT, SHINGUS ??
DUNN, J. H.
PERRY, BENJAMIN
LEWIS, W. C.
STRICKLIN, JOSHUA
GOOLSBY, SIMEON
ALLEN, WILLIAM
BOULWARE, JAMES
SPEAK, GEORGE T.
KILGORE, WILLIAM
BAKER, G. W.
SHURLOCK, ELI B.
MOSELEY, SILAS
MOSELEY, WILLIAM E.
CARROLL, BARWELL
DUBOIS, BARENT
MOSELEY, ELI L.
MERRITT, ANN
LOFTIN, JEREMIAH
CONNER, DANIEL
TATUM, ALBERT
BRASIL, ALLEN
Page 169
DOSTER, JAMES
HENDERSON, B. ?
WILLSON, BENJAMIN
CAMPBELL, JOHN
RAMSAY, THOMAS
STEWART, S.
HENDERSON, RACHEL
HARDEN, WILLIAM
MATTHEWS, ARCHIBALD
LAWSON, MATILDA
HAMBY, DAVID
SANDFORD, ASA
SMITH, PETER W.
WAGONER, BENJAMIN
DILLARD. G. W.
BLACKERBY, WILLIAM
SMITH, G.
HOWARD, NANSEY
GILLILAND, WILLIAM

SMITH, JAS. B.
PEARSON, JOHN M.
PEARSON, W. H.
MOORE, JOHN
CROUCH, PETER S.
YOUNG, BENJAMIN
WILLIAMS, JOSIAH H
GOLDING, IRA
SPAIN, JOHN
Page 170
CEYDONFELDT, S.
BOSTIK, WILLIAM L.
ELLIS, W.
HUNNICUT,
KIMBROUGH, WILLIAM
LYON, DAVID
CLAY, THOMAS
WHITWORTH, R. W.
OWENS, ANDY
ELLIS, M.T.
NALL, M.
BASS, W. F.
DENNIS, W.
PURNELL, H.H.
JOHNSON, CURRY
STONE, CHARLES
BERRY, J.B.
HOWARD, GEORGE
BROOKS, ABRAHAM
CHINN, BENJAMIN
BROWN, EDWARD
WEEMS, WILLIS
PERRY, ISAIAH
SPARKS, N.F.
BURKE, WILLIAM
MAINARD, JAMES
BENTLEY, MOSES
PATILLO, JOHN R.
WRIGHT, S.
Page 171
HERRING,
BROOKS,
JORDAN, JOHN
TOLLASON, WILLIAM
ELLIS, JESSE S.
WRIGHT, JOHN
LOVE, INGRAM
WASHBURN,
SHACKLEFORD, C. S.
TOWNS, C. C.
MASON, WILLIAM
BRYANT, GEORGE

* This page had no number, so author numbered it.

-90-

TALLAPOOSA COUNTY

POWER, FRANCIS
DUDLEY, MARTIN
BOWLING, BARBARA
RAWLS, F.C.
WARREN, WILLIAM
MORRIS, ISAAC, SR.
JONES, THEOPHILUS
MUSICK, R. C.
KIMBALL, ALLEN
BURNS, ALEX.
SMITH, HENRY
BURNETT, ELI
WHITE, JESSE
HARRIS, PETER E.
CARROLL, WILLIAM
THORNTON,
SEWELL, JOHN
Page 172
CLARK, SARAH
COOKSY, JONATHON
BROWN, JAMES
COOPER, JAMES H.
YOUNGBLOOD, JOHN
WALKER, BENJAMIN
DILLARD, NATH.
BROWN, GEORGE
HOLTON ?,
SMITH, ROBERT
DAVIS, JOHN
W--------?, CORNELIUS
JONES, ISAAC
SLAUGHTER,
WYATT, WILLIAM
WYATT, PAUL
GREER, SAMUEL
BALES, SARAH
GREER, JOSEPH
JOHNSON, JOSEPH
FENNELL, G.M.
MARSHALL, WILLIAM
BLACK, THOMAS
SELMAN, DAVID
POLK, WILLIAM
JOHNSON, DAVID
POWER, E. J.
MONK, JAMES
VAUGHAN, JAMES
Page 173
KNIGHT, JOHN
JOHNSON, RODERICK
BREWER, WILLIAM R.
JOHNSON, WILLIAM

PERRIN, THOMAS
BALDWIN, HENRY
LOVELESS, O. H.
COOPER, SIMEON
CARDIN, LEVI
COLLEY, ZACH.
HAMMOND, SAMUEL
TRAYLOR, W. C.
STALNAKER, S.Y.
BOSTWICK, L. C.
SHARP, M.
BRIDGES, JAMES M.
JONES, ZACHY.
NALL, RICHARD
RAY, GEORGE
VARDEMAN, RACHEL
SPRINGER, SEABORN
KNOX, JOSEPH
BIRD, JAMES C.
BRICE, WILLIAM
SANDERS, JAMES
GROSS, BLUFORD
WEBB, EDMUND
+WYATT, ELIZABETH
Page 174
JOHNSON, ALFRED
WILKINSON, EDWARD
GAMMOCK, S. W.
NARON, GEORGE
WAKEFIELD, GEORGE
WARD, ROBERT
McFARLAN, THOMAS
EDLEMAN, ELIJAH
JONES, NATH"L
ROLLINS, HENRY
HAMMER, THOMAS
MASK, DUDLEY
MORDECAI, A.
TAYLOR, JAMES
RUSSELL, WILLIAM R.
ALFORD, L. P.
JOHNSON, BENJAMIN
COBB, WILLIAM B.
CONNERS, TIMOTHY
BUSSY, CHARLES
SPRAGGINS, ORSANIUS
GRIFFIN, THOMAS
PEARSON, M.W.
SENTELL, WILLIAM
OWEN, C. G.
COLLEY, JOHN
STARR, JOSHUA

HARRAL, M.
LANGLEY, ORSEY
Page 175
WALKER, JAMES
KEITH, AP.
WILLIAMS, DANIEL
MORRIS, JOHN
SCOGGINS, G.
EDDINGTON, JAMES
PATTERSON, EMERY
WARD, E. B.
HALL, ISAAC
PERRY, K.
ADAMS, ALF.
GOODWIN, R. G.
EALSEY, ROBERT
WILLIAMS, T.
DARDEN, JOHN
FULLER, ARTHUR
BROOKING, R. N.
SMITH, ISAAC
HASTING, JAMES ?
POWELL, MOSES
POWELL, WILLIAM
HUDGINS, JAMES A.
GOODWIN, W. H.
ROSS, WILLIAM T.
HICKMAN, C.C.
POWELL, TERRY
HUTCHINSON, JOHN
STEWART,
VEASEY, F. H.
Page 176
BURNETT,
DILLARD, JACOB
MYERS, DAVID
IRVING?, JOHN
CLARK, WILLIAM
BULGER,
BAILEY, W. S.
GREEN, LEWIS S.
YOUNG. H. M.
LAYTON, HENRY
JACKSON, CARTER
HANNA, ZACH.
HARLAN, JOHN
CHAPPELL, JAMES G.
WELCH, JAMES
WINSLETT, JAMES
BERRY, LEWIS T.
BAILEY, HENRY S.
BAILEY, S. N.

+notation by this name that she refused to describe the persons in her family but gives a total of 5 in family.

TALLAPOOSA COUNTY

McBRYDE, DUNCAN
CARTER, WILLIAM
HARRIS, MAJORS
HARKINS, JOHN
SHIELDS, THOMAS E.
HASKINS, M. H.
FINCHER, WILLIAM C.
BAILEY, JAMES
EDDINGTON, W. L.
CAIN, JAMES
Page 177-178
CANNIFALL, ELIJAH
EASON, W.
McCOY, B. B.
BROOKS, JAMES
BROOKS, WILLIAM
McCOY, JEFFERSON
PALMORE, F. W.
WALKER, FREEMAN
GREEN, LEWIS
WEBB, WILLIAM
WALDRIP, BENJAMIN
LEABOW, WILLIAM
MOBLEY, JESTIN
PARKER, GEORGE
McCOMBS, JOHN B.
LEACH, WILLIAM
GILES, JAMES D.
WEST, MARY
GREY, SAMUEL
WRIGHT, RICHARD
CANNEDAY, JESSE
NORMAN, JAMES
BAILEY, JACOB
HUNT, G. T.
MASK, B.
ADAMSON, J. C.
FLAKE, J. P.
GRIFFIN, JAMES
BALDWIN, O.
*Page 178
BEASLEY, JAMES
MONK, S. W.
BROOKS, JOHN
LEE, BENJAMIN
HIGGINBOTHAM, W.
KNIGHT, W. G.
LUNSFORD, WILLIAM
ECHOLS, B. W.
HALL, JOHNSON
YARBROUGH, JOSEPH
HAMBY, E.
PEARCE, JOHN

GARDNER, W. W.
GALLOWAY, E.B.
SMITH, SPENCER
PRICE, WILLIAM H.
POWELL, ISAAC
WALKER, R.G.
HARRIS, JESSE
LEDLOW, JAMES
DURAND, JOHN
WHELAS, DRURY
TALLEY, SAMUEL
HARDEY, RICHARD
PEEPLES, RUFUS
EASON, R.W.D.
McLEAN, SAMUEL H.
WILLIAMS, BENNETT
BROOKS, SILAS
Page 179
RUSK, JOSEPH
SWAIN, DAVID
BROWN, JOSEPH
HUTCHINSON, WILLIAM
DICKINSON, WILLIAM
SHADDOCK, ISAAC
PULLAM, WILLIAM H.
STEVENSON, MOSES
DUNN, JOSEPH
CARR, DAVID
MILAN, B.
GULDER, W. R.
DUNN, JOHN
HUTTO, JOHN
GALLOWAY, JOHN
WHITE, ABRAHAM
LAMBERT, SAMUEL
McKINNON, RODERICK
McKINNON, ALEX.
McKINNON, L. G.
COULTER, J. M.
JOHNSON, THOMAS
JOHNSON, FRANCIS
CARTER, WILKINS
LEE, JOURDAN
MONK, SILAS
PHILLIPS, JOSEPH
JAMES, BENNETT
PATRICK, WILLIAM
Page 180
BUCKNER, R. B.
CARTER, CARTER
FLOURNOY, WILLIAM
CASH, JOHN
COOPER, JAMES H.

SMITH, WILLIAM
MORRISON, WASHINGTON
McCULLOCH, JAMES M.
WEATHERLY, WILLIAM
WOOD, C. W.
KIRKLAND, A.
TODD, JOHN
LOCKS, J.I.
FULLER, ABNER
WOODPIN, M.
McKENZIE, JOHN
RESS?, SOPIAS
JOURDAN, JOHN A.
CARR, JOHN S.
MEARS, R. V.
PATE, WILLIAM
SHAW, JOHN
BELL, SAMUEL
ADAIR, JOHN
RODGERS, WILLIAM
WINSLETT, FLOYD
LACKEY, A. A.
MOORE, JOHN
BAILEY, J. M.
Page 181
POWELL, WILLIAM D.
MABRY, R. E.
BLACKMAN, WILLIAM
STONE, DAVID
RASBURY, ISAAC
CANNIDAY, E.
HENDERSON, HENRY
SPARKS, JAMES
LIPHAM, WILLIAM
LUKER, MARTIN
EDWARDS, JOEL
TODD, JAMES
LAND, SOL
MARABLE, JOHN
COKER, THOMAS
BURNETT, THOMAS
LEDLOW, A.
DUNCAN, J. H.
COTNEY, J. D.
COTNEY, J. W.
PEARSON, JOEL A.
WILLIAMS, DANIEL
ROBERSON, L.M.
BUTLER, JAMES
SANDFORD, JESSE
WOOD, LINNY
WOOD, WILEY
WRIGHT, JOHN

* This page also numbered 178   -92-

TALLAPOOSA COUNTY

WHITAKER, JOHN
Page 182
REPITO, PRISCILLA
DAVIS, ASA
DENT, LIDDY
WILLIAMS, ISAAC
SMITH, J. J.
SWAN, JAMES
TANTON, HENRY
BROOKS, WILLIAM
BRAYER, J. H. M.
DONALD, M.B.
JOHNSON, HANNAH
WRIGHT, JAMES
MONTGOMERY, JAMES
NELSON, JOHN
GRAHAM, RUTH
PLYLER, E.
MORRIS, NANCY
SMITH, THOMAS
WALKER, ROBERT
KEITH, L. H.
KEITH, NINIUS
OSBORN, BENJAMIN
HUDSON, THOMAS
DAVIS, R.
OSBORN, JOHN
WARREN, E.
RAY, SOL
WILLIAMSON, B. O.
CLOWER, H.
Page 183
CLOWER, JACOB
JONES, ROBERT
GALLOWAY, H.
NELSON, E.
LEE, B.
JONES, LEWIS
JONES, JOSEPH
NARON, W.
HENSON, JAMES
MACKEY, G. B.
MELEAR, W. S.
PANNELL, THOMAS
WELCH, ELIZABETH
POSEY, BENJAMIN
GILLAM, J. H.
NARON, ELI
YARBROUGH, JOSEPH
WELCH, N.
HOOD, WILLIAM
YOUNGBLOOD, S.
WELCH, EKI
GRAY, R.

CRAVEN, DAVID
GRIFFIN, J. B.
FIELDER, JOHN C.
MESHEAK, D. D.
TOLLEY, WILLIAM
EAST, BEN
STURDIVANT, A. C.
Page 184
SPENSER, HENRY
WALKER, T.
EAST, WILLIAM C.
NARON, JOHN
ROBESON, JESSE
KIRKSEY, G.
HARPER, J. N.
SMITH, JAMES
TRAYLOR, THOMAS
GREER, A. W.
BURNS, SAMUEL
HERRING, JAMES
HARDEN, WILLIAM
BARRINGTINE, W.
FARGASON, JANE
GRAY, H.W.
McBURNETT, W.
TRIMBLE, MOSES
OLDFIELD, P.
DUFFIE, NATHANIEL
GOLDEN, S.
FLORENCE, MARY
JOHNSON, AMOS
POWER, SARAH
JONES, H.
MORRIS, S.
CURRY, JOHN
SIMMONS, V.B.
WEBB, CHARLES
Page 185
POWELL, H.
LEDBETTER, O.
RAY, T.
PLANT, SARAH
ROWDEN, W. H.
KENIBREW, M.D.
KENIBREW, L.B.
BICKERSTAFF, P.B.
WEBB, G. W.
SCOTT, JAMES
DEAN, WILLIAM
BARKER, WILLIAM
BARTEE, A. M.
PEARSON, DANIEL
KITCHENS, W.
MOORE, JAMES

LESTER, JOHN M.
MARTIN, JAMES
KELLAM, E.
McCULLOCH, MARTIN
McCULLOCH, P.M.
SMITH, STEPHEN
McCULLOCH, L.
PRICE, DANIEL
FREEMAN, R.
PARKER, N.
ROGERS, JOHN
ROE, H.J.
MORRIS, CHARLES
Page 186
COLEMAN, W. W.
EDDINGS, P.R.
YARBROUGH, JOHN
HIGHTOWER, J. S.
RAPE, JACOB
THORNTON, L.
NUOMAN, JAMES
EDDINGS, J.A.
DAVIS, JOHN
ROWELL, A.
HIGHTOWER, J.W.
DAVIS, C.
WARD, S.
MOORE, GEORGE
MOORE, WILLIAM
ROBESON, JEPTHA
THORNTON, Y.
MOTTE, BENJAMIN
KNIGHT, THOMAS
BURNHAM, H.
DRYER, E. H.
PATTERSON, JESSE
CARROL, L.

SURNAME INDEX

The numbers following each surname indicate the page number of this volume on which the name may be found. A number in parenthesis following the page number indicates the frequency with which that particular surname is found on a given page.

In using this index, check for all possible spellings of a name as many census enumerators spelled phonetically and not necessarily in the form that a name may occur today.

AARAN:74
AARON:73
ABBOTT:41,69
ABERCROMBIE:76(2),80,84
ABERCROMBY:9
ABERHEART:27
ABERNATHY:13,32
ABLE:64(2),72
ABLES:12,71,72
ABNEY:2,26,29
ABOCRUMBIE:55(2)
ABOCRUMBY:1
ACESINGE?:50
ACKEN:12
ACKER:16
ACKIN:12
ACUFF:14
ADAIR:41(2),52,74(2),85,86,92
ADAMS:11(3),30(2),31(3),33(2),34(2),36,39,45,46,47,50,52,55,58,61,66,72,75,77,83(4),84(2),91
ADAMSON:92
ADCOCK:26,89,90
ADDAMS:22(2),23(2),28,54(2),57
ADEM:78
ADERHOLD:13
ADGUR:89
ADKINS:59,66
ADKINSON:43
ADORN:77
ADRAIN:71
ADRAN:71
AGERBON:68
AIKEN:22,32
AIKINS:37,66
AKIN:73
AKINS:19,20,66(2)
AKRIDGE:38
ALAWYNE:66
ALBERSON:81
ALBRIGHT:10(4),80(2)
ALBRITTON:2
ALDERSON:56
ALDRIDGE:18,65,73,75,76,79(2)
ALEXANDER:1(2),13(3),19(3),20(2),22,34,36,52,67,77
ALFORD:22,23,74,91
ALFRED:11
ALISON:83,88
ALLAN:70(3)
ALLANS:17
ALLEN:3,4,5(3),12(2),13,14(3),17,21,22(3),25,27,30,36,39,42,43(2),50,56(3),64,65,66,70,73,74,75,77,79(2),80,81,83,90
ALLISON:70,89
ALLMAN:68
ALLSOP:40
ALLSUP:12(3)
ALSOBROOK:66
ALSOP:37
ALSTON:6
ALTERS:40
ALVIS:88

AMATHROUGH:51
AMBERSON:18(2)
AMERLINE:10
AMERINE:9
AMIES:26
AMOS:30,39
ANDERHOLE:11
ANDERSON:13,15,18(2),22,23,24,29,36,61,64(2),65,66,67(2),81,82,89
ANDRES:37
ANDREWS:7,10,13,14,15,18(2),22,23,25,27,30,39,46,50(2),70,75,77,87,90
ANGLE:19,39,77
ANNY:65
ANTHONY:26,34(2),36,37(3),38
ANSEL:13
ANSLEY:29,30,58
APLEBY:23
APLIN:56
APPLEBY:59
ARANT:26(2)
ARCHER:82
ARDIS:77(2)
ARGO:30,89
ARINGTON:75
ARMBUSTER:84
ARMSTRONG:5(2),16,44(5),49,51,62,63,66,71,72(2),77,86
ARNETT:66
ARNOLD:1,9,11,13,18,35,38,56,72,86(2)
ARNOTT:37
ARON:74,75
ARRBRIT:74
ARRINGTON:19,58,75
ARTENBURG:17
ARTHUR:26,34,82
ARWOOD:55
ASBELL:16
ASCUTT:85
ASH:35
ASHBY:33
ASHCROFT:69(2)
ASHLEY:12,17,79,84
ASHLY:60,77
ASKEW:6,22,73(2),85
ASLEY:29,60,77
ASMON:47
ATES:38
ATHWAY:4
ATKESON:29
ATKINS:28,36,42,85
ATKINSON:1,28,50,86
ATWELL:4,57,76
ATWOOD:52
AULD:41
AUSTIN:7,43,47,65
AUTERY:80,81
AUTRY:16,22,24,44
AVERETT:4
AVERETTE:4
AVERY:26(2),31,48,60(2)
AWBERRY:34
AWTRY:28
AYER:7
AYERS:8
AYMAN:1

AYRES:21
BABB:3,6,73
BARBBELL:79
BABER:29
BACHANAN:44
BACHELOR:23
BACKSTER:35
BACON:48,73
BADDATT:71
BADGET:14
BAESHART:60(3)
BAGBY:79
BAGERLY:58
BAGGET:23,43,60,74
BAGLEY:16,81
BAGLY:14,82
BAILEY:13,24,28,35(2),42,44,45,56,59,68,71(2),91(3),92(3)
BAILY:1,20(2),81
BAIN:90
BAIRD:8,18,82,83
BAITEY:62
BAKER:3,4(3),8,9,11(4),15(2),17,21,27,28(2),32,35(3),36,37,45(3),49,50,59,64,65(2),70(2),72,73,74,76,84,90
BALDWIN:6,54(2),56,59(3),74,78,91,92
BALDY:3,6
BALES:91
BALEY:52
BALFOUR:85
BALIS:50
BALL:5,7,82(2),83(2)
BALLAD:9(2)
BALLARD:6,7,23,41(2),48,78,79
BALLARD:85
BANCORSE:85
BANCROFT:11
BANE:9,23,61,62(4),81
BANISTER:82
BANKS:7,31,63,64,70
BANKSON:32
BANKSTON:22
BANSTER:52
BAR:49,73
BARAHAN:18
BARBER:29,30,34,84
BARBERREE:22
BARBOR:62,74
BARCLAY:60,65,81(2)
BARCLEY:60
BARD:75
BARDEN:54,70
BARETT:71
BARFIELD:2,4
BARKER:9(3),10(2),24(2),25,33,47,75,93
BARKINS:85(2)
BARKLEY:26,32(4),54
BARKSDALE:4
BARNES:48(2),52,61(2),62,70(2),72,74,80,86,87
BARNET:10(3),18,21,24
BARNETT:19,21,33,35,42,44,67,73,76,78
BARNETTE:41,42
BARNS:72

i

BARNWELL:21
BARON:6
BARR:26,86,89
BARRETT:9,58,68,82(2),85
BARRINGTINE:93
BARRINGTON:34
BARROT:25
BARROW:8,22(3),24(2),26,
    31(2),71
BARRY:1,32(2),34,35,36,38
BARRUM:32
BARTEE:93
BARTLEY:31
BARTON:17(2),27,28,60(2)
BARWELL:47
BASCOMB:55
BASH:16
BASINGAME:77
BASKINS:85
BASLY:11
BASS:1,7,14,21,26,30,49,
    50,61,69,76(2),82(3),
    84,90
BASSETT:21,89
BASTER:51
BATES:1,3,6,14,18,33,34,
    50
BATEY:52
BATILE:5
BATSON:78
BATTLE:2,3,16,75
BATTLES:33
BATTOR:41
BAUGH:4,23(2)
BAUGHTON:2
BAUMAN:7(4)
BAXLEY:7,8,44(2)
BAXTER:46,47,60,63,64,67
BAYLES:61,66,70
BAYLESS:65
BAYLEY:66(2)
BAYLIS:46,70
BEALLE:45
BEAM:34
BEAN:10(2),68(2),69
BEARD:9(2),34,37,44,56,64,
    67,87
BEARDIN:62(3)
BEARUS:87
BEAS:56
BEASLEY:10,92
BEASLY:11
BEASON:2
BEATY:28,51(2)
BEAUCHAMP:3,54
BEAUIN:58
BEAZLEY:32
BEAZON:33
BECK:2,23,27,44,51
BECKHAM:45
BECKUM:13
BECKWITH:76
BECKWORTH:63
BEDWELL:9
BEECHAM:10
BEEDLE:62
BEEN:47
BELCHER:26,47,51
BELEMA:75
BELFLOWER:26
BELIER:42
BELL:3,6,23(2),32(2),34,
    36,40(3),57(2),59,
    66,78,84,92
BELLAH:68,89
BELLAMY:28
BELTON:66
BELYEU:59
BEMON:56
BENEFIELD:9,68
BENNET:16,25,30,55,57,73,
    75,77
BENNETT:3,8,51,70,72(2),

BENNETT cont.:73,79,82
BENNETTE:5
BENNS:56
BENSON:20,32,42(2),43(2),
    60,61
BENTLEY:18,21,28(3),32,
    35,90
BENTLY:1,10(3),81
BENTON:1,2,22,28,72,77(2),
    78
BERAL:65
BERKET:18
BERRETT:71(2)
BERRY:3,14,20,30,47,48(5),
    63,66,79,80,89(3),
    90,91
BERRYHILL:69
BEST:57,80,83(2)
BETHUNE:50,54,83
BETTS:1
BEVEL:8
BEVELL:60
BEVERLEY:37
BEVERLY:5,57
BEVIL:19
BEVIN:36
BIBB:28
BIBBY:27(2),28(2)
BICE:15
BICKERSTAFF:93
BIDDLE:48,56(2)
BIDDY:62
BIECE:45
BIGERSTAFF:24(2)
BIGFORD:6
BIGGER:32
BIGGS:45,63
BILBRO:31(2)
BILLING:45
BILLINGSLEY:19,24,63,69
BILLIPS:42
BINGE:51
BINNOW:47
BINSON:2
BINT:13
BIPIN:51
BIRCH:76
BIRD:22,30,33,41,65
BIRDSONG:24
BIRDWELL:65
BIRKWELL:61
BISHOP:16,28,35,42,48(3),
    50,63,66,75,77(2),
    80,87
BISSEL:2
BITTLE:83(2)
BIZZELL:7(3)
BLACK:5,7,11(3),12,13(2),
    14,17,21,23,33,35,
    36,38(2),60,69(2),
    81(2),89,91
BLACKBURN:25,28
BLACKERBY:90
BLACKMAN:26(3),54,56,57,
    76,92
BLACKMAR:74
BLACKMARR:74
BLACKMON:57
BLACKSTOCK:26,27,38
BLACKSTON:26,27
BLACKWELDER:8
BLACKWELL:19,40(3),52,54,
    80,87(2)
BLACKWOOD:39
BLAGG:68
BLAIR:16,17,20(2),28,29,
    34,77
BLAKE:13(2),44,53,69(2),
    79
BLAKELY:28
BLAKEY:57
BLAKY:3,4
BLALOCK:9,71,78

BLACHET:1
BLANCOT:51(2)
BLAND:23
BLANKENSHIP:24,43(5),88
BLANKS:58
BLANTON:48
BLASENGAM:61
BLASENGAME:26
BLASINGAME:28
BLASON:33
BLAYDES:4
BLEDSOE:11,29,31,84
BLEDSON:28
BLESSING:63
BLEVINS:47(4)
BLOUNT:23
BLY:49
BLYTHE:83,88
BOADLER:65
BOARING:86(2)
BOATMAN:50(2),52
BOATNER:62,66
BOAZ:80
BOBBIT:3
BODIN:66
BOGG:82
BOGGESS:65(2)
BOGGS:5,15,34
BOGS:82
BOHANNON:26,29,51,52,60(2)
BOID:25
BOLE:12
BOLEHER:31
BOLEN:36
BOLES:18,43
BOLEY:26
BOLIN:10,11,50,57,64,66
BOLING:27,31,70
BOLLING:73
BOLLINGER:15
BOLT:70,71
BOLTON:21,75
BOMAN:61,63(3),81
BOND:22(2),60
BONDLEE:33
BONDS:13(2),21,55
BONNER:26,30,31,42,70
BOOKER:32,34,36,39
BOOKHOUSE:50,51
BOON:4,50,78
BOOSER:12(3)
BOOTH:1,25,79,89
BOOTHE:54
BORDEN:12,18
BORDERS:15,25(2)
BORING:30,36,59
BORUM:81,84,59
BOSTICK:31,44
BOSTIK:90
BOSTWIC:23
BOSTWICK:91
BOSWELL:21,48
BOSWICK:3
BOTTON:84
BOUDEN:51(2)
BOUDRE:77
BOULEN:70
BOULDING:27
BOULWARE:90
BOUMIT:65
BOWDEN:4
BOWDON:15,44,51
BOWEN:30,65,71
BOWERS:6
BOWIE:82
BOWIN:48
BOWLES:36
BOWLING:27,91
BOWLS:85
BOWMAN:10(4),15,41
BOYD:3,6,11,12,14,17(3),
    24,45,46,52,74,79,81
BOYDE:57,54,58(2)

ii

BOYTER:6
BOYETT:6
BOYKIN:78
BOYLES:66
BOYLSTON:2
BOYSTON:48
BOYT:41
BOX:18,68,69
BOZEMAN:22(2),41
BRADBERRY:17
BRACEWELL:37
BRADDY:83
BRADEN:49,86
BRADFORD:10,11,41,80,83,
       90
BRADLEY:6,8,18,42,54,55,
       62,63,65(2),75,78
BRADLY:77
BRADS:70
BRADSHAW:45(2),51(2),56,
       72
BRADWELL:18
BRADY:45,86
BRAGAN:23
BRAKEBILL:17
BRALTON:64
BRANAN:42,45
BRANDON:29,37,51(3),56,81
BRANFORD:77
BRANNON:74,77
BRANSFIELD:61
BRANTLEY:23
BRANTLY:2
BRASHER:86
BRASIL:55(2),90
BRAUER:32
BRAWNER:27
BRAZELL:39
BRAZIEL:76(2)
BRAZIER:43
BRECK:68
BREDLOVE:58(2)
BREED:70,71(2)
BREEDEN:11
BREESON:29
BRELAND:8
BRESSE:89
BREWER:38(2),54,57(3),68,
       80,83,88,89,91
BREWSTER:26
BRICE:90,91
BRIDGES:18,22,48(2),62,
       65,78,91
BRIDWELL:87
BRIGGS:27,47
BRIGHT:66(2),82,88
BRIGHTON:69
BRIGMAN:44,76
BRILEY:33,34
BRISON:63
BRISTOE:50
BRISTOW:52
BRIT:74
BRITT:2,57,79,82
BRITTAIN:13
BRITTEN:86,87
BRITTIAN:17,18
BRITTON:26,56(2),57
BROADFOOT:23
BROADNAX:31
BROCK:15,20(2),47(2),
       48(2),49,82,86
BRODDEN:32(2)
BROGDEN:21
BROMELOW:30
BROOG:74
BROOM:6,8
BROOK:49
BROOKING:91
BROOKS:4,5,12,13,22(2),
       26(3),30,36,72,74,
       79,83,90(3),92(4),
       93

BROTHERS:16,32(2)
BROUGHTON:75
BROWDER:1,5,15
BROWN:1(2),2(2),3(2),6,8,
       9(2),10(6),11(3),
       15,16(4),17,19,
       20(2),21(2),25,26
       (2),29(3),30,33,34,
       35,37,42,44,45(2),
       48(2),49(2),50,51,
       58,59,60,61(2),63,
       64,69,71(2),72(2),
       73,75,76(2),77,78,
       79,80,82(2),83(3),
       84,85,89(2),90,
       91(2),92
BROWNING:7,13(2),17
BROYLES:17(2)
BRUCE:49,50,51,54
BRUMBELOE:68
BRUMBY:55,57
BRUNSON:3,61(2)
BRUTON:17
BRYAN:7,43,71,73(2),78
BRYANT:2,3,5,8,12,27,33,
       37(3),51,75,76,77,
       80(3),81,89,90
BUCE:89
BUCHANAN:9,71
BUCK:19,64
BUCKALEW:89
BUCKLEW:26
BUCKHALTER:26
BUCKHANNON:67
BUCKHANON:31,79
BUCKNER:74,92
BUFFORD:24
BUFORD:74(2)
BUGBY:54
BUGG:77
BULER:16
BULGER:42,84,91
BULGES:42
BULL:82(2)
BULLARD:6,33,36(4),41,76,
       79,83
BULLOCK:4,16,55(3)
BULLSIDGE?:12
BUNDON:52
BUNDOND:52
BUNKLEY:54
BURCH:4,9(4),11,21
BURCHFIELD:81,87
BURDEN:18,19,20,71(2),72
BURDENS:19
BURDETT:27
BURDICK:77
BUREN:80
BURGER:89
BURGES:9(3)
BURGESS:1,12,33,36,41,43,
       49,50(2),75,87(2)
BURGETT:61
BURGGES:33
BURHAM:7
BURING:89
BUITT:9
BURK:24(2),75,78(2),87(2)
BURKE:33,90
BURKET:61,62,47
BURKHALTER:68
BURKS:60(2)
BURLESON:8
BURLISON:3,4
BURNES:19,30,69
BURNET:20,27,54
BURNETT:33,35(2),38,39(2)
       49,89(3),91(2),92
BURNHAM:72,93
BURNS:18(2),26,32,53,64
       (3),77,81,88,91,93
BURNSIDE:76(2)
BURNTSIDE:61(2)

BURR:16,76,77
BURRETT:71
BURRIS:49
BURROUGH:35(2)
BURROW:14,44
BURROWS:26
BURRUS:12(2),49,50
BURSON:26(2),35,71(2)
BURT:14,47,52,74
BURTON:20,23(2),71,72,84
BUSBY:8,64
BUSE:36
BUSEY:82
BUSH:1,2,15,54(3),62,66,
       84,87
BUSHBY:56
BUSHY:52
BUSSEL:47
BUSSY:91
BUSTER:48
BUTLER:12,16,23,42,57,89,
       92
BUTT:81
BUTTER:55
BUTTS:15,28,31,56,85
BYAM:47
BYERS:46,87
BYNUM:5,14,80
BYRAN:5
BYRD:7(3),22,42,61,74,77
CABELL:26
CABINESS:3
CADDLEMAN:71
CADE:5,24
CADENHEAD:8,23
CADWELL:11,51
CAGLE:39,47(2),50
CAHEL:9
CAID:72
CAIN:7,34,92
CAISON:1
CALAHAN:23,49,50(2)
CALAWAY:-2,47
CALDHARN:64
CALDWELL:3,15(2),16,22,23,
       25,39,41,66,80,
       83(2),86,87(2)
CALHOUN:24,41,45(2),75(3),
       79
CALLAHAN:49
CALLAWAY:19,54,57
CALLOWAY:6,8,19,57,59,63
CALLWAY:27
CALTON:25
CALVIN:17,44
CALWELL:39
CAMACK:22
CAMARON:72
CAMBELL:37(2)
CAMERON:6,15,18,19,56,83,
       86
CAMMACK:52
CAMON:37
CAMP:10,46(2),71(3),83,84
CAMPBELL:5,7(4),14,24,
       25(2),34,35,36(2)
       38,39,41(2),42,
       43(2),45,49,52,
       58,60,63,64,65,
       71,75,81,82(3),
       83,89,90
CAMPION:16
CANADAY:77(2)
CANDEN:52
CANDLER:30
CANE:89
CANEDY:56
CANIFOX:78
CANNADY:90
CANNEDAY:92
CANNIDAY:92
CANNIFALL:92
CANNON:1,4(2),7,13(2),

iii

CANNON cont.:17(4),32,33,
       35,40(2),52,
       60,90
CANTELE:85
CANTERBURY:90
CANTRELL:12
CANTRILL:17
CAPEHART:29,48
CAPEHEART:48
CAPENGER:47
CAPERS:3
CAPERTON:52(2)
CAPMAN:73
CAPS:26,57,59,74
CAPSHAW:34
CAR:22,47(2),57(2)
CARBERSON:54
CARDEN:16,52
CARDIN:4,91
CARDLE:70
CARDMILL:68,70
CARDWELL:30,87
CARDY:90
CAREY:21
CARGIL:29,54
CARGILE:1,3,65
CARGILL:54
CARLAND:60
CARLEE:68
CARLETON:45,84
CARLILE:26(2),31(3),76
CARLISLE:28(2),77
CARLSON:16
CARLTON:37,38,42,63
CARMIAL:58
CARMICHAEL:30
CARMICHAEL:20,45,66,79,
           82,89
CARNES:19,47
CARNOCHAN:45
CARNS:47,56
CAROT:66
CAROTHERS:11
CARP:63
CARPENTER:13,26,64,82,
         83(3)
CARPLIN:50
CARR:29,32,92(2)
CARRELL:37,38
CARRINGTON:38
CARROL:1,16,43,90,91,93
CARROWAY:50
CARSON:5,46
CARTER:5,6(2),15(2),19,
       26,27(3),29,44,60,
       62,64,69(2),77,79,
       80(3),83(2),84,89,
       92(3)
CARTHEY:15
CARTT:81
CARY:9,56,77
CASADEY:86
CASCE:69
CASE:2,17,33,47,48(2)
CASEL:71
CASELBARY:11
CASERTY:56
CASEY:19(4),44,48(2),63,
      85(3),86
CASH:38,92
CASK:88
CASKEY:72(2)
CASON:24,34,37
CASPER:71(4)
CASS:60,64(2),67
CASSON:12
CASSY:5,7
CAST:16,64
CASTEEL:50
CASTLE:39
CASTLEBERRY:26,37,39,85,
           87(2)
CASTRAL:16

CASWELL:6
CATENHEAD:56(4)
CATER:46,84
CATES:89
CATHEY:82
CATHORN:38
CATLIN:46
CATO:43
CATOSO:4
CATTENHEAD:73,75
CATTERVILLE:1
CAUSEE:51
CAUSEY:27,28(2),42(3)
CAUSY:4
CAVENDER:84
CAVENESS:43
CAVER:80
CAVIN:38(2)
CAVINESS:2
CAWFIELD:71
CAY:77
CEEGLES:51
CEWSLY?:36
CEYDONFELDT:90
CHADWELL:11
CHADWICK:15,20
CHAFIN:22
CHALCER:79
CHALER:10
CHALKER:9,59
CHAMBERLAIN:27,76
CHAMBERS:7(2),12(2),18(2)
        26,60,64,71,
        74(2),75
CHAMBLESS:16(3),62,64,66
CHAMBLY:26
CHAMPION:8,18,28,39
CHANCE:2
CHANCELLOR:43(2)
CHANDLER:3,9,10,13(4),14,
        19,20,21,25,34,
        56,71,80,84
CHANEY:17,34,50,87
CHANNEL:86,90
CHANY:88(2)
CHAPALEER:32
CHAPEL:81
CHAPELL:34
CHAPIN:25
CHAPLE:65
CHAPPEL:24,55,56,58
CHAPPELL:91
CHAPMAN:16,36,40,41(3),
       44(2),45(2),46,
       48,56(2),57,65,
       77(2),79,84,87
CHARMIR:64
CHASTEEN:50
CHAVIN:1
CHEEK:63,64
CHERRALL:81
CHERRY:26
CHESNUTT:37
CHESSON:45
CHESUR:56
CHILDERS:28(2),41,42(2),
        87
CHILDRESS:36,40,61,62(3),
         66,67(2),68
CHILDRISS:12
CHILDS:68,76
CHILES:72,73,79
CHILTON:16(2),80(2)
CHINALT:52
CHINN:90
CHINNAULT:62
CHISHOLM:33,36
CHISLOM:23,65,79
CHISNAT:2
CHISNUT:2
CHISOLM:29,30
CHITWOOD:19,20,47,51,52
CHRISTIAN:21,27,31,39,44,

CHRISTIAN cont.:56
CHRISLER:35
CHURCH:44
CILDER:50
CILGORE:75
CILLERS:73
CILLS:73
CIRKLIN:73
CIRON:38
CLABO:47
CLACK:5,7,65,81
CLACKLEY:57
CLAGBURN:69(2)
CLAGHORN:62
CLAK:9
CLANAHAN:29
CLANTON:33,58
CLAPP:65
CLARK:1,15,16,20(2),26,
     43,48(2),56(2),60,
     61,62,70,79,87,88,
     91(2)
CLARKE:1,14,19,32,33,36,
      38(2),68,72
CLAUNCH:87
CLAY:16,18,22,27,49,54,
    76,90
CLAYTON:9,10,21,22(3),23,
       35,47,49(2),52,71
CLEASE:59
CLEAVELAND:42,43,46(2)
CLEGHORN:45
CLEMENS:18,19,26
CLEMENT:4,30
CLEMENTS:10(2),68,69
CLEVELAND:50
CLIANT:55
CLICK:83
CLIETT:27
CLIFTON:26,28,32(2),35(2)
CLINAS:35
CLINCH:52
CLINE:60(2)
CLOCK:46
CLONCH:41,87
CLOUD:75,78
CLOUGH:55(2),57
CLOWER:93(2)
CLOWERS:86
CLEGHORN:59
COAL:66,68,69(2)
COALMAN:68
COATES:15,33,37,50
COATS:10(3),15,34
COBB:6,14(2),15,18,27,29,
    37,39,65,84,91
COBERN:34(2)
COBEY:82
COBLER:12
COCKERSON:19
COCKRAN:10,16,35,37,82(4),
       83,87,88
COCKRAND:35(2)
COCKRELL:61,72
COCKROSS:54
COCKROSSE:54
COE:19,22
COFFEE:61(2),62,63
COFFEY:43(2)
COFFY:9
COFIELD:31
COFFMAN:35,37,39
COGBURN:59(2),68
COGGAN:35
COGGINS:29,31,62
COGWILL:76
COHAN:76
COHRAN:29
COKER:16,39,42,44(5),52,
     83(2),92
COLBERN:40,66
COLBURN:44
COLBY:1

iv

COLBURN:44
COLBY:1
COLE:2,5,13,46,54(2),57(2)
    60,71,79
COLEAU:58
COLEMAN:6,15,16,19,22,26,
    30,34,37,45(2),55,
    57,71,82,84,85(2),
    93
COLFER:84
COLIN:42
COLLERN:20
COLLEY:27,91(2)
COLIER:75,76
COLLIAR:13
COLLIER:24,33,37
COLLIN:47
COLLINS:4,8,23,32,33,36,
    48(2),59,63(3),
    72,76(2)
COLLINNS:33
COLLUM:89
COLQUEHAUR:77
COLQUIT:59,73
COLWELL:27,34,76(2)
COLYER:26,64
COMBS:23,38(2)
COMIERE:76
COMMELANDER:26
COMPTEN:80
COMPTON:17
CONALLY:70
CONANT:45
CONAWAY:66
CONDREY:2
CONDRY:1,8(2)
CONE:25,43,49
CONEL:54
CONGER:21
CONIFF:46
CONN:20(2),87
CONNALLY:61,64(2),66
CONNEL:55
CONNER:3,6,24,32,33,42,
    56,90
CONNERS:91
CONNOR:68,81,82
CONUS:5
CONWAY:74(3)
COOB:74
COOK:4,5,6(3),15,18,21,
    24,27,29,30(2),32,
    33,35,36,45,46,47,
    51(2),52,54,55(2),
    58,62,66,69,73,86,
    87
COOKSY:91
COOLEY:7,37
COONER:56,59
COOPER:2,3,4,27,33,42,44,
    45,46,47(4),48,50,
    61,63,66,76,82,
    85(2),86,91,92
COPELAND:16,26(2),31(2),
    32,61,69(2),80
COPEY:7
COPLAND:49
COPPORD:17
COR:79
CORBIN:43
CORBIT:42
CORDELL:61(2)
CORE:80
CORLEE:79(3)
CORLEY:26,68(3)
CORMACK:7,79(2)
CORNER:36
CORPREW:26,31
COSNIMS:69
COSTASNEY:58(2)
COSTON:5
COTHERN:38
COTNEY:92(2)

COTTEN:37,45,80,86(4)
COTTINGHAM:4,84
COTTON:3,5,28,30,36,42,
    71,74,79,84
COUCH:4,9,17
COULTER:92
COUNCIL:85,87
COUNSEL:16
COUPLAND:36
COUR:78
COURTLYNNE:37
COUSINS:54,55
COVINGTON:19,34,39,78
COWAN:1,2,10,33,34(2),
    66(2)
COWARD:43
COWART:2,3
COWEN:78
COWSAR:83
COX:3,8,20,29,35,47,56(3),
    64,65,73,78,79,84,86,
    89
COXE:67(2)
COZENS:24
CRADOC:3
CRADOCK:54
CRADDOCK:26,77,89
CRAFT:29,79
CRAGE:47,52
CRAIG:5,38,61(3),75
CRAIGHEAD:71
CRAIN:87
CRAM:46,50
CRAMP:16
CRANE:14,34(2),36,50,54
CRANFORD:42
CRAUD:48
CRAVEN:93
CRAVENS:89
CRAWFORD:1,7,29,33,38,55,
    74(2),76,84,85
CRAWLEY:54,68
CRAYTON:23
CREAL:2(2),8
CRECY:25
CREED:23
CREG:87
CRENSHAW:44
CRESLER:70
CRESWELL:88
CREWES:33,38(2)
CREWS:34
CRIM:57
CRIMMINS:45
CRIPS:66(2)
CRISTIE:21
CRISWELL:16,88
CRITESBURG:55
CRITTENDEN:24
CRITO:88
CROCKER:59
CROCKET:4
CROFT:24,26,35(2)
CROMBY:70
CROOK:16,17(2),69
CROPLAND:64
CROPKIN:47
CROSBY:1,68
CROSS:4,13(2),28,43
CROUCH:40,90
CROUSE:52
CROW:16(2),32(2),51(2),
    56,72,80,90
CROWDER:24,31(3)
CROWEL:75,78(2)
CROWNOVER:10,11,51,52(2)
CROWSLEY:70
CROWSON:43,71,86
CROZIER:13,33
CRUISE:4
CRUMP:50
CRUMPLER:42(3)
CRUMPTON:9,16,39

CRUTCHER:5,63
CRYER:62
CAUCH:6
CUCHESS:4
CUFNER:9
CULBERSON:24(2)
CULBERTSON:24
CULBETH:75
CULBREATH:63
CULLEN:42
CULLENS:72
CULLER:4
CULLINS:83
CULPEPPER:5,30,32,33,24
CULVER:62(2),63(3)
CUMLY:10
CUMMINGS:15(3),41,68
CUMMINS:81
CUNIGAM:55,57
CUNNINGHAM:3,11,12,15(3),
    16(2),22,32,47,
    49,51(5),52(3),
    60,69,82,83,87,
    88(2)
CURDEN:37
CURETON:77
CURIE:2
CURINCE:77
CURL:14
CURLEW:15
CURLEY:48
CURRIE:2(2),7
CURRIER:11,15,21
CURRIN:7
CURRINGTON:2,4(2)
CURRY:9,31,44,54,68,82,93
CURWELL:88
CUSE:68
CUSICE?:5
CUTHBRITT:75
DABBS:89(2)
DABNEY:68
DACEY:38
DAIL:87
DAILEY:89
DALE:1,12,13(2),46
DALLIS:76
DANBY:7
DANCE:75
DANDY:33
DANFORTH:2(2)
DANIEL:3(3),4,5(3),7,20,
    21,23,34,36,49,53,
    54,64,68,71,73(3),75,
    88,89
DANIELL:68
DAWKINS:74
DAWS:83
DAWSON:24,25,41,46,79
DAYMON:58
DANKLER:19
DANNIE:47
DANSBURY:16
DANSBY:6,7
DARBY:57
DARDEN:26,31,69,91
DARKINS:12
DARLEY:86
DARNELL:39
DARTHEL:16
DAUTFORD:31
DAVEAST:32
DAVENPORT:16,34,52,70
DAVIDSON:22,38,52,46,65,
    66,72,74
DAVIS:1,2,3,8,10,12,13,
    14(2),17,19,21(2),
    23,24,26(2),27,31,
    34(3),35,36,38(3),
    39,45,46(2),47(2),
    48,51(3),55(4),58,
    59,60(2),61(6),64,
    73,74,75(2),76,77(2)

DAVIS cont.:78,81(2),84
(2),89,91,
93(4)
DAY:2,5(2),27(2),34,35,
38(2),57,59(2),74
DEA:58
DEACON:48
DEAK:54
DEAL:54,71
DEAN:20(2),24,26,31,35,
37,38(2),39,46,58,
84,93
DEARING:38,73
DEARMAN:9(4),65
DEAROSSON:86
DEAS:54
DEASON:10,42,56,58
DEATON:16,47,52
DEBARDELEBBIN:75
DEBERRY:34
DEBMORE:70
DECKER:3
DEEL:84,86
DEES:85(4)
DEESE:30
DEFRUE:82
DEFUR:9
DEJARNETT:38
DELBRIDGE:56
DELLAH:68
DELOACH:5
DELOSEY:74
DELVIN:60
DEMPSEY:37
DENARD:5
DENMAN:38
DENNIS:24(2),51,60,87,90
DENNY:9
DENORES?:26
DENSKER:58
DENSLEY:58
DENSON:4,17,23,54
DENT:3,37,56,57,93
DEPREST:55
DEPRIEST:9(2)
DERETT:61(2)
DERHAYCE:85
DERICK:60,61,63,64(4),84
DERION:82
DERITY:80
DERKINS:12
DERRICK:63,66
DESHAZO:3,4(2),5
DESUMPER:50
DEVANPORT:54
DEVENPORT:57
DEVERAUX:54(3)
DEVINORE:16
DEW:45
DEWITT?:8
DIAL:16
DICE:50
DICKENSON:16,18
DICKEY:62,80
DICKINSON:34,44,92
DICKSON:7,30,31,33,36,66,
77(2),79(2)
DIFFY:11,14
DIGGINS:7
DILBECK:50
DILL:3,81
DILLARD:45,76,87,90(2),
91(2)
DINGLER:68
DISCON:85
DISMUKE:57
DISMUKES:26
DITTO:67
DITTS:48
DIXON:59,62,81
DOBB:12
DOBBS:49,80
DOBBINS:16,32,42

DOBS:10
DOBSON:32,57(2),70
DOCKERY:36
DOCKREY:39
DODD:17,13,62,85
DODDS:60
DODSON:9,13,16,80,81,82
DOGAN:38
DOGGEN:31
DOHERTY:33,34,35,36
DOLES:59(2)
DOLLAR:38,41,88
DONALD:56,93
DONALDSON:12,19,63,64,
72(4),88
DONEY:81
DONGAN:65
DONOHUE:8
DOOLEY:87(2)
DORMAN:6,28,73
DOROUGH:21
DORSET:23
DORSEY:73
DOSS:10,66,79
DOSSON:39
DOSTER:28,54,90
DOTON:52
DOTSON:75
DOTY:65
DOUGAN:64,66
DOUGLAS:25
DOUGLASS:48,62,71,80(2),
84
DOUGLE:72
DOUTHAL:12
DOUTHARD:13
DOVE:49
DOWD:77
DOWDEY:70
DOWDLE:12
DOWDY:9(2),21,70
DOWNESS:31
DOWNEY:38
DOWNING:16,41,44
DOWNS:26,28,60,72
DOYL:81
DOYLE:16
DOZIER:13,37
DRAIN:48
DRAKE:32(2),50(2),75
DRAKEFORD:55
DRAM:47(3)
DRENNON:74,85(2),86
DREW:40
DRINKARD:63(2),81
DRISCOL:48
DRISCOLL:49
DRISKEL:1
DRISKELL:55,88
DRISKILL:41,87
DRIVER:16,23,31,41,45,58,
84
DRUSICK:55
DRUTON:52
DRYER:93
DUAHOW:10
DUBERRY:69
DUBOIS:90
DUBOSE:2,3(2),4,5(2),6,8
DUCK:27
DUCKWORTH:48
DUDLEY:73,89(2),91
DUFFIE:93
DUGGAN:30
DUKE:18,27,48,52(2),68,79
DUKERSON:83
DUKES:58(2),59,72
DULANEY:80,84,87(3)
DULANY:16
DUMANE:33
DUN:55
DUNCAN:10,17,20,37,39,60,
64,70,79,80,92

DUNHAM:44(2),49
DUNKIN:64
DUNLAP:8,25
DUNMAN:36
DUNN:5,10(5),23,24,28,30,
34,35,37(3),39,60,81,
90,92(2)
DUNNIGAN:36
DUNNINGTON:28
DUPOISTER:30
DUPREE:38,77
DURAN:66
DURAND:92
DURANT:57(2)
DURHAM:75
DURHAJOU:80
DURHAM:8,28,29,75
DURRER:37
DUTTON:52
DWYER:82
DYE:66,82,84
DYER:26
DYKE:32
DYKES:1,5,8(2),26
DYSON:71
EADS:33
EADY:24,25
EALEY:54
EALSEY:91
EALY:54
EARLEY:87
EARLY:84
EARP:36,39
EASLEY:66
EASLY:14
EASON:23,66,92(2)
EAST:20,27,68(3),69,82,
93(2)
EASTERS:63
EASTERWOOD:27
EASTRIDGE:90
EATMAN:34
EATON:21
EAVES:30
ECCLES:55,57,59(2)
ECHOLS:6,26,27,33,43,46,
85,92
EDDINGS:93(2)
EDDINGTON:91,92
EDDY:56
EDEN:42
EDGE:5,9,26,27,28(2),78,83
EDGING:44
EDINGTON:61
EDLEMAN:91
EDMISTON:14,15
EDWARD:75,79
EDWARDS:9,20(2),25,32(2),
35(2),37(4),43,
49(2),50(3),52,65,
68,69,73,76,77,79,
80(2),81,85,86,89,
92
EFRID:6
EFIRT:6
EIDSON:87
EKINGTON:21
ELAM:38
ELDER:36
ELEOTH:83
ELEY:90
ELGIN:63
ELI:59
ELIOT:74
ELKIN:78(2)
ELKINS:27,77
ELLARD:15,87
ELLASON:20,21
ELLEDY:52
ELLIOTT:1,12(4),19,20,
40(3),70,77,83,84
ELLIS:3,4,5,18,25,48,49(3)
50,59,60,71,75,76,

ELLIS cont.:90(3)
ELLISON:9,15,17,27,46,65
ELMO:4
ELMOR:5
ELMORE:2,20,24,55
ELROD:83
ELSEY:51(2)
ELSTON:9(2)
ELSTORE:83
ELTAN:73
ELYOT:4
EMARY:1
EMBERSON:44
EMBREE:41
EMBREY:87(3)
EMRY:60,63,88
EMERSON:6,33
EMERY:65
ENFINGER:75(2)
ENGLAND:16,32,36,61
ENGLISH:57,81,82(2)
ENNIS:19(2),76
ENSLEN:45
EPMAN:45
EPPERSON:89
EPPS:12
ERVIN:26
ERWIN:43
ESPY:43
ESTELL:11
ESTERS:56
ESTES:21,26,31,51,59
ESTILL:81
ETHERIDGE:41
ETHRIDGE:44
EUBANKS:11(2)
EURY:50
EUSN:16
EVAN:65
EVANS:5,7,20,21,24,33,34,
    40,47,54,60,61,62(2)
    63,65,72,75,77,79,
    82(2),83(2),86,90
EVENS:26
EVERETT:52
EVERIT:58,59
EVES:50
EVETT:63
EWEING:30
EWTON:36
EZELL:10
EZZELL:21
FADYERS:8
FAG:57
FAGAN:33,45,81,82
FAGANS:20
FAILES:68
FAIN:45
FAINSTER:66
FAIRCLOTH:8
FAIRES:82
FAISON:6
FAITH:60
FALKNER:70(2),71,72(3)
FANE:83
FANNING:26
FANNINGTON:31
FANSHER:88
FANT:80,82
FARGASON:93
FARIS:86
FARISH:38
FARRIS:30,34
FARISS:55,63
FARIT:82,83
FARLEY:27
FARLY:2
FARMER:7,8(2),27,39,73,74
FARRAR:13
FARROW:74
FARES:75
FARRIOR:5,7
FASON:6

FATHEMS:23
FAUGHSEND?:13
FAUKNER:30
FAULK:3,5,6(2),7(7),79,89
FAULKENBERG:57
FAULKNER:33,34,36,59
FAVOR:39,86,89
FEAGAN:6
FEAN:4
FEARS:31
FEASLE:87
FEATHERSTON:52,70
FEEMSTER:63
FEENEY:31
FELLOWS:37
FEMELE:31
FENDLESON:54
FENDLEY:30
FENLEY:40
FENN:29
FENNELL:61,65,91
FENNER:37
FERGISON:73
FERGUSON:19,39,43,81,85(2)
FERRELL:69(2)
FERRIL:59
FERRILL:26
FERRINGTON:34
FIELD:2,25(2)
FIELDER:26(2),31,34(2),
    40,74,93
FIELDS:16,28,49,63,66
FILE:6
FILES:57
FINCH:22,26,32
FINCHER:16,68,70(2),72,92
FINDER:49
FINDLAY:49
FINDLEY:23,30
FINER:47,49
FINGER:54
FINKES:47
FINLAYSON:42
FINLEY:14,20(2),28,29(2),
    40,44,55,62,64(3),
    66,67
FINN:15,82
FINNEY:28,44
FINRESTONE:38
FISHBURN:75
FISHER:46
FISLAS:52
FITTEN:24
FITZER:39
FITZGERALD:46
FITZPATRICK:25,26,54,55(3)
FLAKE:3,5,79,92
FLANAGAN:23,40
FLANIGAN:19,56,59
FLASS?:89
FLEINKRN:50
FLEMING:33,84
FLEMMING:11(2),12,44,45,
    46,59
FLETCHER:22,24,50,60,61,
    65(2)
FLEULLEN:65
FLIN:71
FLOID:79
FLORENCE:77,93
FLORNOY:3
FLOURNOY:3,23,57,92
FLOWERS:1
FLOYD:4(2),9,22,25,26(2),
    83
FLUMERS:4
FLURNOY:8,31
FLUTING:34
FLYNN:88
FOLLIER:78
FOLSOM:4,8
FONNAN:85
FONSE:62(2)

FONTAINE:48
FORBES:25
FORCUE:43
FORD:6(2),13,26,41,88(2),
    87(2)
FOREHAND:3
FOREMAN:14,23,86
FORGASON:25(2)
FORGUSON:26
FORMAN:80,81,86,87(2),88
FORMBY:25
FORNEY:11
FORSHEE:27,44,89
FORSHEL:85(2)
FORSYTH:51,56
FORT:5
FORTENBERRY:19
FORTNER:77
FORTSON:5
FORTUNE:27,49,77
FOSCUE:43(2)
FOSTA:34
FOSTER:11(2),18,20,31(2),
    33,46,59,61,71,74,
    76,79,84
FOUCH:4
FOUSTER:71
FOWLER:15,32,36,41(3),68,
    76,81,90
FOX:46
FRALEY:8
FRANCE:57
FRANCHAM:5
FRANCIS:11,53,83
FRANELL:49
FRANKLIN:30,43,51,52,76,
    83,84
FRANKS:87
FRASER:5(2)
FRASHER:88
FRASIE:47
FRASURE:47(2)
FRAXIL:52
FRAZIER:32,64,71(2),78
FREDERICK:23
FREELAND:61
FREEMAN:21,23(2),24,25,
    55(2),59,63,69,
    77,93
FREMAND:62
FRENCH:13,51,84,87
FRETWELL:23
FRIERE:80
FIFFINSIDES:52
FRIOR:46
FROST:3,11,37,48,80
FRUIT:49
FRY:37,62,66,67(3)
FRYER:90
FUCKER:49
FUGLE:47
FUGRESON:72
FULCHER:71
FULKS:17
FULLER:24,25,30,35(2),48,
    77,84,91,92
FULLINGAME:14(2)
FULTON:45
FURENTINE:48
FUNDERBIRK:57
FUNDERBURGH:80,82,85(2),88
FUNDERBURK:44
FUNSTEN:49
FURGASON:4,23,24,25,89
FURGESON:49(3),50(2),61
FURGUSON:3
FURLOW:62(2)
GACHET:6
GADDIS:9,41,58,61
GADDY:49,81,86
GAGE:34
GAHAGAN:89
GAILBREATH:63

GAINES:9,18,27,54
GAINEY:13(2),55
GAILAND:12
GAINS:9(3),82
GAITER:64(2)
GAITHER:46,89
GALBREATH:7
GALLAHER:16
GALLATIN:17
GALLOWAY:1,42,64,92,93
GALTEN:81
GAMBLE:33,36,87
GAMBREL:52
GAMBRELL:31
GAMILION:74
GAMMELL:25
GAMMELS:25
GAMMOCK:91
GAN:22
GANDY:24
GANN:39
GANSS:12
GANT:26(2),33,35,36,74
GANTT:28
GARDNER:27(2),45,46,52,57,
77,92
GAREY:80
GARLAND:60(3)
GARMESON:66
GARNER:7,39,74(3),76
GARNETT:36,46,73
GARRAWAY:83
GARREL:73
GARRET:22(2),
GARRETSON:29
GARRETT:12,22,24,30,32(2),
33(2),34,35,36,39,
48,50,51,61,64,65,
66(2),71,76,87(3)
GARROTT:14
GARRISON:49,61,69,72
GARTMAN:58
GARVIN:54
GASET:59
GASKELL:84(2)
GASKIN:39
GASSAWAY:51
GASSOWAY:51
GASTON:46
GATES:30,57,69
GATING:78
GAUGHT:5
GAULK:74
GAULDELONG:5
GAULMAN:25
GAUTNEY:62
GAY:6,19,27(2),68,90
GAYLOR:33
GEDRY:73
GEE:66
GELASPY:68
GELHOURN:75
GENNEL:21
GENTRY:43,52,85,89
GEORGE:2,5,13(2),27,65,87
GERBO:77
GERIT:82
GERMAN:28
GERMANY:27,28(2),59,54,
55(2)
GESHER:10
GIBBENS:4
GIBBINS:2
GIBHART:5
GIBSON:5,6,10,17(2),24,
39,48,51(3),73,84,
90
GIDDINS:4
GIDEON:27
GIE:58
GIFFETT:38
GIFFIN:43
GIGSEY:55

GIL:57
GILAND:50
GILBERT:17(2),22,33(2),
70,75,79
GILBREATH:38,49(4),50(2),
51,63
GILCHRAST:5
GILDER:24,55,59
GILES:23,34,79,92
GILIAN:50
GILILAND:68
GILKISON:19
GILL:15,46,81
GILLAM:89,93
GILLAND:48
GILLAS:86
GILLELAND:27
GILLESPIE:47
GILLEY:52
GILLIAM:33,36
GILLILAND:49(2),80,90
GILLINWATER:4
GILLIS:2,8(2),46,55
GILLMAN:33
GILLY:43
GILMAN:7
GILMORE:25(2),27,33
GINDRAT:55
GINKS:58,59(2)
GINN:25,45
GINNINGS:58(2)
GINYARD:49
GIPSON:21,60,64,74(2)
GIST:25
GIVENS:13,16
GIVINS:81,82
GLADDEN:16,55
GLADNEY:68(2),70,71
GLANDS:76
GLASCOCK:44,64
GLASCOW:54
GLASS:3
GLAYSNER:49
GLEATON:55(2)
GLEN:57,58
GLENN:3,5,14,68
GLOVER:2,3,13(3),24,33(2)
37,66,72
GOBBLE:64
GOBER:21
GODDARD:33
GODFREY:77
GODWIN:1,73,77,90
GOFORTH:62
GOGGAN:52
GOGGANS:48
GOGGINS:27,31,41,80
GOINGS:78
GOLDEN:26(3),55,63,66,
74(2),93
GOLDING:45,90
GOLDMAN:69
GOLDSMAN:30
GOLDSMITH:23,24,25,26(2)
GOLIGHTLY:34(2)
GOOD:28
GOODGAME:41(2),42,84(2),
85
GOODE:57
GOODLETT:11
GOODMAN:23,37,42,68,85,69
GOODMIN:72
GOODNEY:47
GOODSON:39
GOODWIN:24(2),27,48,58,
65,84,85,88(2),
91(2),69
GOOLSBY:1,90
GOOS:29
GORDIN:58
GORDON:30
GORDY:75
GORE:6,12,17

GORIN:85
GORRES:71
GOSA:14
GOSS:60
GOSSET:21
GOSSETT:36
GOULDING:45,81,82(2)
GOVER:83,84
GRADY:13,25,29(3),31,34,
49,51
GRAGG:27
GRAHAM:1(2),9,10(2),12(3),
15,18,19(3),21,32,
41,42(5),43,44(2),
45,51(2),57(2),81,
83(2),84,93
GRAHM:56
GRAMMAR:65
GRANT:7,11,12,22
GRANBERRY:79
GRANBURY:4
GRANTHAM:3,84
GRAS:59
GRAVES:3,28,33,34,42,63,
77
GRAVIS:86
GRAVY:27
GRAY:3,26,29(2),31(2),36
(2),41,44,45(2),49,
74,80,81,83,93(2)
GRAYHORN:79
GRAYSON:60
GREEG:31
GREEN:8,12,28,31,33,35(2),
37(3),39,40,41,46,
47,57,58,61(2),63,
64,68(2),70,73(3),
78,79,87,88,91,92
GREENE:11,12(2),16,17
GREENLEE:11
GREENWOOD:6,41,48,59
GREER:91(2),93
GREEWAY:59
GREGG:18
GREGORY:20,24,29,30
GRESHAM:69,72
GREY:92
GRIER:24,44
GRIFFIN:14,16,17,18(4),20,
22,33(2),36,42,45,
47(3),57,64(3),66,
68,76,68,69,80,86,
87,91,92,93
GRIFFIS:4
GRIFFETH:64
GRIFFETT:38
GRIFFITH:10,31,33,26,81
GRIFFON:38
GRIGERY:52
GRIGG:78
GRIGGS:6,36,38,59
GRIGORY:57,63
GRIGSBY:26
GRIMES:1,3,20(2),42,78
GRIMMETT:34
GRIMSLEY:26
GRINNIT:58
GRISHAM:23,31,35,44
GRISSEL:8,57
GRISSOM:56,62
GRIST:17
GRIZZELL:38,58(2)
GROGAN:34(2)
GROM:73
GROSS:61,91
GRUBBS:7(2),18,20(2),34,85
GRUMBLES:55
GRYMES:24
GUDDEN:55
GUESS:51,52
GUEST:17
GUIN:58
GUINN:87

GULDER:92
GULLEDGE:42,78
GULLION:63
GUNIGHAM:24
GUNN:2,3,23,26(2),30
GUNNERSON:1
GUPPIN:36
GURLEY:45
GUTHERY:10
GUTHRE:1
GUTHRIE:26,35,37,83
GUY:79
GUYLER:48(2)
GWINN:85
HACKER:42
HACKNEY:90
HACKLY:79
HADDOCK:73
HADEN:11,33,57(2),58(3)
HADLEY:31
HADNOT:58
HADFAIR:85
HAFFORD:12
HAGAN:14,41,42
HAGERTY:42,45(3),72
HAGGARD:83
HAGLER:18,85
HAGOOD:17,25(2),27,30
HALCOM:80
HALE:22,33,34,35,39(2),54
       65,81
HALEY:51
HALL:1(3),2,5,11,14,17,
      18(2),24,30,32(2),
      34,36,38,42(2),47,
      48,51(2),75(2),76(2),
      77,79,80,81,83(2),
      85,91,92
HALLMAN:7,37
HALLMARK:84,85
HALSEY:29,75
HAM:1,2,63(2)
HAMBLEN:25
HAMBLETON:53
HAMBRICK:27,28
HAMBRIGHT:11,15,34,39
HAMBY:17,27,89(2),90,92
HAMER:48
HAMET:21(3)
HAMIL:73
HAMILTON:15,37(2),40,41(2)
          45,46,61,64,67
HAMIT:48
HAMLIN:14
HAMMER:41
HAMMERS:89
HAMMETT:86
HAMMIL?:1
HAMMOCK:8,31(3),77,78
HAMMON:47
HAMMOND:31(2),36,52(2),
         80(2),91
HAMMONDS:33
HAMMONS:48,84
HAMMONTREE:86
HAMP:87
HAMPTON:16,17(2),32,39,65
HAMNER:66(3)
HANBY:64
HANCOCK:7,23,25,26(4),31,
         75
HAND:30
HANDCOCK:80
HANDY:11
HANES:32,61,68
HANEY:8,31,61,77,78(2),82
      86,87,88
HANIS:48
HANK:13
HANKINS:47,48,49,80
HANLEY:9
HANNA:15(2),45,91
HANNAH:72,87

HANNER:51
HANNERS:69
HANNON:34,43
HANSFORD:46
HANSE:89
HANSON:1,31,68
HAPE:54
HARABLE:24
HARALSON:89
HARBIN:89
HARBOW:12
HARCROW:68,69
HARDAWAY:78
HARDEN:23,59,78,89,90,93
HARDMAN:1
HARDEY:92
HARDIE:83
HARDIN:1,5,6,15,19,81
HARDWICK:18,78
HARDWICKE:37(3)
HARDY:2,17,28,42,43,44(2)
       56,57,59(2)
HARE:59,81
HAREMAN:33
HARGROVE:16,78
HARGROVES:2
HARGSONER:49
HARGUS:44
HARIES?:83
HARIS:74(2),75,76,78
HARISON:56,73
HARISS:49
HARKIN:35
HARKINS:68,92
HARLAN:91
HARLAND:87(2)
HARLEY:63
HARLIN:40
HARLTON:32
HARMELTON:68
HARMON:27,43,80,88
HARN:83
HARPER:2,5,6,8,17,18,23,
       36(2),56,58,59(2),
       61,64,66,68,70,80,
       81,93
HARRAL:91
HARRIS:3,9(2),10,11(2),
       12,13(2),15(2),16,
       17,20,23(4),26(2),
       30,31(3),32,37,
       39(2),41(2),44,46
       (2),53,54,55(3),
       56,58(2),64,66,68,
       70,71(3),72(2),76,
       79,81,82,83,87,88,
       90,91,92(2)
HARRISON:1(2),2,3(2),15,
         28,40,44,48(2),
         49,58(2),61,73,
         81,85(3),86,
         88(2)
HARRIST:30(2)
HARRISTON:11
HARREL:24(2),25,29
HARRELL:25,42(2),43,75,
        80
HARRELSTON:27
HARRINGTON:26,51(2),72
HARROD:57
HARRY:30,78
HART:20,64
HARTEFIELD:68
HARTLINE:38
HARTLY:74
HARTT:90
HARTWELL:82
HARTY:22
HARVEL:34
HARVILL:57
HARVY:73
HARWELL:30(2),37,43,44(2)
        46,55,76,82,83(3)

HASKERSON:35
HASSETT:49
HASKINS:77,92
HASNER:15
HASSAN:44
HASTEN:62
HASTING:96
HASTY:48,83
HATAWAY:45
HATCH:64
HATCHER:18,44
HATCHETT:43(2),63
HATFIELD:19
HATHCO(P)X:76,79
HATHHORN:55
HATHORN:54,68
HATON:20
HATTAN:45
HATTERWAY:56
HATTON:13,71
HAUGH:25
HAUGHTON:59
HAVERSON:71
HAW:6
HAWK:52
HAWKINS:5,24(2),33,48,52,
        75
HAWKS:77
HAWS:47,78
HAWTHORN:45,69(2)
HAY:26,69
HAYDEN:44
HAYES:19,36
HAYNES:11,18,41(2),45(2),
       86
HAYS:2,3,4,5,6(2),18,28,
     47,50,66,73,79,80,
     81(2)
HAYWARD:79
HAZARD:54
HEACOCK:80
HEAD:2,8,27,52
HEADEN:45
HEADON:68
HEALE:64
HEALEY:26
HEARD:52,69,87,89
HEARN:7,72,78,86(2)
HEARNE:63
HEART:22
HEARTSUGG:1
HEASLIP:86(3)
HEASTERLY:63
HEATH:2,27,28,71,74
HEATON:15(2),19
HEDGE:73
HEDMAN:69
HEDGES:61
HEDSPETH:26
HEELEY:68
HEERIN:75
HEFFLEN:68
HEFFLIN:6
HEFNER:34,37,38
HELEMS:1
HELM:14
HELMES:39
HELMS:36(2)
HELTON:65
HEMMING:90
HENDESIN:19
HENDERSON:12,19(2),26,31,
          33(2),34,35,36,
          37,38,51,52,
          56(2),57,73,75,
          78,80,81,83,
          84(2),85(3),
          89(5),90(2),92
HENDIX:49
HENDON:68
HENDRIC:19(2)
HENDRICK:72,83
HENDRICKS:81

ix

HENDSAN:19
HENDSON:84
HENK:21
HENLY:4
HENLEY:13,
HENRY:5,9,11,27,28(2),41,
    63,65(2),81,85
HENSLEE:34(2),37(2)
HENSLEY:39
HENSON:52(3),55,60,70,71
    (3),72,78,93
HENSSEY:81
HERD:16,20,84
HERINGTON:56
HERNDON:11
HERON:59
HERRELL:84
HERREN:71
HERRIN:32,33,65,66
HERRING:2,3,5(2),6,8,90(2)
    93
HERROD:2
HERRON:2,23,60(2),66
HESTER:11(2),15,52,68,69,
    82
HESTERLEY:84
HESTERN:63
HETTON:45
HEWIT:58
HEWLIN:56
HEWLIT:58
HICKEY:75,76,79,66
HICKMAN:2,37,63,91,42
HICKS:2,30,51,75,43,47
HIGDEN:60
HIGDON:65
HIGGINBOTHAM:92
HIGGINBOTTOM:26,71
HIGGINS:38,60(2),66
HIGH:35(2)
HIGHTOWER:69(2),93(2),22,
    23,78
HILER:47
HILL:3,6,13,18,20(2),25,
    30,33(2),39,42,46,
    50,51,52,55,61,67(2)
    60(2),61,74,76,80,
    82,85(6),86(3),22,
    45,59
HILLE:6
HILLER:23
HILLS:51
HILTON:18
HIND:8
HINDMAN:11,26
HINES:1,11(5),15(2),63(4),
    75,53
HINKLE:80
HINSON:39,54,73
HINTEN:37
HINTON:14
HIPP:39
HIRD:10(2)
HITCHCOCK:79
HITSON:2
HITT:60
HIX:26(2),59,54
HOBBS:81,87,86,50
HOBDAY:42
HOBDY:8
HODGE:22(3),23,69,71,22(2)
HODGES:8,18,22,34,38,40,
    58,78
HOFF:36
HOGAN:21,70,82,88(2),42
HOGE:15,39,48,49
HOGG:33
HOGUE:62
HOKE:11,13(2)
HOLCOLM:51
HOLCOMBE:20,34,50,12
HOLDEN:47,56
HOLEFIELD:26

HOLIDAY:75
HOLIFIELD:72
HOLINSHEAD:36
HOLKINS.74
HOLLAND:1,2,5,8,15,29,62,
    73,74(2),77,50
HOLLANDSWORTH:54
HOLLEDAY:30
HOLLEY:34,84,86,87,89(2)
HOLLIDAY:26,29,30,31
HOLLIMAN:8
HOLLINS:7,11
HOLLINGSWORTH:11,12,13,20
HOLLIS:30,31,84
HOLLMAN:3
HOLLOWAY:39,77
HOLLY:8,11,37,62,87,89
HOLMAN:30,44,45,52
HOLMES:7,8(4),11
HOLMS:11
HOLOMAN:78
HOLOWAY:25,32,70
HOLSEY:29
HOLSTEN:30
HOLSTIN:6
HOLSTON:25,28(4),29
HOLSTUN:30
HOLT:3,5,26(5),59,65(2)
HOLTON:91
HOLTZCLAW:24
HOLYFIELD:13
HONEY:13(3),37
HONEYCUTT:10,33,49
HOOD:29(2),30,48,50,74,93
HOOKER:23
HOOKS:2,27,54(2)
HOOLE:1
HOOPER:10(2),11,20,23,37,
    39
HOOTEN:73
HOPE:38,67
HOPKINS:2,22,73,90
HOPSON:20,71
HORN:76
HORNBUCKLE:62(2)
HORNER:11
HORTON:6,10(2),11,19,22,
    23,24,26,38,46,47,
    49(2),55,59,79
HOSEY:86(2)
HOSLEY:9
HOTNEY:28
HOTZLAW:31
HOUGH:54
HOUGHTON:46
HOUSE:24,28,34,37,38,46,
    52,56,68,70,72
HOUSTON:59,81(2),83(2),
    84,86
HOUZE:31(2)
HOWARD:1,3,9,23,26,27,30,
    42,51,55,58(2),66,
    71(3),72,75,76(2),
    78,90(2)
HOWEARD:30
HOWEL:60
HOWELL:8(2),12,14,18,20
    (3),29(2),33,35,
    42,50,52,66,72(5),
    81,89
HOWELTON:27
HOWLE:23
HOYATE:19
HOYLE:18,65
HUBBARD:14,25,46,87(2)
HUBBART:81
HUCKNEY:29
HUCKSON:50
HUDAMAN:27
HUDDLESTON:69
HUDDON:56
HUDGINS:32,36,91
HUDMAN:26,28,29,45

HUDNAL:58
HUDSON:18,23,38,66,70(3),
    78(2),85,93
HUEY.13,42(2),80
HUFF:35,36,52,79
HUFFMAN:25,69
HUFFNAKER:35
HUFFSTUTTER:53
HUFMAN:58
HUGGINS:33,39
HUGHES:17,18,32(3),35,37
    (3),39(2),41,43(2)
HUGHEY:31
HUGHS:14,15,21,32,62,64,
    82(2),89
HUGINS:28
HULER:47(4)
HULL:38,71,72(2)
HUMBER:68
HUMBOARD:47
HUMPHRIES:29,37,50,78,89
HUNNALY:45
HUNNECUT:70
HUNNICUT:90
HUNT:12,73,74,92
HUNTER:2,7,25(2),26,27,58,
    76,81,89
HURD:23
HURLEY:32,39(3),44
HURN:75
HURRAGE:34
HURST:26,70(2),73,74
HURT:78(4)
HUSE:47(4),65
HUSKERSON:33,40(2)
HUSSEY.28(2)
HUSTOLLS:49
HUTCHINSON:7,88,91,92
HUTCHISON:24,78
HUTSON:5(2),18,19,74
HUTTEN:86
HUTTO:92
HYATT:19(2),85
INGERSALL:77
INGHAM:31
INGLE:50(3)
INGRAM:10,15,16,62,68,69,
    72,75,76,78,79(2),
    89,90
INNMAN:86
INZER:83
IRVING:91
ISBEL:64(2),83
ISBELL:16,53
ISELL:10
ISLEN:56
ISRAEL:35
IVERSON:59
IVEY:27(2)
IVY:4,35,61,65,78(2)
JACK:35,38,81,82
JACKS:35
JACKSON:1,2,3,4(2),5(4),
    10(2),17,19,25(2),
    27(2),29,34,35(2),
    37,38(2),39,47,52,
    54,56(2),58(2),69,
    73,74,77,78,89,91
JACOBS:5,31,52,80
JAGS:51
JAMES:2,26,30,44(2),45,51,
    55,56,84,85,86(2),
    92
JAMIESON:84
JAMISON:22,80
JARMAN:89
JARRETT:72
JARVIS:22,26,27(2)
JARRELL:74
JEARN:6
JEATER:80
JEFFRIES.17
JELKS:73,75

JENKINS:6,18(4),82,84
JENNINGS:18,37,45,46,56,
    70,89
JEOFFS:45
JERNIGAN:3,4(2),5
JERRING:6
JET:50
JETER:24,27,29(3),57
JETIE:6
JETT:38,78,81
JIMERSON:86
JINKS:58
JINNINGS:59
JOB:65
JOBETH:55
JOHNS:7,22(2),68,69,72,74
JOHNSON:2(2),3(6),4,6,7,
    12(2),13(2),14(2),
    15,17,20(2),23(2),
    24,25,26(3),27(2),
    29(4),30(2),31(2),
    32,33,35(2),36,
    37(2),38(3),40(2),
    42(2),43(2),44,
    47(2),48,49,50,
    51,56,61(3),62,63,
    64(3),65(3),66,67,
    69,73(2),74(2),
    75(5),76(2),78(4),
    89(2),90(2),91(6),
    92(2),93(2)
JOHNSTON:10,11(3),13,30
    (2),54(2),55(2),
    57(2),58,59,62,
    80(2),82,84,86
    (2),87(2)
JOINER:4,45,72
JONAS:15
JONES:4(2),7(2),10,11(3),
    12,15,16,19(2),22
    (2),23,25,26(7),
    28(3),27,29,30,31(2)
    32,38,39,40,42(2),
    43(5),44(3),45,47,
    49(3),50,51,55(2),
    56(3),58,59(3),60
    (2),61(6),62,63(2),
    65(3),66,68,69,71,
    72(2),73(2),75(2),
    76,80,82,83(2),84,
    85(3),87,88,91(4),
    93(4)
JORDAN:12,17,20(2),41,44,
    54(3),59,63,86(2),
    89,90(2)
JORDEN:74,75,76
JORDON:68,69,83
JOURDAN:25(2),26,30,92
JOURDIN:28
JOWERS:69
JOY:35
JOYCE:75
JOYNER:76
JUMPER:44(2)
JUSTICE:5
KAREKINS:81
KASKEY:54
KAY:2,39
KEADEHAMER:54
KEAHEY:83
KEARNES:3
KEATERS:81
KEENER:8,48,50,54(2)
KEETON:35
KEIGS:63
KEITH:16,32,45,50,91,93(2)
KELLAM:93
KELLER:21
KELLERSON:26
KELLEY:55,59,66(2),81,84,
    87
KELLY:8,10,11,13(2),16(2),
    17,20(2),23,28,35,

KELLY cont.:38,41,43(3),
    51,62,75,84
KELLUM:31,79
KELSO:63
KELY:54
KEMBLE:13
KEMP:10,19(3),24,29,50,
    52,55,90
KENADAY:75(3)
KENADY:3,6(2),19,22
KENARD:68(2)
KENDADY:6
KENDAL:26
KENDRICK:27,80
KENDRICKE:82
KENDRIE:22
KENEDY:9,23
KENIBREW:93(2)
KENMORE:76(2)
KENNADA:26
KENNADY:64
KENNAMON:62
KENNAMORE:60(8)
KENNEDAY:38
KENNEDY:15(3),20(3),24,
    32(2),33,35,44,
    45,66,67,68,70(2)
    80,87(2)
KENNERLY:80
KENNEYMORE:79
KENNINGTON:5
KENSEY:23
KENT:3,37,72,76
KENUM:19
KERKLEY:70(2)
KERKSEY:54
KERR:10,71,87
KESLING:17
KESS:20
KETCHUM:7
KEY:23,56,58,61
KIBBER:78
KID:71
KIDD:23,45
KIDWELL:58
KIER:13
KIETH:81(2)
KILCHINS:66
KILCREAST:59
KILEREALT:55
KILFOYLE:66
KILGORE:14,26,83,90
KILLABREW:26
KILLIAN:51(2)
KILLINGWORTH:3
KILLOUGH:80,81,86(4)
KILPATRICK:5,8,69,87(2)
KIMBALL:89,91
KIMBELL:34
KIMBREL:45
KIMBRELL:81
KIMBROUGH:89,90
KINCAID:40
KINDRED:75,78
KINDREN:73
KINDRIC:73
KINDRICK:42
KINER:3,5
KING:6,7,8(2),10,20(2),
    24,32,38,48,50,51,
    52,55(2),62,63(2),
    64,66(2),74(2),76,
    77,78,84,88(2),90
KINGAID:84
KINGKADE:24
KINSEY:30
KIRKENDALL:40
KIRKLAND:1(2),61,65(2),
    83,89,92
KIRKLEY:81
KIRKPATRICK:2,6,9
KIRKSEY:63,66,93
KITCHENS:93

KITE:65(2)
KNIGHT:8,28,69,72,76,88,
    91,92,93
KNORS:83
KNOTT:87
KNOWLES:71,74
KNOX:28,31,88,91
KRAFT:35
KUPS:87
KUTS:7
KYLE:46
LACEY:26,49
LACKEY:10,15,21,83,92
LACY:28,39,49,75
LAGRONE:84
LAID:2
LAIN:12
LAIRD:11
LAJURIE:84
LAKE:71
LAMAR:5
LAMB:34,41,69(5),84
LAMBERT:10,16,19,22,72,
    83(2),86,88,92
LAMEASTER:39
LAMPKIN:49
LAMSTER:65
LANCASTER:7,71
LANCE:43
LAND:58,92
LANDERS:10(2),52
LANDON:39
LANDRUM:3,7,34
LANE:10(2),83,84,87
LANEY:26,28,56,76,77,78,
    89
LANFORD:56,59
LANG:6,22
LANGFORD:59,89
LANGLEY:29,89,91
LANGLY:24(4)
LANGSTON:26
LANIER:45,49,70,77
LANKFORD:40(2),49,51,52(2)
LANSDAL:9
LANSDALE:81
LANSDEL:9,21
LANTRIP:16
LANTRON:9
LANTSIS:16
LAPAN:55
LAPRADE:45
LAPUST:51
LARD:88
LARKINS:55
LARLEY:55
LAROE:81
LARRISON:12
LARSESENT:79(3)
LARTON:56
LASAGE:20
LASETER:61
LASLEY:54
LASONBY:55
LASOR:65,74
LASSETER:90
LASSITTER:78
LASTER:7
LASTON:47
LATHAM:47
LATIMORE:68,72
LAUDERDALE:41(4),90
LAUFOR:52
LAUGHLIN:20(2)
LAURENCE:55,56,58(2)
LAURIE:33
LAUSON:76
LAUTER:54(2),56
LAVENDER:8
LAW:29,60(3),61,64
LAWHON:23
LAWLER:36,84,85,86
LAWRENCE:29,31,35(3),74,

xi

LAWRENCE cont.:79,80
LAWSON:11,17,24,28,35,
    47(2),56,81(3),82,
    89,90
LAY:34,36(2)
LAYMAN:35
LAYSE:11
LAYTON:54,91
LEA:39,41(2),42(2),45
LEABOW:92
LEACH:18,20,92
LEAK:44
LEALAND:5
LEAR:88
LEARS:77
LEARLEY:81
LEATH:11(3),32(2),87
LEATHERWOOD:11,14,33
LEBAN:24
LEBIN:13(2)
LEDBETTER:1,19,20,42,69
    (2),75,83,84,
    87,89,93
LEDFORD:86
LEDLOW:92(2)
LEE:4(2),6(2),7,8(3),17
    (3),18,22(4),27,29,
    30(2),31,32,33,35,38,
    40,42,48,51,58,60(2),
    62(2),63,68,69(2),72
    (2),81(3),83(2),85,86,
    87(2),92(2),93
LEFEW:64
LEFTWICH:80
LEGALE:82
LEGAR:77
LEGARE:78
LEGG:32,38
LEGGET:73
LEGGITT:39
LEGRAND:57
LEITH:34
LEMON:48,49
LENDVILLE:72
LENNAHAN:12
LENOARD:2
LEOPARD:41,70(3),76
LEROY:47
LERVENT:79
LESICER:76
LESLEY:83
LESTER:75,85,93
LETCHER:85
LETT:11
LEUPEN:88
LEVAN:78
LEVERET:24
LEVERETT:68,75
LEVERTON:59
LEVERITT:87
LEVI:86
LEWIS:1,2(2),3,4,5(2),6
    (2),8,11(2),15,16
    (2),17,18,19(3),26,
    32,34(4),38,41(5),
    43(2),46,47,48,58,
    64(2),65(2),70,73
    (4),75,76,78,80,
    84(2),86,90
LIGHTFOOT:43
LIGHTNER:5
LIGHTSEY:86
LIGON:24
LIKENS:84
LILLE:11
LILLEY:61
LILLY:39
LILMAN:14(2)
LINDLEY:11
LINLEY:12
LINDSAY:30,28,84
LINDSEY:4,6,25,30,43,85(2)
LINNY:26

LINSAY:69
LINSEY:83
LIPHAM:42
LIPSCOMB:8
LIPSEY:75
LISENBE:58
LITLE:28
LITTLE:2,10(3),17(2),18,
    34,42,47,48,63,66,
    88
LITTLEFIELD:17(2),49,50
LITTLEJOHN:81(2)
LIVELY:45
LIVINSTON:26
LIVINGSTON:42,45,51,76
LIVLY:12
LIZMORE:52
LLOYD:14(2),17
LOCK:76
LOCKE:5
LOCKLAY:4
LOCKLER:28
LOCKETT:62
LOCKHART:73,79
LOCKLY:4(2)
LOCKS:92
LOCKWELL:79
LOCKWOOD:90
LOE:58
LOFTEN:26
LOFTIN:35,46,90
LOFTIS:58
LOFTON:26
LOGAN:11(2),17,24,43(4),
    46,65,79,80
LONG:3,6,34,48(2),63,68,
    73,79,84(2),85,86(3)
LONGSTREET:45
LOONEY:44,49,61
LOOPER:39(2)
LOOSER:28
LORENZ:82
LORINAS:52
LORTEN:56
LOT:9
LOTT:10(3),28(2)
LOVE:13,16(2),17,26,33,
    36,45,62,77,90
LOVEJOY:45(3),46
LOVELACE:5(2)
LOVELADY:47
LOVELESS:5,66,89(2),91
LOVEN:69
LOVETT:83
LOVINGS:49
LOVINS:49
LOVITT:75
LOWE:60,74,79(2),81
LOWERY:78
LOWRIE:81
LOWRY:33(3),34,35,44(2),
    50,51(2),52,67(2),
    81
LOYD:14,15,23,26,75
LUCAS:57,62,69,77,87
LUCK:87
LUKE:55
LUKER:92
LUMMUS:67
LUMPKIN:24,31,49,75,76
LUNDEL:69
LUNDIE:83
LUNEAU:58
LUNSFORD:68,92
LUSTER:22
LUSK:34
LUSTRE:11(2)
LYLE:22,24,28,30,46,69
LYLES:30
LYMAN:28
LYNCH:54,76
LYNES:35
LYON:90

LYONS:48
LYSTER:2
MABRY:10,18,92
MABSON:66
MACHERN:84
MACKAY:1,36,37
MACKEN:32(2),33
MACKEY:33,66,67,78,79,93
MACKIN:32,33,37
MACKLIN:81
MACON:56,58
MADDEN:75(2),81
MADDISON:82
MADISON:15(2)
MADDOCKS:33
MADDON:14,80
MADDOX:6,14(3)
MADKING:2
MADOWS:48
MADUX:22
MAGEE:68
MAGELL:18
MAGERS:47,48
MAHAN:41(2),42
MAHAFFY:19
MAHEFFY:52
MAHON:84
MAHONY:12
MAHURD:44
MAINARD:89,90
MAJORS:62,64
MALLETT:69
MALLORY:14,15(2),85
MALLOY:6
MALONE:34,47,48(2),49(2),
    50(3),76,84(3)
MALORY:84(2),88
MALY:9
MAN:55,77
MANGHAM:73,74,76,77,79(2)
MANGNUM:26,29
MANGRUM:70
MANLEY:65(2)
MANN:1,4(2)
MANNING:19,43,60,65(2),
    72(2),83,90
MANSFIELD:22,58
MANYHAM:14
MAPLES:35
MARABLE:9,88,92
MARBURY:41
MARCHEL:77
MARCUM:74
MARING:85
MARION:12
MARK:24
MARKET:44
MARLOW:90
MARONEY:65
MARONY:30
MARS:27
MARSH:12,65(3),66(2)
MARSHAL:57
MARSHALL:28,31,52,91
MARSHEL:78
MARSHELL:88
MARTEN:31,86,88
MARTILLA:14
MARTIN:2,3(2),5,6(2),11,
    13,15,16,19,20,22,
    25,28,31,33(3),35
    (3),36,39,40,41(2),
    42(2),49(2),58,61
    (2),62(5),63,64,65,
    72,73(2),75(2),76
    (2),80(2),82(2),85,
    88(3),93
MARTINDALE:22
MARTON:64
MASER:80
MASHBURN:83(2)
MASINGALE:45
MASK:26,91,92

MASON:18,25,26,37,46,56,
    86,90
MASSEY:13,78,81
MASSIE:50
MASSY:2
MASTERS:23,46
MASTIN:46
MATHENY:51,52
MATHES:9
MATHEWS:21,22(2),34,38,
    47,64,66,73,79
MATHIAS:2
MATHIS:20,55,58,59
MATLOCK:37
MATSEN:65
MATSON:82(2)
MATTHES:11
MATTHEWS:1,2,27,35(2),37,
    90
MATTOCKS:35
MATTON:15
MATTOX:9,13,25(2),78
MAUGHAM:73
MAULDING:81
MAXEY:31
MAY:14,25,47,57,65,82(2)
MAYBERRY:7
MAYER:55
MAYES:50
MAYFIELD:9(2),12,50,60,80
MAYO:62
MAYS:9,48(3)
MAXWEILL:77
MAXWELL:19(2),47,85
MEAD:13
MEADERS:18
MEADOW:18
MEADOWS:22(2),26(2),31,
    39,45
MEANS:34
MEARS:92
MEASELY:20
MEASLES:42
MEDLEY:6(2),30,58
MEDLOAK:39
MEEKS:19,52,80
MEHANE:56
MEHONE:59
MEIGAURT:75
MEIGS:73,76
MELEAR:93
MELONE:54
MELTON:11,17,18,43,59,88
MENAFEE:23
MENEFIELD:59
MERCER:23
MERRELL:61,86
MERRIL:1,24,29
MERRITT:39,46,90
MERWEATHER:55
MESHEAK:93
METCALF:17,72,87
METCALFE:66
MIAMS:59
MICHAEL:47,49,52
MICHEL:72
MICHELL:5,6
MICKEY:60
MICKLE:68(2)
MICKLES:68
MICOSZOLZKI:33
MIDDLETON:33
MIHAN:56,59
MILAM:19(2),31,88
MILAN:92
MILENDER:81
MILES:26,54,59(3),74,76,
    78,89
MILFORD:67(3),79
MILHAM:57
MILLER:2,8,9,10,12(3),14,
    21,24,29,32(2),33
    (2),35(2),36(5),

MILLER cont.:37,38(3),41
    (2),43,49(2)
    50,55,59(2),
    61(2),64,68,
    69,70(2),72
    (2),80(2),
    82,83(2),85
    (3)
MILLAGAN:29
MILLICAN:62,83
MILLS:6,58,61,64,67,73,74
MILLSAPS:65
MILTON:17,27,74
MILROY:75
MIMMS:26
MIMS:58(2),59,77(2),78
MICHEN:3
MINFIELD:58
NIMGO:48(2)
MINGS:56
MINICKS:62
MINSHAW:7(5)
MINTER:19(2)
MIRAN:6
MIRES:82
MISBON:68
MISE:71
MISELL:10
MITCHEL:10,15,18,23,25,
    47,49(3),54,77
MITCHELL:4,7,15,29,30,33,
    41,49(2),55,57,
    58(3),61,75,77,
    80,82,84,85,86,
    88
MITCHAM:89
MITCHUM:28
MITHROE:47
MIZELL:76
MIZLE:79
MIZZLE:41
MOBLEY:9,25,26,27,31,44,
    56,92
MODESETH:45
MOFFET:78
MOFFIT:14
MOFFITT:14
MOLEY:19
MOLTON:75
MOMAN:30
MONAGAN:35
MONAHAN:40
MONIEES:68
MONK:26,34,44,50,91,92(2)
MONROE:48,54
MONTANE:79
MONTCRIEF:5
MONTGOMERY:14(2),18,45,
    69,81,88,93
MORE:76
MOREHAM:56
MOODY:14,16,17,30,74(2),
    86
MOON:2(2),42
MOONEY:36,43,48,63(2),74
MOORE:2,4(2),8,10(2),12
    (2),15,16(2),17,18,
    19,21,22,23,24,25
    (3),26,30,31,35(3),
    39(2),43,44(3),48,
    54,56(4),58,59,60,
    61,63,66,69(2),70,
    71(2),73,76,77(2),
    80(2),82(2),83(2),
    85,86(2),89,90,92,
    93(3)
MORAGNER:11
MORAN:30,45
MORDECAI:91
MORELAND:12,20,57,67,73,
    76
MORGAN:2,11,17,18(8),31,
    43,48(2),50(3),

MORGAN cont.:52(2),62,63,
    79(2),80,89
    (2)
MORILAND:18
MORRELL:79
MORRICE:23
MORRING:13
MORRIS:11,13,15(2),17,19,
    24,26(2),41(2),43
    (3),44(3),46(2),49,
    60,61,63,65,71,72,
    78,81,82,84,87,91
    (2),93(3)
MORRISON:1,2,5,8,12(2),13,
    38,57,61,70(2),
    71(2),83,92
MORROW:61(3),72,83,88
MORRY:40
MORTON:7,63(3),64(6),68
MOSELEY:35,36,90(3)
MOSELY:1
MOSLEY:85
MOSS:40(2),41,84
MOTE:19,77
MOTES:3,7,15,58
MOTLEY:56
MOTTE:93
MOULTON:72
MOUNT:16
MOUNTAIN:34
MUCKLEROY:12(3)
MULDER:54
MULDREW:70(2)
MULIGAN:25
MULINAX:25(2)
MULLICAN:24
MULLIGAN:32
MULLIN:59
MULLINS:10(2),15,50,55
MULLOLLY:70
MUNDAY:41,87
MUNK:76
MUNKUS:68
MUNROE:5,81,82
MURABLE:25
MURCHISON:43(2)
MURE:39
MURPHEY:14(2),31
MURPHY:4,8(2),20,26,38,40,
    42,50,52,57,60,63,
    72,77,78,86,88
MURRAY:41(2),77,80,89,90
MURRELL:26,38
MURRY:7,19
MUSE:23
MUSELWRITE:9
MUSGROVE:48,52
MUSIC:28,71
MUSICK:30,91
MUSKETT:37
MUSSEL:25
MUSSELWHITE:83
MUZLE:78,79
MYER:84
MYERS:41(2),44
MYRICK:66,73(2)
MYZE:25
McAKER:16
McADAMS:11(2),34,37(2),84
McAFEE:83
McAGEE:14
McALESTER:82
McALLISTER:2,63
McARTHUR:44,45
McBEE:10,12
McBETH:54
McBRAYER:17
McBRIDE:14,25,33
McBRIER:50(4)
McBRYDE:1,4,92
McBURNETT:71,72,93
McCABRON:38
McCAHER:10

xiii

McCACHRAN:1
McCAHRAN:9
McCAIN:26,30,80,87(8)
McCALE:1
McCALES:86
McCALL:5,8,16
McCALLINS:16
McCALLISTER:56
McCALLY:16
McCALPIN:12,57
McCALUM:10(2)
McCANDLISH:19
McCANE:26,73
McCANN:46
McCANNON:43
McCARREL:3
McCARRELL:34
McCARTER:87,88
McCARTY:3
McCASKILL:72
McCATS:22
McCAULESS:60
McCIBBIN:16
McCINON:79
McCLAIN:31
McCLANE:2-,54(2),76
McCLELLAN:16,22,31,85,87(2)
McCLEMORE:51
McCLENDEN:26,28
McCLENDON:27(2),54,59(2),69,72(2),89
McCLEOD:54
McCLINDEN:75
McCLUNEY:17,33
McCLUNG:85(2),87
McCLURE:7,44
McCOMBS:92
McCONNEL:17
McCONNELL:36,66,82
McCONNELY:77
McCONTHEY:86
McCORKILE:6
McCOY:23(2),24,30(2),31,32,35,46,69,70,78,85,92(2)
McCOWAN:27
McCRACKEN:33,75
McCRARY:3,59,78
McCREA:86
McCREDY:66
McCRELESS:71
McCRIMMONER:29
McCRORY:57
McCUCKING:74
McCULLERS:43,71
McCULLOUGH:3,22(3),26,33(2),83,85
McCULLOCH:35,92,93(3)
MCCURDY:23,52
McCURRY:14(2),15
McDANIEL:7,16,25,26(2),30,32,34,35,42,44,64,69,78,90
McDONALD:1,3,4,5(2),8,15,26,27(2),28,29,43(2),44,50,51(2),68,69,71,85
McDONOUGH:65
McDOOGALD:78
McDOUGAL:38
McDOUGALD:45
McDOUGALL:72
McDOUGLE:37
McDOW:13,70,81
McDOWELL:2
McDUFFEY:33
McDUFFIE:44,62(3),73,77,85
McDUFFEY:33
McELDRY:82
McELHENNEY:84
McELHENNY:84

McELHENY:80
McELRATH:36,40,41
McELROY:81
McERVIN:90
McFARLAN:91
McFARLAND:46,52
McFARLANE:66
McFARLIN:59
McGAGE:14
McGAHA:61
McGAN:59
McGARROW:26
McGEE:10,77,78
McGEEHEE:57,84
McGEHEE:6,33,36(2),37,39,73,84
McGILL:55,57
McGILVARY:3(2),4,6
McGINNIS:36(2)
McGINTIE:26
McGLEN:69
McGLINNIS:12
McGOUGH:42,43
McGOWAN:86
McGOWYER:82
McGRADY:85
McGRAGAN:37
McGRATH:59
McGREGOR:23
McGRUDER:1,55
McGUFFEN:85
McGUGAN:32
McGUIRE:25,59,80,84(2),90
McGUIST:19
McHALL:54
McHARGUE:26
McHAUL:55
McHENRY:22
McINNIS:5,7(2)
McINTIRE:25
McINTYRE:2,44
McINTOSH:1,6(3),13,55
McICER:36,89
McKAIN:64
McKAMIE:26
McKAN:67
McKARNEY:17(2)
McKASHLER:14
McKASKEL:6,57
McKAY:2(2),7,10,22,54,55,59,74,79
McKEE:29,44(2),65,70,86
McKELLAR:7
McKEM:77
McKENNON:76
McKENSAY:71
McKENZIE:1(2),3,5,41,52,84,92
McKEONS:23
McKERLEY:29(2)
McKEY:26,30,82
McKINCY:60
McKINEY:71
McKINIS:57
McKINLEA:59
McKINLEY:23,25,29,31
McKINNES:69
McKINNEY:30,41(2)
McKINNISH:32
McKINNON:1,58,92(3)
McKINSY:25
McKISICK:26
McKISSACH:73
McKITHEN:7
McKNEELY:28
McKNIGHT:28(3),68(2)
McKORKLE:13
McKORLEY:9
McLAIN:7
McLANE:39
McLAUGHAN:33
McLEAN:1(3),4,5,6,7,25,92
McLELAND:80

McLELLAN:12(2)
McLELLAND:80,88(2)
McLEMON:42,60
McLEMORE:13,23,90
McLENDON:2,4,7(2),8,26
McLEOD:1,7,8(2),21,41,82,83
McLERKIN:82
McLEROY:23
McLURAIL:86
McLURE:80
McLUSKEY:18
McMAHAN:13,15,33,34,36,39
McMANN:84
McMANUS:45
McMEANS:83,87
McMICHAEL:18,48,65,77
McMICHAELS:10
McMILLAN:3,4,6(2),41(2),45
McMILLEN:84
McMURRAY:2,3,68
McMURRY:5
McNABB:61
McNAIR:7,41
McNEAL:55,57
McNEELY:43
McNEIL:1,6,7
McNEILL:43,46
McNEW:36,52
McNIEL:3
McNIELL:82
McNIELY:23
McPEARSON:60
McPHAIL:1,71
McPHERSON:7,29,47(2),70(2),86
McPHURSON:4
McQUAIG:12,20
McQUEEN:44
McRAE:1,3,5
McRATH:37
McREA:26,43
McREYNOLDS:65,80
McRIGHT:11,40,82,83
McROBERTS:15
McSPADEN:52(2)
McSWAIN:54,71
McSWAN:2
McTEER:34
McTHRASH:19
McTYRE:75
McWHORTER:26,30,54,70
McWILLIAMS:80
NABORS:12(3),14,18(2),20(2),41(2)
NAGER:16
NALL:90,91
NALLY:20,45
NANCE:79(2),88(2)
NANTZ:35
NAPIR:74
NAPPER:15
NAPPIER:14
NAPPIR:18
NARON:68,89,91,93(3)
NASH:2(2),11,26,42
NATIONS:49,73
NAULS:76
NAYMAN:15
NEAL:14,21,32,56,59,63,85
NEALE:35
NEELEY:64(4)
NEELY:9
NEIGHBORS:26,29
NELMS:79
NELSON:1,12(2),13,20,24,32,34(2),35(2),36,38(2),48,51,54,87(2),93(2)
NETTLES:26
NEUGENT:59
NEVENS:16

xiv

NEVES:89
NEWBERRY:33,35
NEWBURY:6
NEWELL:30
NEWKIRK:52
NEWMAN:6,7(2),31,35,47,52,
    62,63,65(2)
NEWSOM:44,70
NEWTEN:28
NEWTON:20(2),74
NEYMAN:21
NICHLES:66
NICHLESON:49,50,52
NICHOL:64
NICHOLS:7,16,26,27,31,36,
    37(2),38(2),40,
    47(2),48(2),51,54,
    64,65,67
NICHOLSON:44,56,57
NICKERSON:79
NICKLES:15
NICKS:76
NICKSON:75
NIECE:5
NIEL:25
NIGHT:11,12,30,64,69,79
NIPPER:20
NILES:76
NILVELS:7
NISBET:7
NISBETT:11
NIX:41(3),55(2)
NIXON:63,69
NOAH:17
NOBLE:4,17,27,58(2),63(4)
NOBLES:52
NOBLETT:20
NOEL:68
NOKERN:39
NOLAN:55
NOLAND:18,50
NOLEN:25(2),29(3),30(3),
    58
NOLIN:1,2,4,54,57(2)
NORMAN:61,62,92
NORRIS:2,9,12,15,22,23,26,
    28,29,30,55,56,81
NORRY:31
NORTHAM:68
NORTHCUT:81(2)
NORTON:2,3,4,8(2),23,52
NORWOOD:24(2),82
NOTT:86
NUCKLES:58,77
NUNN:29,55,56,68,71
NUNNALLY:13,64
NUNNALY:46
NUOMAN:93
OATES:22
O'BANION:16
O'BAR:60(2)
OBION:24
OCHTERTONE ?:1
O'CONNER:23
O'DANIEL:56
ODELL:18,35,37(2)
ODEN:39,63,74,84,85(2)
ODIORUR?:45
ODOM:2,3
ODUM:11,78
OGLETREE:41,42,88
O'HARA:29,30
OHARRA:44,45
O'HARROW:72(2)
OLDFIELD:93
OLIVER:13,14(2),27(3),32,
    44,48,55,62,70,79
ONEAL:13,14,32
ORAM:45
ORE:60
O'REAR:12,78
ORR:69
ORSON:36

OSBORN:62,93(2)
OSBORNE:33,38,68
OSBOURNE:23,24(2)
OSBURN:75,87
OSSINGTON:16
OSWORT:53
OTT:3
OTWELL:27,28,72
OTWILL:72
OUSLEY:56(3)
OVERMAN:84
OVERSER:57
OWEN:39(2),58,70,73,91
OWENS:10(3),12,13,14,20,
    21(3),23,26,33,38,
    53,54,56(2),58,69
    (2),75(3),78,83,
    85(2),90
OWINS:7,88(2)
OWSLEY:38
PACE:14(2),20,45,61,64,
    78,87
PACKER:1,4
PADGET:58,59(2)
PAGE:17(3),25(3),39,60(2)
PAIN:50
PALEY:14
PALMER:19(2),39,73(2)
PALMORE:12,28,92
PALSON:67
PANE:52
PANKING:52
PANNELL:93
PANTER:51(2)
PARIS:4,66(3),69,72
PARISH:12,22,45,60,61(2)
PARISS:63
PARK:73,83
PARKER:1,12,23,24(2),29,
    31,32,33,35(3),39
    (2),45(3),46,47(2),
    50(2),52,54,55,62
    (2),63,65(2),67,69
    (2),70,71,72(3),73,
    74,77,84,92,93
PARKHILL:65(3)
PARKISON:18
PARKS:14,19,24,65,67,74
PARMER:4,5,51,63
PARNEL:15
PARNELL:26
PAROM:59
PARRAMORE:4
PARSON:57
PARSONS:36
PARTON:17,62
PARTRIDGE:90
PASCALL:27
PASCHAL:41
PASS:24
PASWELL:15
PATE:41,42,44(3),62(3),
    68,85(2),92
PATEN:47,49,52
PATERSON:19,78
PATEY:35
PATILLO:59,90
PATRIC:48
PATRICK:10,25,39,66(4),92
PATRIDGE:27,28
PATTEN:27,39
PATTERSON:2,25,28(2),29
    (3),30(2),36,
    39,43(2),46,57,
    64,81(2),83(2),
    89,91,93
PATTESON:63
PATTILLO:77
PASSMAN:7
PATTON:23,35,88,89
PATY:10,33(2),36
PAUL:57
PAULDING:44

PAULIN:3
PAULK:77
PAULMER:20
PAYNE:32,37,84
PEA:19
PEABODY:76(2)
PEACOCK:42
PEARCE:13,19,76,92
PEARSE:11
PEARSON:8,22,26(2),28,37,
    38,41,49,52,80,86,
    90(2),91,92,93
PEAVY:45
PEDDY:58
PEEBLES:6
PEED:74
PEEDEN:38
PEELER:70,72
PEEPLES:42
PEERSON:68(2)
PEIRCE:75
PELHAM:14,18
PELMAN:68
PEMERTON:26
PEN:51,74
PENDEGRASS:22,60(2),62(6),
    85(2)
PENICK:46
PENLAND:19
PENN:22,34,37
PENNEGER:32
PENNINGTON:45,69
PENNOYER:76
PENNY:24,51
PENOUGH:69
PENSON:69,70
PENTON:26(2)
PEOPLES:8
PERESTON:81
PERIN:84
PERKIN:52
PERKINS:2,9,38,60,73,81
PERMENTER:75
PERREN:83
PERRIN:91
PERRY:10,11(2),12,21,34,
    37,54,55,59,68(3),
    69,73(3),75(2),77,
    85(4),87,90(2),91
PERRYMAN:20,27,43
PERSON:6(2),37
PERSONS:75,77
PETERS:15,27,43,60
PETERSON:41(2),57
PETEY:5
PETIS:77
PETT:63(2)
PETTEWAY:56
PETTIS:87
PETTIT:1,17(4),77
PETTON:60
PETTY:3(2),72
PEVOUGHN:68
PHELPS:28
PHILIP:78
PHILIPS:3,6,7,23,32,41(2),
    42(4),43(2),48,64,
    65,68,77(2)
PHILLIPS:16(5),17(3),18,
    19,26,27,28,35,
    47,56,58,62,68,
    87(2),92
PHIPS:9
PHIRY:9
PICKENS:15,44
PICKET:6(2),57(2)
PICKLE:36
PIERCE:44,54,61
PIGGERS:51,58
PIGGINS:54
PIKE:12
PIKETON:9
PILCHER:64

PILE:60
PILES:82
PILGRIM:18
PILKERTON:9(2)
PINCKARD:68
PINCKET:12
PINE:32
PINKARD:55,68
PINKERTON:7(2)
PINKSTON:44,58
PINSON:13,42,49
PINSTON:80
PIPKIN:6(2)
PIPKINS:65
PITMAN:73,79
PITS:23
PITTS:5,14,26,35,36,47,48,
    50,54,57,60,63,74,
    79
PLANT:48,93
PLATT:10
PLOUGHMAN:80
PLUNKET:42
PLYLER:93
PO:51
POAG:74
PODY:41
POE:13(3),16,42,61,80
POINER:26(3)
POK:73
POLK:91
POLLAIC:38
POLLARD:6,34(2),38(3),45,
    66
POLLOCK:14,63
POMENTS:59
POMROY:77
POND:43
POOL:17,21,68(4),77(3)
POPE:4,10
POR:17
PORCH:90
PORE:72
PORTER:8,14(2),15(4),18(2)
    29,73,83(2),84
PORTOWINE:77
POSEY:9(2),10,17,18,44(2)
    69,93
POSTER:77
POTTER:39,49
POTTS:6,32,56
POUNDER:21
POUNDS:10
POWEL:55,86
POWELL:1,3,7,8,17(2),30,
    32,42,43(2),64,69,
    83,88,91(3),92,93
POWER:66,91(2),93
POWERS:17,20(2),30(2),38
POWRIDGE:57
PRATER:12(2),41,44,88
PRATHER:23
PRATT:23,66
PRESLEY:25,36,74
PRESNELL:9(3),68
PRENTIS:63
PREST:74
PRESTON:21
PREVETT:11
PRICE:16(4),17(2),22,36,
    38,40,41,55,58,59,
    64(2),75,76,81,86,
    92,93
PRICHARD:18
PRICHETT:61
PRICKETT:35,68
PRICKOLT:35
PRIDDY:72,77
PRIDE:75
PRINCE:47,48,77
PRINGLE:79
PRINTISS:44
PRISOCK:10

PRITCHETT:44,82(2)
PROCTOR:11
PROTHRO:29,70
PROVENCE:36
PRUET:26,78(3)
PRUETT:29,70(2)
PRUIT:13(2),14,15(2),25
PRUITT:9(8)
PUCKETT:12,34,49
PUGH:55(3),57
PULLAM:92
PULLEN:39(2),56
PULLIN:5(2)
PULLINS:55
PUPNAM:29
PURCELL:8
PURNELL:90
PURRSELL:8
PURSER:39
PURSEY:22
PUTMAN:16,63,71(3),72
PUTNAM:10
PUTTS:43,46
PYLANT:24,43
PYRUS:4
QUADDLEBUM:55
QUARLES:38
QUARLS:55,57
QUATTLEBAUM:28(2)
QUATTLEBUM:31
QUEEN:63,65
QUINN:1,35,42
RACER:58
RACHELS:3(2)
RACKLEY:87
RADEL:79
RADFORD:41,78,85
RAE:37
RAELY:13
RAGAN:6,15,21,40,70
RAGANS:48
RAGLAND:58,62,67,81,84
RAGSDALE:20(2),44,61,63(2)
RAIFORD:5,16
RAINES:2,33,38(3),60
RAINEY:29,46,60
RAINWATER:38,47
RAINS:6,15,58(2),65
RAKER:11
RALBON:68
RALLS:74
RALSON:19,42
RAMAGE:22,25
RAMBO:26
RAMMAGE:26
RAMSEY:7,30,50(4),54(2),
    64,66,75,84,90
RAMSY:29,74
RAND:51
RANDALL:2,58,80(2)
RANDALS:61
RANDELL:83,84(2)
RANDLE:35
RANDLES:65
RANDOLPH:37
RANES:62,63
RANEY:20,62(2)
RANFROW:77
RANSOM:33,62
RAPE:93
RASBERRY:89
RASBURY:89
RATCLIFF:75
RASCO:87
RATSFORD:26
RATTEN:70
RAWLINGS:37,40
RAWLS:4,22,91
RAUSE:6
RAVAN:82
RAY:12,16,35(2),36,37,
    42(3),43(2),50(2),
    55,56(2),81,91,93

RAYBORN:66
RAYBURN:32
RAYFIELD:85(4)
RAYSON:15
REA:29,30,31
REACE:48
READ:4,38,49,50,59,60,64,
    76
READER:8(2)
READING:36
READY:45
REAGAN:15
REALS:70
REASON:88
REAVES:13,35,50,88
REAVIS:3,63,85
RECINE:11
RECTOR:61,63,64(2),65
RED:1,74,78
REDDEN:89
REDWELL:37
REDWINE:73
REED:17,18(2),23,31,32,34,
    39(2),48(4),51(2),
    75(2)
REESE:20(2),22,25(3),26,
    49,76,84
REEVES:13(4),21,26,28,30,
    37,69,70(2)
REHAUG:71
REID:9(3),11
REIVES:1
REMLEY:12
RENDLEY:36
RENFRO:12,13,14(3)
RENFROE:74
RENNS:65
RENTFROW:83
RENTON:39
REPOE:74
REPPETOE:81
RESPESS:83
RESS:92
REVILL:33
REVIS:61
REYNOLDS:13,17,20(2),34,
    42,62,70(2),72(2)
    80,84
RHEA:65,84
RHINEHART:80,81,84
RHODAM:9
RHODEN:85(2)
RHODES:21,81
RICE:29,64(2),80
RICH:17,73
RICHARD:80
RICHARDS:3(2),7,23,24,31,
    42,43,74
RICHARDSON:4,10,23,38,77,
    78
RICHBURG:64
RICHE:61(2),64
RICHERSON:50
RICHEY:15,16,17(4),18(2),
    49,87
RICHIE:80
RICHUSON:48
RICKS:23,24,50(2)
RIDEOUT:83(2)
RICKETTS:65(2)
RIDDLE:15,24,52,86(3),87
    (2)
RIDGEWAY:25,27,63
RIDINGS:34
RIDNER:14
RIEVES:22,25,26
RIEVIS:5
RIGBY:58(2)
RIGSBY:71(4)
RIGGINS:61
RIGGS:14,20,39
RIGHIGHT:76
RIGHT:74(2),9,58,63

RIDER: 8(2)
RILEY: 80,87,76
RINEHART: 12,85
RINK: 50
RINOLA: 52
RION: 47
RIORDEN: 38
RIPLEY: 21
RISEN: 35
RISER: 84
RISSELL: 36
RITCHIE: 86
RITE: 47,48,77
RITTER: 76
ROACH: 1,3,47(2),50
ROAD: 26
ROBBINS: 42(2),43,61
ROBERSON: 30(2),31(3),52, 92
ROBERTS: 2,9,12,13(2),19, 20,21,32,38,39, 40,49(3),50,52,55, 57(3),62,69(2),72, 73,74,78,81
ROBERTSON: 4,9,41,42(4),43, 78,86
ROBESON: 25,26(3),29(2),30, 37(2),39,80,82,83, 93(2)
ROBINS: 65,66
ROBINSON: 3,5,11(2),13,14, 16,18,19,20(3), 21,22,23,24,25, 35(2),39(2),42, 43(2),55,62(2), 64(2),65,73,75, 78(3),87,90
ROBISON: 1,83,85(3)
ROCKER: 55
ROCKMAN: 4
ROCKMORE: 76
RODEN: 14(2),49(3),50(2), 53,62,65(3)
RODES: 49
RODGERS: 27,29,44,45(2), 82(2),86,92
ROE: 3,6,93
ROGERS: 6,16,24,37(2),46, 48,51,56,62,68,93
ROJERS: 70
ROLLASON: 42,43
ROLLIN: 41
ROLLINS: 91
ROMAN: 61,62
RONALDS: 51
ROOF: 56,57
ROONEY: 19
ROPER: 9(2),20(2),32,38, 50(2),63,79
ROSE: 22,45,48,60,64
ROSS: 21,22,27,32,33(3), 49(2),71,91
ROSWELL: 62(2)
ROTCH: 26
ROTTEN: 54(2),68
ROOUNDTREE: 7,26,29,30(2)
ROUSE: 3,45
ROUSEAU: 35
ROUT: 73
ROWAN: 47(2),51,52(3),87
ROWDEN: 93
ROWE: 36,37(2),44,45(4), 80,81
ROWELL: 70,93
ROWEN: 35
ROWLAND: 12
ROYAL: 59
ROYALL: 62
ROYSTER: 19(2)
ROZELL: 80,86
RUAKS: 13
RUBEL: 82
RUCKER: 72

RUDWELL: 33
RUFF: 22
RUGELY: 37
RUMEL: 86
RUMPH: 5,54
RUNELS: 74
RUNNELS: 24,25,56,57,75
RYNYAN: 81(2)
RUSE: 51(2),73,78
RUSH: 11,38,55
RUSHAM: 71
RUSHING: 42
RUSK: 28,92
RUSSELBNE: 57
RUSSEL: 43,48,49(4),52,56, 73,76,78,85
RUSSELL: 15,17,24(2),26(3), 33(3),48,64,66, 72,75,76,90,91
RUSTON: 70
RUTHERFORD: 9,21,76,78(2)
RUTLAND: 29,30,58
RUTLEDGE: 27,34(2),36,83
RUTLIDGE: 27,56
RYAN: 1,10,70,83,84
RYALS: 36
RYLAND: 45
RYLANT: 42
SADLER: 20,51
SAINT: 74
ST. CLAIR: 20,38,64
SALE: 72
SALLEY: 27,54,56
SALTER: 10,42(3)
SAMMONS: 38,60
SAMPLES: 13,49
SAMPLEY: 7(2)
SAMPLY: 1
SAMPSON: 30
SAMS: 11,42
SAMSON: 11
SAMUELS: 16,29
SANDEFER: 32
SANDERS: 1,9,13,22,26,27, 33,36,48,57,59, 56,62,89(3),90, 91
SANDFORD: 90,92
SANDLIN: 33
SANFORD: 3(2),5(2),24,45 (2),59,83
SANLIN: 32
SANSOM: 34
SAPATER: 17(2)
SARGENT: 4
SARLES: 60
SARTIN: 80
SARTON: 50
SATCHER: 80
SATTEMORE: 20
SATTERWHITE: 28,29(2),78
SAULS: 3
SAUCIE: 7(2)
SAULS: 7,50
SAULSBURY: 1
SAUNDERS: 6(2),45(2),48
SAUNDIN: 55
SAVAGE: 14,19(2)
SAWARIT: 83
SAWEARINGANN: 77
SAWLS: 50
SAWYER: 15,70(2),81,82,84
SAXON: 26,29,33,44,86,89
SAYMON: 35
SAYRE: 57
SCALES: 79,83
SCARBOROUGH: 19,73,75
SCARBROUGH: 20,73
SCHERCK: 17
SCHLEY: 77
SCHOOLER: 62
SCISSON: 80,88
SCOTT: 6,10,12(2),14,22,

SCOTT cont.: 30,33,37,43, 48(2),49(3), 50,54,56,58, 59,81,84,93
SCRIMMONS: 81
SCHRIMSHAW: 66
SCOGGINS: 91
SCREWS: 4
SCROGGINS: 18(2),55,56,63, 73,74,75,90
SEALES: 83
SEALS: 3,4,57
SEALY: 72
SEARCY: 4(2),7
SEARS: 70
SEAT: 40
SEATON: 79
SEAY: 81,82,86
SECKORY: 68
SEESON: 80,81
SEGANS: 15
SEGLER: 26
SEGREST: 56
SEIGNER: 56(3)
SEIGNS: 55
SEIGREST: 57
SELARS: 3
SELF: 14(2),15(3),16
SELLARS: 15
SELLERS: 45
SELMAH: 27
SELMAN: 91
SEMMES: 3
SENTELL: 90,91
SESSION: 20
SESTRUNK: 59
SETCHER: 44
SEWALLER: 18
SEWART: 70,71
SEWEL: 78
SEWELL: 36,38,82,91
SEXTON: 66,71
SEYMORE: 5
SHACKLEFORD: 30,38,42,90
SHADAWICH: 73(4),77(2)
SHADDEX: 14
SHADDOCK: 92
SHADRIACK: 53(2)
SHADWICK: 75
SHAFFER: 84(2)
SHAMBLIN: 12(2)
SHANDFIELD: 68
SHANK: 76
SHANKLE: 48
SHANKS: 3
SHANNON: 25
SHARBUTT: 72
SHARD: 59
SHARP: 6,7,13,19,26,31,50, 55,66,73,74,79,91
SHARPE: 24,33,36,37,50
SHARRED: 75
SHAW: 2,7,24,25,26,28,29, 41,46,56,60,61,92
SHAWTER: 56
SHEARD: 12
SHEARER: 12(2),51
SHEARMAN: 74(2)
SHEASTLER: 81
SHED: 33
SHEEZOG: 38
SHEFFIELD: 17
SHELLEY: 80,81,85
SHELMAN: 23
SHELNUT: 68,69
SHELTON: 27(2),32,41,43(2), 48,52,57,58
SHEPARD: 23,29
SHEPHARD: 4,76
SHEPHERD: 1,2(2),3,4,11,54, 57(2)
SHEPP: 72
SHEPPARD: 17,22,45

SHERLY:27
SHERRARD:29
SHERRELL:32
SHERROD:70
SHERROR:26(2)
SHIDY:33
SHIELDS:92
SHINAULT:49
SHIP:71,72
SHIPMAN:7
SHIPPEN:12,18(2)
SHIPTER:74(2)
SHITWOOD:52
SHIVERS:76,78
SHOCKLEY:34,36,39(2),76,
    82
SHOEMAKE:48,68
SHOEMAKER:34
SHOOK:35
SHORES:66,76
SHORT:30(2),32,86
SHORTER:1
SHORTRIDGE:81
SHOTE:50
SHEPHERD:3,4,44,12
SHOUTTS:82
SHROPSHIRE:85,90
SHRUM:48
SHUFFIELD:17,50
SHUMAKE:8
SHURANS:68
SHURLOCK:90
SIBERT:50
SICILY:18
SIDES:13,49(2),50(2),87,
    88(2)
SIKES:31,42,59
SILAS:76
SILLS:77
SIMENGTON:30
SIMINGTON:31
SIMMES:5
SIMMONS:12(2),13,14,15(2),
    20,23,25,32,40,54,
    55(2),57,58,76,82,
    83(2),86(2),89(2),
    93
SIMON:49
SIMONS:53
SIMPKINS:7
SIMS:14,18,28(2),65(2)
SIMPSON:3,15,25(2),49,55,
    61(3),70(2),76(2)
SIMS:6,17(2),18,19,20,25,
    28,51,61(3),73,80(2),
    83
SINCLAIR:62
SINES:84
SINGLETON:18,26
SINQUEFIELD:3
SINSON:2
SINT:65
SIPSEY:15(2)
SISMORE:10
SISSON:80(2)
SISTON:47
SITROUT:7
SIVLEY:61(2)
SKELTON:15,16
SKINNER:10(2),14,39,45(3),
    57(2),69,70
SKIPPER:7
SKIRLOCK:57(2)
SLACK:17
SLAPPY:4,78,79
SLATON:21,39
SLATTER:5
SLATTONGS:35
SLAUGHTER:4,26,31,75,89
    (2),91
SLAUTER:54,56
SLAYTON:23,47(4)
SLEDGE:59

SLOAN:29,63
SMALL:18
SMALLEY:51
SMALLWOOD:36,60
SMART:30
SMEALY:51
SMEDLEY:51(2)
SMIDLEY:36
SMILLY:7
SMITH:1,2(2),3(2),4(2),5,
    6(4),8(2),9(2),10,
    11(4),12(2),13,14
    (3),15(2),17,18,
    20(6),21,23(3),
    24(3),25(4),26,27
    (2),29(3),30(6),31
    (2),32(6),33(2),34
    (3),35(3),36,37(4),
    38,39(9),40,41(3),
    42(4),43(7),44,46,
    47(2),48(2),49(3),
    50,51(2),52,53(2),
    54,55,56(4),58(3),
    59(4),60(6),61,62
    (4),63(6),64(7),66,
    67,68,69(5),70(3),
    71(3),72(4),73(4),
    74(4),75(2),76(2),
    78,80(3),81(2),82
    (5),84,85(2),86(2),
    87(2),89(2),90(7),
    91(3),92(2),93(4)
SMITSON:73
SMOOT:81
SMYTHE:18
SNAPE:82
SNEAD:77
SNELL:85
SNIDER:35,49,76
SNIPS:8
SNOW:12,68
SNYDER:15(2)
SOCK:82
SOCKE:41
SOLNE:86
SON:2
SORREL:28
SORRELL:28(2)
SORELLS:12
SOUTH:52,86
SOUTHERLAND:62(7),64
SOWELL:24,37
SPAIN:37(2),38,90
SPARKS:16,19(2),20,23,82,
    90,92
SPARKY:26
SPARM:26
SPANN:35
SPARKMAN:85
SPEAK:90
SPEAKS:41
SPEARMAN:1,32,39(3)
SPEARS:5,31,42,44,45,68,
    69,70(3)
SPENCE:37,75,87(2)
SPENCER:2,11,16,45,61,79
SPENSER:93
SPERLING:27
SPERRY:69(2)
SPIER:75
SPIGNER:44(2)
SPIKES:28,30
SPILLARS:74
SPINKS:59
SPIVEY:41(2),68
SPORE:56
SPRAGGINS:28,91
SPREWELL:83
SPRING:39
SPRINGER:86,91
SPRINGIN:50
SPRUEL:14
SPURLOCK:1,4(2)

SQUIRES:2
STACY:58
STAFFORD:50(3),58
STALLING:32
STALLINGS:22,28,72,75
STAMPS:22,41
STANDEFER:36(4)
STANDIFER:38(2)
STALNAKER:29,91
STALS:2
STANFIELD:90
STANFORD:5,24
STANLEY:23,25(2),42,51,64
STANSEL:11
STANTON:59
STAPLES:24,29,61
STAPS:23
STAR:56
STARK:45
STARKE:45
STARKIE:26
STARNES:26,60,65(4)
STARR:2,25(2),91
STARRIS:80
STATON:6,18
STEAD:20
STEADMAN:86
STEEL:47,56
STEELE:64,66
STEGALL:14
STELE:31
STENNETT:81
STEPES:11
STEPHENS:7,14,18,25,26(3),
    28(3),30(3),34,
    38(2),40,47(3),
    50(2),56(2),59(2),
    60(2),61(2),63,
    66(2),73,86,89
STEPHINS:77
STERNS:89
STEVENSON:7,92
STEWARD:65
STEWART:3,4,10,20,23,24,
    25,26,27,43,44(3),
    45,46,49,50,51(3),
    59(2),69,70(2),
    71(2),72,73,77,
    78(2),90,91
STIDAM:87
STIDHAM:41
STIFLE:71
STIGGINS:55
STILES:48
STILL:62
STILO:28
STINER:11(2)
STINNET:48
STINSON:26,35,57
STITT:68
STOCKDALE:16
STOCKS:86(2)
STOCKSTILL:50
STOKES:14,26(2),44(3),75,
    78
STONE:2,4,11,24,31,40,53,
    55,68,69,83,87(3),
    90,92
STONECHER:70
STONER:47
STORES:58(2)
STOREY:26
STORRS:26
STORS:1
STORY:24,36,63,76
STOVALL:1
STOVER:85
STOUDENMIER:54(2)
STOW:89(2)
STOWARS:48
STOWE:1
STRACENER:21
STRADFORD:55

STRAND:38
STRANGE:51,57
STRATFORD:73
STRATTON:20
STRAYHORN:25,28
STREET:5,37,66,87
STREETER:6(2)
STREETMAN:6
STRENGTH:90
STRIBLING:71
STRICKLAND:3,32,36,77,83
STRICKLIN:52,70(2),90
STRINGFELLOW:43,46,87
STRIPLAND:6(2)
STRIPLEN:70
STRIPLIN:19
STRIPLING:3
STRODER:31
STRONG:31,71
STROTHER:19,27,29(3)
STROUD:24,71,76
STROZIER:22
STUART:12,14,18(3),20(2),
        47,74(2),76
STUBBLEFIELD:43,54
STUBBS:6,75
STUDHAM:28(2)
STURDIVANT:93
STURGIS:60,78
STURKIE:26
STURNS:75
STURRIT:85
SUBLETTE:11
SUDDETH:74
SUETS:74
SULLIVAN:13,16(2),34(2),
        45,61,65
SUMNER:22
SUMMERKAMP:2
SUMMERS:63,67
SUMNER:35,84
SUMMEY:13
SUMTER:14
SURRY:68
SUTER:42
SUTHERLAND:51
SUTTLE:42
SUTTLEMEN:32
SUTTLEMEYER:38(2)
SUTTLES:42
SUTTON:3(2),7,11,27,47,61,
        64,65(2)
SWADER:51(2),62(2)
SWAFFORD:22,36,52,62
SWAILS:4
SWAIN:42(2),92
SWAN:18,93
SWANSEY:40
SWEARINGIN:60
SEEENEY:25,29
SWEET:70,71(2)
SWEETON:64
SWENY:25
SWINDLER:63
SWINGIN:66
SWINNEY:2
SWINT:25
SWITZER:23
SWORDS:19,66
SYCLAY:39
SYLVESTER:2
SYTHE:52
TABOR:4
TACO:65(3)
TAFF:73
TAILOR:33
TALBOT:54(2),57,59
TALIFERIO:84
TALLEY:13,79,92
TALLY:8,26
TAMLIN:76
TANIER:73
TANKERLY:14

TANKERLEY:13
TANKERSLEY:26
TANNER:76
TANT:50,51(2),65(2),88
TANTON:51,93
TAPLEY:29
TAPP:38
TARDY:45
TARGINTON:59
TARKENTON:54
TARPLEY:55
TARRANTT:82
TARVER:57(2),70,78,89
TARVIN:55
TATAM:54
TATE:4,19,29,34,38(2),51
        (3),60,73(2),84
TATUM:10(3),58(2),87,89,
        90
TAWBS:73
TAYLOR:1,4(2),10,11,12,
        15,18(2),19,20,23
        (2),24(2),25,26(4),
        28,29(4),30,31,34
        (2),36,40(2),44,
        45,46,47,48,49,50,
        51,54(3),57,58,61,
        62,64,65,68,69(2),
        71,77,78(2),80,81,
        83,84,85(2),86,87,
        89,91
TEACH:27
TECEARGE:50
TEDDER:57
TEDWELL:11
TEAGUE:9(4),11,14(4),18,
        21,36(4),50
TEAL:1,7,28,89(2)
TEEL:73
TEMPLE:43
TEMPLES:55
TEMPLETON:15
TENNESON:33
TENNISON:10(2)
TERRELL:66(2)
TERRIL:3
TERRILL:78
TERRY:41,44,57,80,84
THACKERSON:12,18
THARD:11
THARP:3,4,7
THARPE:49
THAXTON:24,31
THIELA:27
THIGPEN:1,74
THOMAS:1(2),2,3(2),8(8),
        12,22(3),24(3),26
        (3),29,31,36(2),41
        (2),45(3),46,50,51
        (3),54,60(2),64,
        66(3),71,72(3),74,
        76,78,79(3),82,87,
        88,90
THOMASON:17,40,52,71
THOMASTON:29,94
THOMPSON:7(2),9(2),13(2),
        15,18(3),20,21
        (3),22(2),24(2),
        26,27,28(2),29,
        31(2),33,34(2),
        36,38,40(2),42
        (2),43(2),49,54
        (4),55(2),57,58,
        59,64(2),69,71,
        73,74,76,77(3),
        79,80,81,82,84
        (2),85(3),86,87
        (2)
THOPSON:52
THORN:25
THORNBURG:66
THORNE:8
THORNELL:43

THORNTON:5(2),23(2),24(2),
        25,29(2),31(2),
        38,45,56(2),73,
        76,77,91,93(2)
THORP:12
THORPE:33
THRADER:14
THRASH:31
THRASHER:46,49(3),70
THREDGILL:71,74
THRESHER:9(3)
THRIFT:84
THURMAN:31,49
THWART:44
TICENOR:2,23
TIDEWELL:14(2)
TIDMORE:39(2)
TIDWELL:48,60,61,62,65(2),
        66,76
TIGON:66
TILLAY:64
TILLERY:73
TILLESON:39
TILLEY:2
TILLMAN:32,51
TILLORY:90
TILLY:35
TILMAN:74
TILTON:11
TIMERMAN:23
TIMMONS:35
TINDAL:55
TINDALL:7
TINDLE:71
TINER:32
TINGLE:13,49
TINSLEY:37
TIPTON:60
TITTLE:13
TOD:57
TODD:25,30,52,66,75,92(2)
TOKE:51
TOLAFAIRO:62
TOLBERT:10,21,27(2),32,63,
        70
TOLES:79
TOLLASON:90
TOLLESON:31
TOLLEY:93
TOMASON:11
TOMLIN:77,85
TOMPKINS:5,6,75,80,81
TOMSERY:1
TONAHAM:72
TOPP:38
TORBERT:59
TORRENCE:4
TOWERS:70
TOWLE:50
TOWLES:30(2),34
TOWLS:89
TOWNES:14
TOWNS:14,15,23,67,90
TOWNSEND:42,45(2),77,81,88
TRAMMEL:6
TRAMMELL:29(2),30(2),83
TRANAM:59
TRANOM:58
TRAUNT:70
TRAXLEY:29
TRAYACK:38
TRAYLOR:9,71,78,91,93
TRAYWICK:3
TRAYWICKE:76
TREADGIL:57
TREADWELL:1,3,12,28
TREDWELL:11(2),69
TRESLE:86
TREUTLEN:5
TRICE:25,26
TRIMBLE:26,93
TRIPLET:86
TRIPLETT:65

TRIPP:32,34
TROTTER:73,76
TROUP:65
TRUMAN:4(3),6
TRUP:80(2)
TRUSS:87
TUBMAN:72
TUCK:41
TUCKER:3,6,22,23(5),26,
    37(2),51,60,63,64,
    65,78
TUFF:35
TUGGLE:53
TULLIS:41
TULLUS:25,57
TUNNEL:14
TUNNELL:14(2),43(2)
TURKE:77
TURMAN:27
TURNER:1,6,9,12,14(2),16,
    25(2),26,27,28,30
    (2),33,34,37,39,
    44(2),48,56(2),57,
    58,61,64,73,74(2),
    75,80(2),85
TURNIPSEED:9,15(2)
TURNLEY:33(2)
TURPIN:59
TUTT:26
TWILEY:68
TYLER:65
TYREE:71
TYSON:31,78
TYUS:4
UBANKS:42
ULAN:41
ULARD:41
ULREND:45
UNDERWOOD:33(2),42,44,54
UPSHAW:5
UPSON:30
UPTON:50(2),60
URQUHART:3
URSERY:70
URSURY:70
URY:6
USERY:66
USTON:52
UTSEY:7
VALENTINE:8,34
VANBIBBER:46
VANCE:47,52,70(3),73(2)
VAN CLEAVE:62
VANDERVERT:40
VANDIGRIFF:53
VANDIVER:34
VANDYKE:35
VAN MOSBY:12
VANN:2,4,28,37(2),41,55,
    56
VARDEMAN:42,91
VARDENA:12
VARDIMAN:85(2)
VARNEEM:15
VARNELL:36(2),85,86(3)
VARNER:26,33,40
VARNUM:14,16(2)
VATILLA:14
VAUGHAN:34,41(2),63,91
VAUGHN:15,57,58,68
VAUGHT:15
VEASEY:57,91
VEEZY:26
VENABLE:51(2),52(2)
VENAWAY:78
VENIBLE:48
VENTERS:5,27
VENTRESS:1
VERNON:26,27
VERNONS:4
VESSELS:22
VESTAL:13
VEVERETT:37

VIARS:8
VICARS:6
VICE:14,71,82
VICKERS:22,29,87
VICKERY:56
VINCENT:4(2),6,31,37
VINES:10,13,14,15,21(3),
    83,89
VINEYARD:21(3)
VINSON:77
VINTNERS:10
VINYART:85
VOWEL:10(2)
VOYLE:16(2)
VRITCH:20
WADDELL:32,81
WADDILL:17
WADDLE:32,39
WADE:8,16,21,28,50,69,74,
    75(2),77
WADKINS:3,5,13,55,79
WADSWORTH:82(2)
WAFER:58,71
WAGGONER:56
WAGNON:39
WAGONER:90
WAITES:34
WAKEFIELD:16,69,91
WALDEN:10,26,36
WALDRIP:9,92
WALDRON:82
WALDROP:24
WALKER:4,9,10,11(2),13,
    17(2),18,19,23,25,
    26,31,37,43,45,47,
    48(2),49(2),50,52,
    54,55,58,61(3),
    62(2),63(2),68(3),
    73,70,74,71,77,78,
    80,82,85,91(2),92
    (2),93(2)
WALKLY:2
WALL:10,25,35,43,44
WALLACE:10(3),21,22(2),
    25,74
WALLIS:5,15,25,26(3),63,
    69(2),79,84(2),85
WALLS:13
WALLY:3,22
WALSTON:20
WALTERS:38
WALTHOL:27
WALTON:29,88
WARD:6,7(2),29(3),30(2),
    31(2),37,46,48(5),
    50,51(2),52,60(3),
    68,69,73,76,81,84,
    85,89,91(2),93
WARDEN:21
WARDLAW:27,29,82
WARDWORTH:71
WARE:16,18,26,39(2),57,72
WARHAM:16
WARLOCK:76
WARNOCK:14
WARREN:5(3),8,21,31,46,
    47(2),52,91,93
WARSON:29
WASHBURN:90
WASHINGTON:16,18,39,51,
    74,85
WASSEN:47,52
WASSON:21
WATERS:35,36,39,53,61
WATES:15
WATKINS:10(2),39,41,42,
    75,81,83,84(2)
WATLEY:26(2),30,58,86
WATSON:3,6(3),7,16,18,19,
    21,26(2),31,33,34,
    40(2),42,57,63,64,
    71,73,79,82(3),83,
    85,86

WATT:37,77(2)
WATTERS:26,85,86(4)
WATTS:10,11,21,22,39,48(2)
    65,84,86,87(2)
WATTY:1
WATWOOD:69
WAUGH:80
WAYD:1
WEAKLEY:33
WEAR:20,32,36,87
WEATHERFORD:4,87
WEATHERLY:14(2),16,82,92
WEATHERS:31,68,69(2),82
WEAVER:12,14,17,32(2),35,
    42(2),44,51,57,83,
    88
WEBB:12,19,25,28,29,31,32,
    34,36,49,62,63,72,91,
    92,93(2)
WEBBER:62
WEBLEY:69
WEBSTER:17,22
WEDGES:44,62
WEDGEWORTH:61(2)
WEED:29
WEEKS:54
WEEMS:17,38,41,90
WEIR:9,14(2),35
WELCH:22,26(2),28,32,39,
    45(2),49,77,81(2),
    85,91,93(3)
WELDEN:30
WELDON:69
WELLBORN:2(4),3
WELLMOTH:64
WELLS:2,12(2),19,28,34,36,
    52,66,70,75
WELSH:20,22
WEPON:70
WESSON:34,81
WEST:39,42,61,63,64(2),75,
    78,82,89,92
WESTER:27,32,38(2)
WESTBROOK:38
WESTBROOKS:35
WESTMORELAND:31,36,39,45,
    57
WESTEN:39
WESTERN:39,63
WESTON:16,17(4),39
WETHERSBY:75
WETHERTON:55
WHALES:64
WHALEY:22
WHARTON:32(2),34,37,40
WHATELEY:42
WHATLEY:17,75,76,77(3),78,
    89
WHEAT:22
WHEELER:3,5,19(2),30,37,
    72
WHELAS:92
WHELASS:87
WHIFFIN:46
WHISNANT:37
WHISTELLE:5
WHITAKER:25,61(4),93
WHITE:1,2,4,5,9,11,16,17
    (2),18,19(5),20,25,
    35(2),36,40,41(2),
    43,48,49(3),51(2),
    52,54,57(3),60,69,
    71(3),73(2),74(4),
    76(4),78(2),79(2),
    80,89(2),91,92
WHITECOTTON:60
WHITEHEAD:24,47,50,65
WHITES:13
WHITESIDE:19,20,21
WHITESIDES:13
WHITINGTON:24
WHITLEY:41,59
WHITLOCK:20,66

WHITMIRE: 35
WHITMORE: 35
WHITSON: 40
WHITSTONE: 41
WHITT: 33
WHITTEMORE: 4
WHITTEN: 23, 37
WHITTENBURGH: 83
WHITTLE: 3, 76
WHITWORTH: 66(3), 90, 62
WILAFORD: 24
WILCHER: 66
WILCOX: 74
WILDER: 29, 32, 37, 54, 60, 82, 89
WILDMAN: 16, 60(3), 62, 64
WILDON: 72
WILEMAN: 60
WILEY: 3, 23, 24, 26, 62, 76
WILHITE: 36
WILKERSON: 9(2), 27, 28, 69, 78
WILKES: 7, 41
WILKINS: 7, 8, 11, 30, 46(3)
WILKINSON: 2, 16, 17, 25, 32, 42, 55, 56, 91
WILKISON: 26(2), 27(2)
WILKON: 38
WILKS: 4, 70
WILL: 18
WILLBORN: 52(2)
WILLIAM: 62
WILLIAMS: 1, 2, 3(3), 4(4), 5(5), 8(3), 9(2), 10, 11, 12, 13(2), 15(3), 16, 18(3), 19(2), 21(2), 23, 25, 26(8), 28(4), 31, 37, 39, 40, 42, 43(5), 44(3), 45, 47, 51(2), 54(4), 56(2), 57, 58(2), 62(4), 63, 65(3), 66(2), 68(2), 71, 73(2), 74, 75, 76(3), 77(2), 78(3), 79, 80, 88, 89, 90(2), 91(2), 92(2), 93
WILLIAMSON: 9(4), 10, 12, 13, 25, 29, 30, 34(2), 35, 36, 73, 82, 83, 93
WILLIFORD: 51, 76
WILLINGHAM: 10, 14, 30, 68, 69, 72
WILLIS: 2, 5, 6, 10, 11, 16, 17, 18, 27, 31, 39, 43, 44, 59, 66, 68, 71
WILMOTH: 39
WILLMOTH: 64
WILLOBY: 27
WILLOUGHBY: 66(2)
WILLS: 17, 74, 76, 81, 88
WILLSON: 47, 74, 75, 90
WILSON: 2, 11(2), 13, 15(2), 18, 19(3), 20(3), 23, 24, 26(2), 27, 28(2), 32(2), 33, 35(2), 37, 38(3), 39, 40, 42, 43(2), 44(4), 45, 46(2), 47, 49, 52, 54, 55, 57, 58(3), 60(3), 64, 69(2), 71, 80, 81, 82(2), 83, 84(4), 88(2)
WILT: 18, 34, 35
WILTEN: 38
WIMBERLY: 4
WINGATE: 58
WINGO: 89
WINSLETT: 23(2), 27, 41, 91, 92
WICKER: 58, 77

WICKES: 31
WIGGES: 48
WIGGINS: 7
WIGGS: 66
WIGHLTE: 14
WIMBERLY: 4, 59, 77
WINBURK: 31
WINBUSH: 22, 25
WINDHAM: 2, 7, 44(3)
WINDSOR: 64, 66, 68, 70
WINDURN: 77
WINGATE: 58
WINIKEL: 58
WINKLE: 61
WINN: 14
WINSTETTE: 1
WINSTON: 47
WINTERS: 39
WISDOM: 39
WISE: 4, 27
WISMAN: 12
WISNER: 16
WITHAM: 79
WITHERINGTON: 74
WITHERSPOON: 48
WITHROW: 51(2)
WITSTER: 74
WITT: 47, 51
WITTON: 42
WITZELL: 33
WOLENS: 79
WOLF: 19(2), 20
WOMACK: 14, 46
WOMBLE: 77
WOOD: 4(2), 7, 8, 13, 18, 22, 25, 27, 31, 37(2), 44, 45, 46, 64, 65, 68(3), 73, 75(2), 85, 86(2), 89, 92(3)
WOODALL: 60, 67
WOODARD: 38, 55
WOODBY: 7
WOODEN: 89
WOODLAND: 38
WOODLEY: 13(2), 34, 39
WOODPIN: 92
WOODRUFF: 14, 17, 59, 69
WOODS: 2, 10, 61, 64, 65(3), 69
WOODSON: 19(2), 38
WOODWARD: 11, 32, 38, 82, 85
WOODYARD: 26, 27
WOOLARD: 66
WOOLEY: 63
WOOSLEY: 62
WOOTEN: 42
WOOTON: 2, 63(2)
WORDSWORTH: 64
WORLD: 4
WORLEY: 71
WORLICK: 4
WORMACK: 14, 15
WORREL: 42
WORSHAM: 76
WORTHINGTON: 9, 15, 21, 88
WORTHY: 26
WRAY: 89
WRIGHT: 5, 15, 18(5), 24(3), 26(3), 30, 48(2), 50, 51, 52(2), 60(4), 61, 65, 66, 69, 76, 78, 83, 89, 90(2), 92(2), 93
WYATT: 17(3), 27, 66, 83, 91(3)
WYLY: 13
WYNATT: 83
WYNN: 27, 45, 56, 73
YANCEY: 45, 59
YANCY: 70, 73
YARBOROUGH: 26, 27(2), 35, 46, 80, 86
YARBROUGH: 26, 86, 92, 93(2)
YATES: 51, 68, 69, 87
YEARGAIN: 48

YEATMAN: 15(3)
YORK: 9(2), 42, 74
YOUNG: 2(2), 12, 13(3), 14(4), 17, 58, 62, 63(2), 68, 69(2), 70, 80, 89(4), 90, 91
YOUNGBLOOD: 16(2), 29, 30, 54, 58, 75(2), 91, 93
YOW: 52
ZOLLARD: 51

xxi

www.ingramcontent.com/pod-product-compliance
Lightning Source LLC
Chambersburg PA
CBHW031424290426